BOB DAVIES

BOB DAVIES

A BASKETBALL LEGEND

BARRY S. MARTIN

 RIT PRESS

ROCHESTER, NEW YORK

RIT Press
90 Lomb Memorial Drive
Rochester, New York 14623-5604
http://ritpress.rit.edu

Book and cover design by Marnie Soom
Cover photo from "Basketball's Li'l Abner" feature, *Liberty* magazine (see p. 24).
Printed in the U.S.A. by Thomson Shore

ISBN 978-1-939125-29-3 (e-book)
ISBN 978-1-939125-28-6 (print)

Library of Congress Cataloging-in-Publication Data

Names: Martin, Barry S., author.
Title: Bob Davies : a basketball legend / Barry S. Martin.
Description: Rochester, New York : RIT Press, [2016] | Includes
   bibliographical references and index.
Identifiers: LCCN 2016008660 (print) | LCCN 2016010175 (ebook) | ISBN
   9781939125286 (pbk. : alk. paper) | ISBN 9781939125293 (e-book)
Subjects: LCSH: Davies, Bob, 1920–1990. | Basketball players—United
   States—Biography.
Classification: LCC GV884.D367 M37 2016 (print) | LCC GV884.D367 (ebook) |
   DDC 796.323092—dc23
LC record available at http://lccn.loc.gov/2016008660

For our son, Shawn

CONTENTS

CHAPTER 1

HALLEY'S COMET

A RECORD-SETTING 18,341 BASKETBALL FANS JAMMED INTO NEW York City's Madison Square Garden on March 19, 1941, for a National Invitational Tournament (NIT) game. They were looking forward to watching the Seton Hall College Pirates, riding a 42-game win streak (one shy of the then second-best all-time collegiate record), take on the Rhode Island State University "Two Points a Minute" Rams, the nation's highest-scoring team.[1]

Late in the game, Seton Hall star Bob Davies dribbled with his right hand to the foul line, bounced the ball *behind* his back to his left hand, and blew straight past the man guarding him for a lay-up. He had introduced in the "basketball capital of the world" the behind-the-back dribble, the stuff of which legends are made.

Stunned fans, most of whom had never seen this ball-handling trick, roared in approval. Future NBA player Andrew "Fuzzy" Levane, then a starter for the St. John's University Redmen, leaped from his seat. A priest in the act of winding his watch tossed it in the air. Men threw their hats. Allegedly, a spectator suffered a heart attack. [2]

A *Newark* (NJ) *News* staff correspondent was the first sports reporter to characterize Davies' stunning performance as legendary. "All stops were out today," this observer opened his story, "as basketball historians scoured their adjective storehouses for new ways of explaining Bob Davies, the blond thunderbolt of Seton Hall." The writer dubbed Bob "the Nijinsky[3] of basketball." He described the spectators "alternately spellbound and frenziedly cheering" Bob who

1

was "leaping like a hooked tarpon, dribbling behind his back, looking in one direction and passing in another...."[4]

"You can take the whole Hollywood lexicon of superlatives and still be at a loss for words to describe the utterly fantastic operations of the Harrisburg Houdini," raved a veteran *New York Herald-Tribune* reporter. "The things Mr. Davies does with a basketball have to be seen to be appreciated, but even then you don't believe them. You think it is a mirage or some optical illusion made possible by sideshow mirrors. To put it feebly, the Seton Hall acrobat is a whole show by himself."[5]

"Halley's Comet has a rival today," exclaimed sports writer David Eisenberg. "Bob Davies is the new satellite, and the firmament across which he blazes in brilliant hue, is a basketball court."[6]

"That sealed my popularity, so to speak, in the New York area," commented Bob, "and as New York goes, so goes the country."[7]

Rather than celebrate his coronation as a sports legend and his team's 70–54 NIT victory, Bob visited Assistant Athletic Director Father James A. Carey in his hotel room, drank a Coke and ate a sandwich, returned to his room, and fell asleep.[8]

Five years later, African-American Jim Dilworth, who, as a junior high school student, had witnessed Davies' NIT histrionics, dribbled behind his back in the Colored (now Central) Intercollegiate Athletic Association (CIAA) tournament.[9]

Three years after Dilworth, Holy Cross College basketball magician Bob Cousy unveiled his behind-the-back dribble. All his life, Davies remained philosophical about Cousy receiving credit for inventing the behind-the-back dribble, pioneering the penetration (moving the ball deeper within the defense by dribbling and passing to create a closer shot opportunity) and transition (fast breaking for an open shot) styles of play, and creating several innovative passes. After Davies retired, Cousy benefited from the expansion of the National Basketball Association (NBA) to the west coast and an exponential increase in its national TV coverage. Cousy hired an agent, co-authored five books and was the subject of three more, plus a plethora of *Sports Illustrated* magazine articles. On the other hand, Davies never retained an agent and has been featured in only six national magazine articles, one each in *Liberty, Newsweek, PM, Sport, Basketball Digest,* and *Sports Illustrated,* and a book chapter in Charles Salzberg's excellent *From Set Shot to Slam Dunk: The Glory Days of Basketball in the Words of Those Who Played It.* [10]

Undeservedly, the legendary Bob Davies, one of the greatest players in the history of collegiate basketball, has been almost forgotten. *Sports Illustrated 100 Years of Hoops,* however, in 1991 recognized his status as "a critical transition figure" and one of the eight most influential players in the first century of college basketball. The other seven cagers in this group are U.S. Senator Bill Bradley (Princeton University); the dominating center of the 1990s, Patrick Ewing (Georgetown University); the precursor of seven-footers, Bob Kurland (Oklahoma A&M); the first great player of the modern basketball era, Hank Luisetti (Stanford University); the basketball showman of showmen, Pete Maravich (Louisiana State University); the extraordinary vertical leaper, David Thompson (North Carolina State University); and the dynamic center, Bill Walton (UCLA).[11]

The name Bob Davies, however, was well known in mid-20th-century basketball circles. He received the sixth-most votes for *Sport* magazine's All-Time All-American College Basketball Team selected in 1955. DePaul University center George Mikan, the greatest basketball player of the first half of the 20th century, received the most votes, followed by Stanford University forward Hank Luisetti, who fathered the one-hand push shot and several innovative passes. The recent 1950 Holy Cross graduate Bob Cousy was the only guard selected for the *Sport* team, and the 1954 National Player of the Year, LaSalle University forward Tom Gola, was chosen for the fourth slot. Davies received two fewer votes than Pittsburgh University forward Charles D. "Chuck" Hyatt, who, in the 1920s, had been College Player of the Year, national scoring leader, and a three-time First Team All American.[12]

Bob Davies has also been recognized as one of the greatest professional basketball players.

Davies' Naismith Memorial Basketball Hall of Fame plaque recognizes him as the "first Super Star of Modern Professional Basketball."

The renowned Boston Celtics coach Red Auerbach identified Bob

Davies, "the creator of the behind-the-back dribble," as one of eight legendary players who had made an indelible mark on the game of basketball. The other seven cagers were Hank Luisetti for introducing the one-handed shot, George Mikan for making the hook shot a deadly offensive weapon, Wilt "The Big Dipper" Chamberlain for popularizing the dunk, Kareem Abdul-Jabbar for the sky hook, Bob Cousy for popularizing the behind-the-back dribble, Oscar Robertson as the model for the do-it-all guard, and Sam Jones for crafting the bank shot off the backboard. [13]

Fifteen years after Davies' retirement from professional basketball, the NBA in 1970 honored him as one of the top ten players during its first quarter century. Other members of the NBA Silver Anniversary Team included guards Bob Cousy, Bill Sharman, and Sam Jones (Boston Celtics), centers George Mikan (Minneapolis Lakers) and Bill Russell (Boston Celtics), and forwards Bob Pettit (St. Louis Hawks), Dolph Schayes (Syracuse Nationals), and Paul Arizin and Joe Fulks (Philadelphia Warriors).[14]

Unfortunately, recognition as the greatest guard of his collegiate era and one of the greatest in the early NBA years did not guarantee Bob Davies lasting fame. He never played west of Denver in the continental United States. "Nobody really knew about me except the other players," Davies said in 1977. [15] The reason: he played for the Rochester Royals in upstate New York before the NBA became a fixture on national television. When Davies retired in 1955, the league numbered eight teams with the westernmost in Minneapolis, Minnesota, the southernmost in Baltimore, Maryland, and the easternmost in Boston, Massachusetts. During his last two seasons, a total of 32 NBA games were nationally televised, mostly in the northeast and midwest.[16] Ironically, the last major national media story about Bob Davies, a 1980 *Sports Illustrated* (circulation 2,287,159) article, focused more on his character than his basketball exploits, and identified him as the prototype for the mythical sports-hero role model character Chip Hilton featured in 23 juvenile fiction books. [17]

"For me, the love was in the game," said modest Bob Davies. "I love basketball and I wanted to see it get better. If somebody else got the credit for some of the things I did, that's okay. I have to admit, I would rather have the credit come where it should, but at least the game was the final winner."[18]

Three quarters of a century, the usual period between appearances of Halley's Comet, has passed since Bob Davies shocked the Mecca of Basketball with his ball-handling wizardry. There are few, if any, alive who can claim *I was there that night*. As Joe Gergen commented in *Newsday* after Davies died in 1990: "The NBA, indeed all basketball, is in his debt." It is time that Bob Davies is again acknowledged for his contributions, not only to basketball as an innovative player, but to society as a real sports-hero role model.[19]

NOTES

1   "Bob Davies: Davies, Harrisburg Court Player All-American," Bob Davies Scrapbook, Joseph M. O'Brien Historical Resource Center, Naismith Memorial Basketball Hall of Fame, Springfield, MA (hereafter cited as BDSHOF); National Collegiate Athletic Association, *Official 2007 NCAA Men's Basketball Records Book*, 53.

2   Joe Gergen, "Of Showtime And the Real Chip Hilton," *Newsday,* April 26, 1990; Dan Parker, "Garden Goes All Out for Seton Hall and Davies," *New York Daily Mirror,* March 22, 1941; "the basketball capital," Arthur Daley, "Basketball Is In!" *Sport,* Jan. 1947, 15. "legend … 3(d): one around whom such stories and traditions have grown up: one having had a special status as a result of possessing or being held to possess extraordinary qualities that are usu. partly real and partly mythical." Philip Babcock Gove, Ph.D, ed.-in-chief, *Webster's Third New International Dictionary Of The English Language Unabridged*, 1290. "legendary adj.: of, relating to, or having the characteristics of a legend," Ibid.

3   Russian ballet dancer Vaslav Nijinsky was admired for his seemingly gravity-defying leaps and was regarded as the early 20th century's greatest male dancer.

4   "All stops": "Davies Awes Record Garden Crowd: Seton Hall Ace Has Field Day on Court," *Newark (NJ) News*, March 20, 1941.

5   "You can take": Everett B. Morris, "Seton Hall Five Routs Rhode Island State, 70–54; LIU Also Gains," *New York Herald-Tribune,* March 20, 1941.

6   "Halley's Comet": David Eisenberg, "Davies Season's Standout Cager:

Setonian Fine Shot, Passer and Dribbler," *New York Journal-American*, March 20, 1941.

7   "That sealed": Charles Salzberg, *From Set Shot to Slam Dunk: The Glory Days of Basketball in the Words of Those Who Played It*, 49.

8   Joe Cummiskey, "Bob Davies Also Good Ball Player," BDSHOF.

9   Joe Goldstein, "Davies dribbles his way into history," http://espn. go.com/classic/s/goldstein_behind_the_back.html.

10   Bill Reynolds, *Cousy: His Life, Career, and the Birth of Big-Time Basketball*, 18, 76–77; http://sportsillustrated.com/vault/search?term=Bob+Cousy. For books by and about Bob Cousy see Bibliography listings under Cousy, Devaney, Gelman, Kirkpatrick, and Reynolds.

11   "a critical transition figure": Alexander Wolff, *Sports Illustrated: 100 Years of Hoops*, 88; Ibid. 82, 86, 90, 96, 98, 100, 108, 110.

12   "Basketball's All-Time All-America," *Sport,* March 1955, 21–23; George Beahon, "In This Corner" column in Rochester Royals Scrapbook 1954–55 Season, Joe Cronin Collection, Joseph M. O'Brien Historical Resource Center, Naismith Memorial Basketball Hall of Fame, Springfield, MA (hereafter cited as RRSHOF with season designation); Gerald Eskenazi, "Pro Basketball: Tom Gola, a Philadelphia Basketball Legend, Dies at 81," *The New York Times* (hereafter *NYT*), Jan. 27, 2014; http://www.hoophall. com/hall-of-famers/tag/charles-d-chuck-hyatt.

13   "the creator": Red Auerbach with Joe Fitzgerald, *On And Off The Court*, 25; Ibid, 24.

14   *Sporting News, Official 1971–72 National Basketball Association Guide,* 138–9.

15   "Nobody really": Don Bowman, "Davies: Basketball's celebrated unknown," *Ft. Meyers (FL) News-Press*, July 27, 1977.

16   Paul Pinckney, "In the Pink," *Rochester Democrat and Chronicle* (hereafter *"D&C")*, Dec. 13, 1953; "Celts Top Bullets On TV, 106–105, *D&C,* Dec. 13, 1953; Al C. Weber, "Royal–Celtics TV Game Launches Season Oct. 30," RRSHOF 1954–55.

17   Jack McCallum, "A Hero For All Times," *Sports Illustrated*, Jan. 7, 1980, 50–56, 58–60; *'80 Ayer Directory of Publications*, 639.

18   For me": Don Bowman, "Davies: Basketball's celebrated unknown," *Ft. Meyers (FL) News-Press*, July 27, 1977.

19   *New Encyclopedia Britannica*, 5th ed., *s.v.* "Halley's Comet"; "The NBA": Gergen, "Of Showtime," *Newsday*, April 26, 1990.

HARRISBURG HOUDINI

MARBLES ACE

The Davies Comet first burst upon the American sports firmament in 1931 when, as an 11-year-old, Bob finished third in the National Marbles Tournament. During the Great Depression, millions of youngsters played marbles, the truly All-American sport, open to everyone regardless of sex, race, creed, color, or economic status. Any child could afford common clay marbles, costing a penny a handful, and could scratch a ring on a sidewalk or in the dirt. The *Scripps-Howard* newspaper chain sponsored a national marbles competition open to boys and girls ages 6 to 14. In 1930, three million American youth participated in school and then city or county elimination tournaments. Leonard Tyner, a 13-year-old African-American orphan, won the 1936 national championship.[1]

Competing against 5,700 boys and girls, Bob Davies won the Harrisburg, Pennsylvania, city tournament in June 1931. He had developed a back spinner that enabled him to keep his shooter marble in the ten-foot diameter ring and continue shooting and knocking out his opponents' marbles. The player who knocked out the most marbles won the game.[2]

"Boys and girls of the *Harrisburg Telegraph* Marble Tournament," intoned the nascent sports-hero role model Bob Davies, "it gives me great pleasure to be with you here today, as the city champion. I am leaving tomorrow for Ocean City [New Jersey] with but one thought in mind and that is to capture National honors for our great city. I know

The All American Edris and Esther Davies family gathered for their only family portrait at the time of Bob's marriage to Mary Helfrich: From left, Top Row: father Edris, Bob, mother Esther, Tom, Bill; bottom row: Bettye, Ed, and Dick (Aug. 8, 1942, Courtesy of Mary Davies)

all of you will be rooting for me to come through. May the best kid win."

Cheering on Bob the next day at the railroad station, a hundred well wishers yelled in unison: "Bring back the bacon!"[3]

In Ringer Stadium on the Ocean City boardwalk, Bob, wearing a sweater emblazoned *Harrisburg,* parlayed his skill at pitching a penny closest to a wall into winning the lag by tossing a marble nearer than his competitor to a line ten feet away and earning the first shot in the game. He captured the Mideastern League title with 20 victories and 5 defeats.[4]

"Robert Davies is a real contender," said a tournament referee. "He's a true blue sportsman and he deserves to win. He certainly has been doing some fancy shooting."[5]

Performing in front of 10,000 spectators, Bob, the youngest and smallest competitor, lost in the semifinal round to the eventual national champion. "I have had the time of my life, thanks to the *Harrisburg Telegraph*," said Bob upon returning to the Pennsylvania capital city laden with, instead of bacon, four pounds of candy, a bronze trophy, and 150 marbles.[6]

DEPRESSION LIFE

Bob was growing up during the worst economic depression in modern American history. Approximately one-third of the breadwinners in the United States and 40 percent of those in Pennsylvania were out of work. Nationwide, one in ten families lost their home to foreclosure. Unemployed men sold apples on street corners. Little boys stole chunks of coal from railroad cars to heat their homes and pilfered bottles of milk from front porches for their hungry sisters and brothers. In Washington, DC, 100 miles from Harrisburg, U.S. Army soldiers used bayonets and tear gas to disperse 23,000 destitute and desperate World War I veterans who had marched on the nation's capital seeking early payment of a bonus so that they could feed their families.[7]

The year after Bob's fancy shooting in the National Marbles Tournament, his father, Edris, lost his job. A bank foreclosed on the Davies home, and the family lived three months with grandparents in nearby Hummelstown. It was not a good year, either, for Bob in the marbles ring. He lost the Harrisburg tournament final round in "four stirring ring battles" to two-years-older Bill Canning. "Fine work, Bill," said competitor and sportsman Bob. "I'll be out again next year to try to win the title again."[8]

Although Edris Davies found work as an accountant with the Works Projects Administration (WPA), which provided employment on public construction projects, his paycheck and monthly food allotment were insufficient to provide for a growing family blessed with four fine boys. As the oldest son, Bob did his best to help his family. He sold magazines and doughnuts door to door, clerked in a neighborhood store, and delivered groceries, charging ten cents a trip and earning 50 cents on an especially profitable day. He dutifully and unselfishly turned over all earnings to his parents. Every nickel and dime helped—a loaf of bread or a can of pork and beans cost five cents, a box of breakfast cereal ten cents, and four cans of soup or two dozen oranges 25 cents.[9]

"I don't know how mother kept us fed," said fourth-oldest brother Ed, "but she always had food on the table." Mrs. Davies walked a mile and three-quarters, sometimes through snow or rain, to a discount food store, bought groceries, including day-old bread and evaporated milk that she watered down for extra portions, and pulled the bags uphill in a child's play wagon to the family home. [10]

The Davies children passed down clothes to the next oldest until worn out. The only girl, Bettye, donned her brothers' worn-out blue jeans to play with neighborhood kids. Dick, the youngest child, wore Bettye's pink pants for outdoor activities because his bigger brothers' hand-me-downs were torn to shreds. [11]

"We wouldn't have survived without mother," said third-oldest son Bill. "She didn't know what it was to quit. She taught us to stick to it, never give up." [12] Faith in God helped sustain the family. Esther Davies, proud of her Pennsylvania Dutch heritage, had her children baptized as Lutherans and every Sunday walked with them to church. The kids attended Sunday school classes and then, as their mother sang in the choir, sat in the front pew during the adult service. One Christmas Day, Mrs. Davies cried because she and her husband could not afford presents for the children.[13]

"But we had a happy childhood and enjoyed each other," recalled Bill. "We really loved each other and our parents. There were some other kids in the neighborhood who ate well and had all the material things they wanted, but they said they'd rather be in the Davies family."[14]

MORE MARBLES

Due to junior high school track and baseball team commitments, Bob, again the Harrisburg marbles champion, arrived late at the 1934 Pennsylvania State Marbles Tournament. He played as many as 15 games a day to catch up and defeated all challengers to win the state title. In Illinois, ten-year-old George Mikan won his county marbles tournament and met baseball hero Babe Ruth. Gangly George, almost as tall as the Babe, would become known as the "Babe Ruth of Basketball" and frequently frustrate Bob Davies' NBA championship ambitions. George, however, did not win his state tournament.[15]

Competing again in the National Tournament in Ocean City, Bob won the preliminary Midwestern League, but lost in the semifinal round. "I got a twitch in my thumb," said right-handed Bob. The Columbia Broadcasting System (CBS) introduced a pint-sized competitor's name to the nation's radio listeners. Future Brooklyn Dodger shortstop Harold "Pee Wee" Reese, nicknamed after his favorite marble, finished second overall. In little more than a decade, Bob Davies and Pee Wee Reese would play significant supporting roles in the integration of American professional sports.[16]

DISCOVERING BASKETBALL

By the time that he competed in the 1934 National Marbles Tournament, Bob had been playing basketball about five years. Before the stock market crash in 1929, his parents could afford the Harrisburg Central YMCA 25-cent weekly membership fee. Assistant Y Director Walter E. Kirker introduced Bob to the hoop sport. After Mr. Davies lost his job, however, Bob, too poor to pay YMCA dues or buy a basketball, and without access to a gym, had to figure out a way to play his favorite sport. He and his friends marked off a court in an alley, nailed a five-gallon paint can to a board on a telephone pole, and used a tennis ball. On this alley court, Bob developed juke moves, keeping the ball away from three or four other youngsters. When it snowed, the boys shoveled off the court and kept playing. [17]

RACIAL RELATIONS

The two Harrisburg high school basketball teams played home games in the Chestnut Street Market House second-floor Madrid Palestra Ballroom, where on other nights African-American musical talents like Louis "Satchmo" Armstrong, Count Basie, Duke Ellington, and teenager Ella Fitzgerald performed. Unable to afford basketball game tickets, Bob peeked through a crack in the ballroom door. His field of vision encompassed only the backboard and three feet either side of the foul lane at one end of the court. [18]

"I'd see these great black players jump in the air, throw the ball, hit somebody with a pass, or shoot the ball, and I guess that stuck in my mind," said Bob. "I think that's what helped me to become a playmaker. I always figured that it was best just to get the ball down the court, get there first, and get in a two-on-one situation where I could pass off for a goal rather than score myself." Peeking through the crack, he probably saw black players laying up (not yet dunking) the ball with their hands closer to the rim than whites, taking horizontal jumping shots, and making no-look, hesitation, leaping one-handed, and behind-the-neck and back passes.[19]

As a young boy, Bob appreciated the creativity, artistry, grace, and rhythm of African-American basketball. "He watched the blacks because they did more stuff than the whites," said his widow Mary.[20]

"When it's played the way it's spozed to be played," points out celebrated African-American author and University of Pennsylvania All-Ivy League basketball forward John Edgar Wideman, "basketball happens in the air; flying, floating, elevated above the floor, levitating the way oppressed peoples of this earth imagine themselves in their dreams."[21]

The Davies children walked to and from school through a racially mixed neighborhood. About 6,000 (7½ percent) of Harrisburg's 80,000 residents were African Americans. Public schools, streetcars, movie theatres, and the Catholic and Episcopal churches were integrated. An African-American doctor served pro-bono as physician and trainer at high school sporting events that both blacks and whites attended. At Edison Junior High School, the track team comprised 60-yard-dash man and long jumper Bob Davies, seventeen other whites, and seven blacks.[22]

But traces of Jim Crow, named for a stereotyped 19th-century black man song-and-dance act, existed in Harrisburg, located 35 miles north of the Mason-Dixon Line that symbolized the boundary between pre-Civil War northeastern Free states and southern slave-holding states. "Jim Crowism," a racist system embodied in law (state statutes, zoning and other local ordinances, deed covenants, and judicial decisions) and custom (law enforcement policies, private rules, and social pressure), was based on the concept of white supremacy and primarily

Youthful track star Bob Davies, first row, third from left, participated on inte-grated sports teams while attending Edison Junior High School and John Harris High School in Harrisburg, PA. (c.1934, Harrisburg School District)

directed against blacks.[23] Harrisburg African-Americans worshiped in their own Baptist and Methodist churches, belonged to their own YMCA, and transacted business at an African-American savings and loan association. Eleven hotels hosted whites and one welcomed blacks. Blacks were not allowed to use public swimming facilities, try on clothes in white-owned stores, or sit at the bar in white taverns but could take out beverages and food.[24]

TEAM BASKETBALL

Bob enjoyed his first team basketball experience. A small and quick seventh grader, he was second leading scorer on the undefeated, inte-grated Edison Junior High School junior varsity squad. It is part of the Bob Davies legend in Harrisburg that, while his family tempo-rarily resided in Hummelstown, he walked and ran approximately ten miles each way to and from Edison Junior High School so that he could continue playing on this team until the season ended. [25]

But Bob's eighth- and ninth-grade junior high school varsity basketball team experiences were not encouraging. "I remember Bob,"
said Harris Freedman, an opposing junior-high squad member. "He
was so small he didn't get to play, but he could really handle the ball.
I thought he was the ball boy." [26]

Buried on the bench in ninth grade as 14th man, Bob became
extremely frustrated. His father told him to stop pitying himself and
work harder on improving his skills. Thanks largely to the encour-
agement of Coach Shorty "The Meteoric Midget" Miller, a 5' 5", 145-
pound Penn State University All-American Second Team quarterback,
Bob persevered and progressed to be the junior high varsity's number
one substitute.[27]

The discouraging trend continued in high school. As a five-foot,
90-pound sophomore, Bob began the season as 12th man on the
John Harris High School junior varsity basketball team, and played
very little in games. He admired African-American varsity star Dick
Felton's speedy, high-jumping and quick-passing style, and tried to
imitate him. Near the end of the season, Bob earned a starting position
and the honor of junior varsity team captain. Half a century later he
believed that this accomplishment may have been the most satisfying
experience in his extraordinary basketball career.[28]

Eight inches taller his junior year, Bob made the varsity team. One
of his best friends, African-American Walter "Ducky" Brown, threw
behind-the-back passes, and Bob made unconventional, leaping over-
hand passes. Bob always acknowledged that he patterned his style of
play after Dick Felton and Ducky Brown.[29]

As a senior, skinny 5' 11", 142-pound team captain Bob Davies led
the John Harris High School Pioneers to an unexceptional five win
and seven loss record and a Central Pennsylvania Scholastic League
fifth place finish. As leading team and second highest league scorer
with an 11.2 points-per-game average, Bob garnered All-League First
Team honors. His school yearbook memorialized him as "one of the
greatest players ever developed in the region."[30]

In the unofficial Harrisburg city championship game against
archrival William Penn High School, Bob turned in the best performance of his high school career. The William Penn cagers could not

Bob Davies, the Harrisburg Houdini, earned All-Central Pennsylvania Scholastic League First Team Honors and stunned opponents with spectacular passes. (1937, Harrisburg School District)

stop him, so they fouled him. Three opponents fouled out pummeling him. He did not complain and sank all 13 free throws. "His coolness at all times was largely responsible for the John Harris High win," noted a Harrisburg sports writer.[31]

HIGH SCHOOL LEGACY

The John Harris High School yearbook editors described the well-rounded Bob Davies: "Personality, athletic ability, and popularity all rolled into one bundle of white-headed fury. That's 'Bob,' who is well liked by all and is a good student as well as an excellent athlete." The second four-sport letterman in John Harris High School history, Bob, as captain and shortstop, steadied the baseball team; played a flashy end and tackled with devastating effect on the football team; and, in track and field, high-jumped five feet five inches and narrowly lost a 50-yard dash to the Harrisburg city record holder.[32]

Athletes at rival William Penn High School admired Bob and compared him to Jack Armstrong, the All-American boy. During the 1930s, American boys and girls listened to the tremendously popular, nationally broadcast Jack Armstrong juvenile adventure radio series. Jack, a fictionalized ideal teenager, natural leader, and incredible athlete, traveled around the globe, tracking down evil-doers in a hydraplane, and, when home, single-handedly won games in the last minute for his high school team. Kids mailed in Wheaties box tops for premiums such as a "Dragon's Eye Ring," "Hike-O-Meter," or explorer telescope just like Jack Armstrong used.[33]

Unlike Jack Armstrong, however, Bob was not a sensation at every sport. Bob tried ice-skating, but gave it up because he could not master the Ice Follies maneuver of skating with his feet placed laterally to his body. "I guess if I couldn't be with the best," Bob said, "I didn't want to play."[34]

COLLEGE BOUND

The Davies family was enthusiastic about sports, but also recognized the value of higher education. Bob's parents, who never had an opportunity to attend college, convinced him that college graduates had a better chance of keeping their jobs in an economic downturn. Bob buckled down his junior year and devoted more time to his studies. He did not know how he could pay for a college education, but he was determined to get one. [35]

No collegiate basketball power recruited the Harrisburg Houdini. Only Franklin & Marshall (F&M), a small liberal arts college in nearby Lancaster, Pennsylvania, expressed an interest in him. He received a tuition-only scholarship and waited on tables to earn his breakfast. Weekends he hitchhiked home, 35 miles each way, and returned to school with ten peanut butter or single-slice baloney sandwiches for the upcoming week's lunches and dinners. Hitchhiking, working, studying, and playing up-tempo basketball, he often felt tempted to snack on a sandwich but disciplined himself so that his food supply lasted all week. Friday's sandwiches were often moldy.[36]

Filled out to 6' 1" and 165 pounds, Bob led the Eastern Pennsylvania Collegiate Basketball Conference Freshman League in scoring with a

22 points-per-game average and the F&M Blue and White freshman team to an undefeated, 11-win season. In his highest scoring effort, 31 points against Lebanon Valley College, his teammates near the end of the game kept feeding him the ball, but he refused to shoot and passed it back to them. According to the F&M yearbook, Bob "netted two-pointers with deadly accuracy, displaying remarkable floor work, both as a play-maker and the most important cog in the frosh whirlwind attack." After watching Bob embarrass the opposition with his speed and skill, Muhlenberg College (Allentown, PA) varsity basketball coach Doggie Julian (later Bob Cousy's Holy Cross mentor) said that Bob Davies was the best young player he had seen in 20 years. [37]

But Bob did not enjoy his experience at Franklin & Marshall. Unable to afford textbooks the first three months of school, he failed algebra and biology and was placed on academic probation. He really wanted to play baseball, but F&M did not have a team, so on weekends he joined a semi-pro town team. He decided to withdraw from F&M because certain recruiting promises had not been fulfilled.[38]

That summer Bob played shortstop for the semi-professional Palmyra and Highspire town teams in the Lebanon Valley and Dauphin County Leagues. Impressed by his slick glove work, fielding range, accurate throwing arm, and .341 batting average, major league scouts tried to sign him to a professional baseball contract, but he rejected their overtures because he was determined to complete his college education.[39]

Boston Red Sox scout Jack Egan suggested a practical solution. He signed Bob to an option contract and arranged a Seton Hall College baseball scholarship for him. Under the contract terms, as permitted by the National Collegiate Athletic Association (NCAA), the Red Sox paid Bob a bonus and $300 ($5,040 today) each year, and he agreed to work out with the Seton Hall baseball coach his first 30 days in school, play on the college baseball team, and, if he decided to play professional baseball, join the Red Sox. Egan felt sure that Bob would tire of studying and eagerly report for the next spring training.[40]

NOTES

1   "Birth Announcement," *Harrisburg (PA) Evening News,* Jan. 16, 1920 (DOB
     Jan. 15, 1920); "Jeffries Wins Title In Marbles Tourney," *NYT,* June 27,
     1931; http//akronmarbles.com/players_ history_ the_ game_ of_ ringer.
     htm; Michael C. Cohill, e-mail to author, Dec. 29, 2013; "8 Survive
     Marbles Test," *NYT,* June 25, 1931; "Chicago Boy Wins Title At Marbles,"
     NYT, July 3, 1936.
     The National Marbles Tournament, still held annually in Wildwood,
     NJ, claims to be the nation's longest-running youth sports event. John
     W. Miller, "These Children of the Digital Age Play for All the Marbles,"
     Wall Street Journal, June 16, 2014.
2   "Lincoln Boy Wins City Marble Title; In National Series," *Harrisburg (PA)*
     Telegraph, June 15, 1931.
3   "Boys and girls" and "Bring back": "City Marble Champion Leaves For
     Ocean City," *Harrisburg Telegraph,* June 20, 1931.
4   Wellington G. Jones, "Marble Champion From City Holds Lead In
     League," *Harrisburg Telegraph,* June 23, 1931; Bill Davies, telephone
     conversation with author, June 18, 2013.
5   "Robert Davies": Wellington G. Jones, "Tops Mideastern League With 20
     Ring Victories," *Harrisburg Telegraph,* June 24, 1931.
6   "Wellington G. Jones, "Harrisburg Boy Is Eliminated In Marble Play,"
     Harrisburg Telegraph, June 25, 1931; "I have": "Marble Prizes To Be
     Presented Winners In City," *Harrisburg Telegraph,* June 27, 1931.
7   Page Smith, 8 *Redeeming The Time, A People's History Of The 1920s And*
     The New Deal, 295, 299, 301, 336–39; "The Great Depression," http://
     www.portal.state.pa.us.
8   Bill Davies, telephone conversations with author, May 21 and 30, 2008;
     "Fine work": "Steelton Boy Captures City Marble Title," *Harrisburg*
     Telegraph, June 17, 1932.
9   Bill Davies telephone conversations with author, May 21 and 30,
     2008; Smith, *Redeeming Time,* 612–13, 840–42; Mary Davies, telephone
     conversation with author, May 16, 2007; Ralph Hyman, "The Davies
     Story: Hero-Worshiping Father Raised His Own Hero: Robert Edris
     Davies," *Rochester (NY) Times-Union* (hereafter cited as *T-U*), March 10,
     1953; http://www.thepeoplehistory.com/30sfood.html.
10   "I don't": Ed Davies, telephone conversation with author, April 7, 2009.

11   Bettye Davies Frierson, telephone conversation with author, April 8,
     2009; Dick Davies, telephone conversation with author, April 4, 2009.

12   "We wouldn't": Bill Davies telephone conversation with author, May 21,
     2008.

13   Bill Davies, telephone conversation with author, Sept. 14, 2011.

14   "But we had": Bill Davies, telephone conversation with author, April 6,
     2009.

15   "Robert Davies City Champion," *Harrisburg Telegraph,* June 12, 1934;
     "Harrisburg Lad Wins Marble Tournament," *York (PA) Dispatch,* June 11,
     1934; "Harrisburg Boy In Title Race," *Harrisburg Telegraph,* June 28, 1934;
     George L. Mikan and Joseph Oberle, *Unstoppable: The Story of George
     Mikan, The First NBA Superstar,* 3–4.

16   "I got": Mary Davies, telephone conversation with author, Feb. 8, 2011;
     "Husing Again to Broadcast Marble Tourney Finals Here," *Ocean City
     (NJ) Sentinel-Ledger,* June 8, 1934; Gene Schoor, *The Pee Wee Reese Story,*
     20.

17   Jack Freed, "Bob Davies Recalls Start at City 'Y,'" *Harrisburg Patriot,* May
     7, 1971; Tom Lassiter, "Hall of Fame Basketball Player Bob Davies Dies
     At 70," *Sun (Ft. Lauderdale, FL) Sentinel,* April 23, 1970; Mike McKenzie,
     "Bob Davies: A Pioneer in the Backcourt," *Basketball Digest,* Jan. 1975, 60.

18   Jim Newkirk, "Day or Night, Old City Market Was Social Center,"
     Harrisburg Patriot, Sept. 19, 1977.

19   "I'd see": Salzberg, *Set Shot,* 47; Ibid., 45–46; Bob Davies, interview by
     Charles Salzberg, Coral Springs, FL 1986, tape recording and Bob
     Davies-edited transcript, Joseph M. O'Brien Historical Resource Center,
     Naismith Memorial Basketball Hall of Fame, Springfield, MA.

20   Jack Barry, "Davies' Dreams Came True Thanks to Hard Practice,"
     BDSHOF; "He watched": Mary Davies, telephone conversation with
     author, July 26, 2010.

21   Wideman quote from Kareem Abdul-Jabbar with Raymond Obstfeld,
     On The Shoulders Of Giants: My Journey Through the Harlem Renaissance,
     137; https://en.wikipedia.org/wiki/John_Edgar_Wideman.

22   Dick Davies, telephone conversation with author, Jan. 29, 2009; Work
     Projects Administration (WPA), *Pennsylvania: A Guide To The Keystone
     State,* 237–38; Calobe Jackson Jr., telephone conversations with author,
     Oct. 20, 2010 and March 4 and 26, 2013; Calobe Jackson Jr., e-mail

messages to author, March 6, 2013, and Feb. 14, 2014; Edison Junior High School track team picture, courtesy of Harrisburg School District, Harrisburg, PA.

23   C. Vann Woodward, *The Strange Career of Jim Crow: A Commemorative Edition,* passim; Stetson Kennedy, *Jim Crow Guide: The Way it Was,* 7, 26, 34, 73, 75, 190, 205.

24   Calobe Jackson Jr., telephone conversation with author, July 22, 2008.

25   Bill Davies, telephone conversations with author, May 21 and 30, 2008.

26   "I remember": Harris Freedman, telephone conversation with author, July 22, 2008.

27   Salzberg, *Set Shot,* 46; "Shorty 'The Meteoric Midget' Miller," http://www.collegefootball.org/famersearch; "Services Tomorrow For 'Shorty' Miller," *Harrisburg Patriot,* Sept. 22, 1966.

28   Salzberg, *Set Shot,* 46; Hyman, "Hero-Worshipping," *T-U,* March 10, 1953.

29   Nick Horvath, Jr., "At 60, Bob Davies Still Looks Like Top Cager," BDSHOF; *John Harris High School Pioneer* (1936): 89, 90.

30   "one of": *John Harris High School Pioneer* (1937): 188; ibid., 190–91.

31   Harris Freedman, telephone conversation with author, July 22, 2008; "His coolness": "J-Harris High Five Rallies to Win 30–26," *Harrisburg Patriot,* March 11, 1937.

32   "Personality": *John Harris High School Pioneer* (1937): 64; ibid., 184, 189, 192, 197; "Lancaster High Track Team Wins," *Harrisburg Patriot,* May 3, 1937; Hyman, "Hero-Worshipping," *T-U,* March 10, 1953.

33   Ronnie Christ, "Davies may have been the first 'magic man', " *Harrisburg Patriot-News,* April 27, 1990; Bruce Anderson, "His Career Still Reads Like a Novel," *Miami (FL) Herald,* April 6, 1980; John Dunning, *On the Air: The Encyclopedia of Old-time Radio,* 352–55; http://en.wikipedia.org/wiki/Jack_Armstrong, _the_All_American_Boy.

34   "I guess": Jack Barry, "Davies' Dreams Came True Thanks to Hard Practice," *Boston Globe,* BDSHOF.

35   Hyman, "Hero-Worshiping Dad," *T-U,* March 10, 1953.

36   Mary Davies, interview by author, Lake Mary, FL, Dec. 3, 2007; Bill Davies, telephone conversation with author, May 21, 2008.

37   "Lebanon Valley Passers Top F. and M. 63–48 Score," *Lancaster (PA) Daily Intelligencer Journal,* Feb. 18, 1938; "netted two-pointers": "Freshman

Basketball," Franklin & Marshall College *1938 Oriflamme,* 97; Elliot
Cushing, "Sports Eye View," *D&C,* Nov. 16, 1948.

38   Mary Davies, telephone conversation with author, Jan. 22, 2009;
Robert Edris Davies Franklin & Marshall College 1937–1938 transcript
(admitted Sept. 16, 1937), Registrar Office, F&M College, Lancaster, PA;
Bus Funk, "Cruising Around," *Harrisburg Patriot,* May 13, 1938; Charles
Wimbert Taylor, "A History of Intercollegiate Athletics at Franklin and
Marshall College" (Master's Thesis, F&M, 1962), 120–21.

39   Bus Funk, "Cruising Around," *Harrisburg Patriot,* Aug. 17, 1938.

40   Salzberg, *Set Shot,* 46–47; "Davies to Seton Hall," BDSHOF; Ellen L.
Summers, NCAA Librarian, e-mail message to author, Sept. 22, 2005;
Samuel H. Williamson, "Seven Ways to Compute the Relative Value
of a U.S. Dollar amount, 1774 to the present," Measuring Worth, 2015,
URL:www.measuringworth.com/uscompare/ (hereafter cited as
"Measuring Worth").

LI'L ABNER AND THE WONDER FIVE

FRESH OFF THE CENTRAL PENNSYLVANIA BASEBALL DIAMONDS, Bob Davies, in September 1938, walked onto the Seton Hall College campus in South Orange, New Jersey, wearing baggy socks and football shoes without cleats. Students in physical education class immediately noticed his serious demeanor mastering gymnastics and boxing techniques. They nicknamed him "Abby" because of his resemblance to the lovable, homespun cartoon character *Li'l Abner*, who was an innocent paragon of virtue in a wicked and threatening world. Seton Hall's publicity director commented that Bob, "a modest, unaffected guy," with his "shock of yellow hair" and high winter boots, was a dead ringer for the popular comic strip character. A major magazine, *Liberty*, with a circulation of 2,302,298 copies weekly (second in general circulation to the *Saturday Evening Post*), published a highly complimentary article about Bob entitled "Basketball's Li'l Abner."[1]

Five hundred thirty-two white male students attended Seton Hall, a Catholic liberal arts college, located 14 miles west of New York City. Despite the school's small enrollment, its administration sought national prominence through success in athletics. The best-known Catholic university in the United States, Notre Dame, was a major football power. New York metropolitan area schools, such as Saint John's University, New York University (NYU), City College of New York (CCNY), and Long Island University (LIU), were drawing large crowds to Madison Square Garden for basketball doubleheaders. Hoping to take advantage of this opportunity, Seton Hall hired

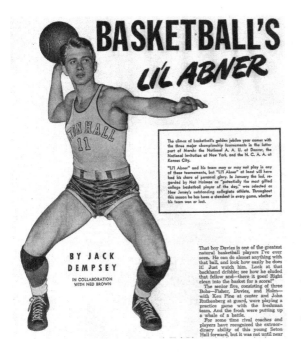

Liberty, *a major national magazine, published a feature article likening Seton Hall College basketball star Bob Davies to the lovable cartoon character "Li'l Abner." (1942, Liberty Library Corp.)*

Hall of Famer John "Honey" Russell, generally regarded as the best professional defensive player of his era, as basketball coach.[2]

BEHIND-THE-BACK DRIBBLE

Shortly after arriving on the Seton Hall campus, Bob saw the Paramount Pictures B-minus romantic comedy *Campus Confessions*, starring future World War II pinup girl Betty Grable and Stanford University All-American basketball player Hank Luisetti. Basketball did not yet enjoy enough status compared to the major sports of baseball, college football, boxing, and horse racing to warrant a national hero like Babe Ruth, Red "The Galloping Ghost" Grange, Jack "The Manassa Mauler" Dempsey, and Triple Crown Winner "Man O' War." If basketball had been more popular, 6' 3", 185-pound Hank Luisetti would have been recognized as its national idol. Dating the modern basketball era from the births of the NIT (1938), the National Basketball League (1938), the eight-team NCAA Tournament (1939), and the National Association of Intercollegiate Basketball (NAIB)

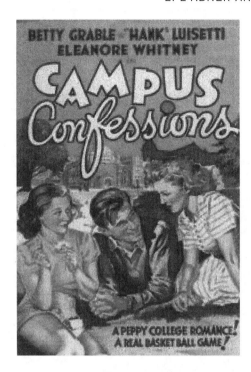

Stanford University All-American Hank Luisetti's performance in the movie Campus Confessions *inspired Bob to create his behind-the-back dribble. (1938, Universal Studios Licensing LLC)*

tournament (1939) for smaller universities and colleges, Luisetti was clearly the first great modern basketball player. During a December 29, 1936, game against Long Island University, Hank amazed a Madison Square Garden crowd with one-handed shooting, creative dribbling, and innovative passing. Luisetti finished his collegiate career as a three-time All-American, two-time college player of the year, and all-time leading college scorer. [3]

According to best-selling author James Michener, seeing Hank Luisetti play basketball constituted "a revelation." Michener watched in disbelief as Luisetti sank staggering, delayed shots, hanging in the air, changing direction, and banking the ball softly into the hoop. "We were seeing the end of a basketball era," wrote Michener, "the beginning of a new world.... It demonstrated that there is always the possibility someone will come along who will be able to do old things in bold new ways." Hard on Luisetti's heels, legendary Bob Davies with his bold innovations would prove to be another such basketball "revelation."[4]

Bob Davies created a sensation in the 1941 National Invitational Tournament (NIT) in Madison Square Garden when he introduced the behind-the-back dribble to a national audience. Here, he executes the dribble on the famous Boston Garden parquet floor for a Wheaties Breakfast cereal TV commercial. (1954, Courtesy of the General Mills Archives/Courtesy of Mary Davies)

Luisetti was actually the player who invented the behind-the-back dribble, albeit different than Davies' version, but Luisetti never received credit for this accomplishment because he may have done it only once in a game. A January 31, 1938, *Life* magazine article picture panel illustrated what Luisetti called a reverse dribble. Bouncing the ball about knee-high with his right hand, Luisetti, with his feet close together, pushed the ball straight down and moved ahead as he slightly changed direction, brought the ball behind his back as he continued changing direction, reversed it to his left hand, and continued at an angle to the basket for a lay-up. In the movie *Campus Confessions*, released in September 1938, Luisetti did not reverse dribble but did dribble the ball behind his back without moving and also through his legs. [5]

After studying the *Life* magazine illustrations and watching Luisetti dribble (not Betty Grable's gorgeous gams) in *Campus Confessions*, Bob Davies decided that he could become America's greatest basketball player if he could dribble behind his back at full speed, going toward and around the man guarding him, and then repeat the move past any other opponents who tried to stop him. "If it involved a ball and took five steps," said Bob's sweetheart and future wife, Mary, "he would figure out how to do it in three steps."[6]

Practicing in his room, Bob, with his right foot on the floor, bounced a ball to his knee-high right hand and then, as he moved forward, behind his back and up to his left hand before his right foot again hit the floor. As he fell asleep, Bob visualized performing this maneuver when pressured on the right side by a defender, and going past him straight ahead without breaking stride. According to Bob's brother Dick, who had a two-week tryout with the Boston Celtics and practiced against Bob Cousy, the Davies behind-the-back dribble differed from Luisetti's and Cousy's in that Davies continued essentially straight ahead rather than veering at an angle.[7]

FROSH FREAK

Armed with his secret weapon, baseball recruit Bob Davies walked uninvited into the Seton Hall freshman basketball team tryouts. Coach Honey Russell watched Bob uninhibitedly running around like a wild gazelle and bumping into other players, and thought that Bob was playing a joke on him. Worse, in Russell's opinion, Bob dribbled a lot, and Russell despised dribblers because most of them refused to give up the ball until they were prevented from further dribbling. But Bob was different; he dribbled with a purpose—to set up passes to open teammates. Recognizing Bob's unmistakable basketball instincts and talent, Coach Russell kept him on the freshman team as ninth man and started trying to tame him into a conventional basketball player. [8]

Even though Bob had played freshman basketball at Franklin & Marshall the previous season, he did not sit out a year before playing for Seton Hall, an independent college unaffiliated with the NCAA or an athletic conference. A transfer student's sports eligibility depended on school policy, not NCAA rules. Smaller colleges typically allowed transfer students to compete immediately after enrollment. Under the NCAA Home Rule approach, institutions also determined their own total year eligibility standards. The four-year limitation was not yet universal. Bob played on a Franklin & Marshall freshman team and on a Seton Hall freshman and three varsity basketball teams for a total of five collegiate seasons. His future NBA nemesis, George Mikan, completed a five-year law program at DePaul University, another non-NCAA affiliated Catholic institution, and played one freshman and four varsity seasons. Both young men were genuine student-athletes. Davies eventually earned a master's degree in physical education and Mikan a bachelor of civil law degree.[9]

During Christmas vacation, Bob publicly unveiled his "dipsy doodle dribble" in the John Harris–William Penn high schools' alumni game in the Harrisburg Central YMCA. "Bob began to dribble down the court with his right hand," wrote Bus Funk in his *Harrisburg Patriot* "Cruising Around" column, "and when a guard closed in on him, he made a motion as though he would pass the ball backward to a mate, but instead of doing that, he twisted the ball around his back to his left side and continued to dribble down the court without missing a stride…. It was the slickest thing your motorman has seen on the hardwood for many a moon."[10]

Back at Seton Hall after Christmas vacation, Coach Russell continued trying to slow down dynamic Bob, who played at too fast a pace for most of his teammates. Accustomed to an up-tempo, fast-breaking style, Bob felt lost in Russell's disciplined half-court offensive system, in which players then designated forwards brought the ball up court and initiated set plays. (Taller players who rebounded and defended the opponent's big men were then designated as guards; beginning in the mid-1940s, the designations were changed and guards handled the ball while forwards played in the front line.) Once Bob demonstrated that he could consistently execute the fast break, however, Coach Russell, to his credit and future success, changed his approach and allowed the freshman team to play Bob's way—fast and creatively.[11]

For the sake of the team's half-court offense, however, Russell insisted that Bob develop the standard outside shot of the day, the two-hand set shot. The Seton Hall freshmen defeated pop singer Kate ("God Bless America") Smith's Celtics, one of the best professional teams, and Bob closely observed their star, Hall of Famer set shot artist Bobby McDermott, and copied his form. Davies held the ball about a foot from his chin with the tips of his fingers spread comfortably and thumbs almost pointed toward each other on the ball's end panels. He tucked his elbows close to his body in a relaxed, comfortable position and adopted a boxer's stance with knees flexed and with his weight mostly on his slightly advanced left foot. Focusing his eyes on the front of the rim, he stepped forward with his left foot, as if to start dribbling, and quickly recoiled if his defender backed up and allowed him room to shoot. With a flick of the wrists in a rotary motion, he rolled the ball outward off his fingertips and released it. He followed through—hands high, palms outward, and feet slightly off the floor. The arc of the shot depended on the defender's closeness and the distance to the hoop. It took him four seasons of practicing to perfect the shot. [12]

"Bob could get off a set shot without it being blocked easier than jump shooters without getting their shots blocked," said younger brother Dick Davies, a high scoring jump shooter for Louisiana State University (LSU). The two-hand set remained the standard outside shot until the early 1950s. With the advent of the jump shot, however, players used it or the one-hand push shot as their primary outside offensive weapon. Most players needed too much time to release a set shot, and few made a satisfactory percentage. Atlantic Hawks player-coach Richie Guerin may have taken the NBA's last "Forgotten Shot" in a 1970 playoff game.[13]

On defense, Bob liked to steal the ball. He was a diver and wore leather knee guards. Very perceptive about committing himself, he tried to take advantage of his opponent's ignorance of his where-abouts as well any dribbling or ball handling weaknesses. Although Coach Russell wanted his man-to-man defenders to stay close to their assigned opponents, he made an exception for Bob, who, with his quickness and superior reflexes, usually recovered if fooled and seldom hurt the team's overall defensive effort.[14]

By mid-season, Bob worked his way into the freshman starting lineup as a forward. Six-foot Bobby "Turnip" Holm and 6' 2" John

The Wonder Five - from left Ken Pine, John Ruthenberg, Bob Fisher, Bob Holm, and Bob Davies, coached by John "Honey" Russell, won forty-three consecutive games. (c. 1942, Artist Louis Raggi/Monsignor William Noel Field Archives & Special Collections Center, Seton Hall University)

"Big John" Ruthenberg filled the guard positions. Mighty-mite 5'9" forward Robert "Little Bobbie" Fisher and 6' 3" center Ken "Porky" Pine rounded out the quintet. After Bob led the frosh to a scrimmage victory over the varsity, Coach Russell awarded him a basketball scholarship. Nicknamed the "Wonder Five," the freshmen quintet won 14 games and lost one by only a point.[15]

SOPHOMORE SEASON

At the beginning of their sophomore season, Coach Russell held the Wonder Five in reserve and substituted them as a unit. After star first-string center 6' 5", 245-pound Edward "Big Ed" Sadowski was injured mid-way through the season, the Wonder Five started the remaining games. Playing home contests on local armory and high school courts, the Seton Hall Pirates compiled a 19–0 record, including victories over St. Bonaventure College, Canisius College, University of Florida, and Tulane University. In the season's final game against the Scranton (PA) University Tom-Cats, "Dazzling Davies" dribbled behind his back, but the befuddled player guarding him lunged past on the wrong side and surprised Bob so badly that he missed a lay-up.

R. DAVIES

Bob Davies entered Seton Hall on a baseball scholarship, and was an All-Star infielder for the Burlington (VT) Cardinals in the semi-pro summer Northern League (c. 1941, Monsignor William Noel Field Archives & Special Collections Center, Seton Hall University)

Although the Pirates were the only major undefeated college team in the country, the Premo Power Poll ranked them 12th. Maintaining an impressive 87 cumulative grade point average in the classroom, "Basketball's Li'l Abner" led the Pirates in scoring, averaging 11.8 points per game (PPG).[16]

After hitting .381 for the Seton Hall varsity baseball team, Bob spent the summer with the Burlington (VT) Cardinals in the semi-professional Northern League a.k.a. "the League with the College Atmosphere." As permitted by the NCAA, players earned as much as $125 ($2,130 today) a month, about the same as a bus driver and a little more than an assembly-line worker or coal miner. Sportswriters marveled at second baseman Bob's ability as the pivot man on double plays. "Davies can play that position like a million bucks," wrote a scribe. "He's the sweetest thing these eyes have seen around the second sack in many a moon." Although he hit only .242, Bob led the league in triples and turning double plays. Chosen as the Cardinals' Most Valuable Player (MVP) during their successful pennant drive, Bob played in the Northern League All-Star Game. At this point in his life, Bob wanted to make the diamond his career.[17]

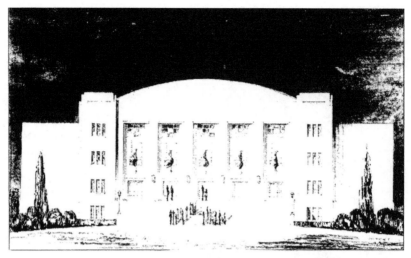

The Seton Hall Walsh Gymnasium was also known as "the house that Bob built." (c.1940, Monsignor William Noel Field Archives & Special Collections Center, Seton Hall University)

43-GAME WIN STREAK

During the Wonder Five's 1940–41 junior season, Seton Hall opened its $800,000 ($13,500,000 today), 3,200-seat Walsh Auditorium-Gymnasium, also known as "the house that Bob built." Newark Diocese Archbishop Thomas J. Walsh, the gym's namesake and president of the Seton Hall board of trustees, presided over games from a half-court balcony seat above the 90-foot-long by 50-foot-wide basketball court. He invited Bob to visit his residence and gave him cash as Christmas and Easter presents. Yet Archbishop Walsh, Seton Hall President Monsignor James Kelley, Assistant Athletic Director Father James A. Carey, and other priests never tried to convert Bob to Catholicism, and he worshipped regularly in a Lutheran church.[18]

The Seton Hall Pirates swashbuckled into the 1940–41 season on a 23-game win streak. Team captain Bob Davies began wearing jersey 11, and kept that number the remainder of his basketball career. He dribbled behind his back in a few games, but never more than once, because Coach Russell, although he recognized the publicity value, believed that the trick had little practical utility. On his 21st birthday, Bob fooled his Villanova University Wildcat defender with the move and scored. "What made it a double gift," said Bob, "was the fact we beat an undefeated club."[19]

While grammar-school student Bob Cousy cavorted on a New York City playground, Bob Davies, despite having "uncommonly small" hands and fingers, created several innovative passes, as well as the modern penetration and transition styles of play. "He changed the game," said Seton Hall and NBA star Frank "Pep" Saul. "When others were just beginning to think of what could be done with a basketball, Bob Davies was out there doing it." Bob dribbled behind his back, through his legs, and also in reverse, shifting gears and changing hands on the ball without slowing down. He did the change-of-pace dribble. He passed behind his back with either hand; looked one way and passed another (no look); jumped, faked a pass in one direction, and delivered it in another (hesitation); looked ahead and passed backward; hung in the air and passed behind his neck; twisted in the air, freezing his defender, faked a shot, and passed; and flicked the ball off his elbows. According to a couple of sports writers, Bob Davies "was born with the peripheral vision of a forward artillery observer and the reflexes of a ballet star" and could "do everything with a basketball but make it say 'uncle'."[20]

Across the nation, moviegoers and sports page readers discovered Bob Davies' ball-handling magic. His legerdemain inspired comparisons to Hank Luisetti's sensational Madison Square Garden performance against Long Island University four years earlier. An Associated Press (AP) reporter commented that "a real hero of the hardwood" like Luisetti or Davies "whose fame spreads outside his own territory" only appeared every two or three basketball generations. Audiences for a month in more than 7,000 movie theaters gasped as they watched Bob dribble behind his back in a *Pathé News* sports newsreel shown between Warner Brothers' double-feature films. *PM (Picture Magazine)*, with a circulation of 165,000, published a story with a picture of his behind-the-back dribble and compared him to *Harold Teen*, a popular syndicated adolescent cartoon character and movie-musical and radio-series hero. Although no national sports or basketball magazine existed, a Buffalo, New York, newspaper reported that Bob's talents were being "expounded at length in magazine layouts and the movie sports reels."[21]

"I like all this fuss being made over me," Bob told a reporter. "Who wouldn't? Yet, don't forget this point. Basketball is still a five-man game and those other players on this team are playing heads-up, adroit ball and to them belongs a share of the credit for the success and spotlight I'm being centered in today."

"You know these boys I'm playing with," he continued, "are the finest unit and the best drilled in the country. This isn't a one-man ball club. Get that idea out of your mind. Honey wouldn't stand for it. He's for unity. Bob Fisher, my co-forward, Center Ken Pine, Guards Bob Holm and Johnnie Ruthenberg—and our second team—are vital factors."[22]

With the high-flying Pirates winning streak at an impressive 40 games, a minute remaining on the clock, and trailing by three points, Bob Davies' field goal and free throw tied the score, and Ken Pine's free throw clinched a 39–38 victory over the University of Scranton.[23]

With Seton Hall trailing the University of Baltimore Bees by a point, and ten seconds remaining on the clock, Baltimore guard Wiseman near mid-court attempted to inbound the ball. Bob Davies laid back, anticipated an angled throw-in, and intercepted the pass. As he dribbled across the half-court line, the timer erroneously blew the horn. Bob ignored the reflex to stop, continued on, and made a lay-up. The referee allowed the field goal because under the rules a game ended with the referee's final whistle. "That play saved our record of two unbeaten seasons, for a total of 42 straight victories," said Coach Russell. "It was a thriller." Bob, who led all scorers with 15 points, considered this game the best of his college career.[24]

Li'l Abner's brilliant intuitive reaction preserved Seton Hall's chance for an NIT bid. Tournament promoters claimed that every coach who had seen both Davies and Luisetti regarded them as equals. CCNY coach Nat Holman, however, called Bob "THE BEST" collegiate or professional basketball player. Honey Russell also rated Davies better than Luisetti because he believed that Hank was fundamentally a scorer, and pointed out that Bob was a scorer, a good defender, and a playmaker who threw perfect, easy-to-handle bullet passes.[25]

The NIT "Halley's Comet" Seton Hall–Rhode Island State game featured Bob Davies and 5' 10", 170-pound Stanley "Stutz" Mod-zelewski, the nation's previous-season leading collegiate scorer. Hit-ting 70 percent of his field goal attempts, Bob outscored Stutz 19 points to 12 and also contributed 9 assists. Newspaper photos showed Bob leaping "like a kangaroo" at the inner foul circle edge, with his knees looking as high as an opponent's shoulders, and sinking a one-hand shot released from his forehead, as well as jumping at the end of a foul line with his body turned toward the center of the court, and releasing from shoulder height a one-hand bounce pass leading to an easy basket. Not only did the crowd set a Madison Square Garden attendance record, Seton Hall and Rhode Island State's combined 124 points and the Pirates' 31 field goals established Garden single-game records.[26]

When Honey Russell substituted for Bob with two minutes remaining in the game, Rhode Island State players joined the crowd in giving him a long ovation. *New York World-Telegram* sports reporter Tim Cohane, inventor of the nickname "Seven Rocks of Granite" for Fordham University's great football linemen, anointed Bob "Basketball's young Barnum" after the great showman and circus owner Phineas T. Barnum and selected Bob as the "Star of the Week" for convincing a record crowd that he was "one of the greatest basket-ball players who ever walked on to a court." *New York Times* reporter Arthur Daley described Bob as "the closest approach to Hank Luisetti ever to show in the Garden and in some few times of court deport-ment... a trifle better than the peerless Stanford wonder." Sports col-umnist Dan Parker of the *New York Daily Mirror*, a widely-read Hearst morning tabloid, wrote that the time had come for Luisetti "to step down from his throne and hand over his scepter to Bob Davies, the new Bey [governor] of Basketball."[27]

In the next NIT game, the Seton Hall Pirates faced Coach Clair Bee's Long Island University Blackbirds. In ten seasons, Bee's basket-ball teams had won a Helms Foundation National Championship,[28] completed two undefeated seasons, and compiled a 43-game win streak. Playing in the Brooklyn College of Pharmacy matchbox gymna-sium, the Blackbirds won 139 consecutive home games. Bee invented

This rare action photograph shows acrobatic Bob Davies electrifying a Madison Square Garden fans with a leaping one hand shot. (March 20, 1941, Queens Borough Public Library, Archives, New York Herald-Tribune Photograph Morgue Collection)

the one-three-one zone defense and recommended the three-second foul lane rule. His 82.4 career winning percentage is second-best best in NCAA history for major college coaches, behind Sam Burton (West Texas A&M) and ahead of Adolph Rupp (University of Kentucky), Mark Few (Gonzaga) and John Wooden (UCLA).[29]

Bee scouted the Pirates in their game against Rhode Island State for five minutes. "They're a one-man team," he said. "Stop the one man and you stop the team." Asked how he planned to hold down the Harrisburg Houdini, Bee replied: "Hit him with an ax." [30]

Trash talk was not yet in vogue in college basketball, but Bee pushed the envelope a bit. "I told my players to talk to him all the time," said Bee. "You know, Shoot, Bobby! Dribble, Bobby! Things like that. No profanity, understand. I didn't tolerate that."[31]

Bob ignored the Blackbird jabber. He did not respond in kind, and on a national stage established himself as a good sportsman and a true role model. Honey Russell thought that Bob showed tremendous poise under the circumstances. He concentrated on passing to open teammates, but they either dropped the ball or missed easy shots. He committed three fouls in the first 12 minutes and left the game. He made one field goal in seven attempts and converted two foul shots. With eight minutes remaining, over-eager Bob committed his fourth and final foul (the rule changed to five in 1945). He sat hunched on the bench, head bowed, fighting back tears. The ovation for him lasted five minutes. But Bob considered it the worst game that he ever played.[32]

The Wonder Five's 49–26 loss ended their win streak tied with LIU at 43 games, sixth longest in NCAA Division I history. In the consolation game, the Pirates faced CCNY and their 5' 10," 170-pound playmaker William "Red" Holzman, later Bob's Rochester Royals teammate and a successful NBA coach. Bob and Red each tallied 11 points, as CCNY crushed Seton Hall, 42–27.[33]

Notwithstanding Seton Hall's two humiliating losses, Li'l Abner's electrifying performance against Rhode Island State made him the hottest commercial commodity in college basketball. He had achieved national sports hero status in the basketball capital of the world. Handsome as a movie matinee idol, Bob almost followed in legendary Hank Luisetti's cinematic footsteps. Paramount Pictures' talent scout Boris Kaplan tried to schedule an interview with Bob to discuss a movie role, but he was not interested. [34]

And Bob turned down another money-making opportunity. Major corporations hired talented basketball players as full-time employees who maintained their amateur status playing on the company team. An Ohio tire manufacturer offered Bob a job with an opportunity for advancement. Although strapped financially and doing odd jobs around Walsh Gymnasium for a small stipend, and walking a mile and a half in order to save a three-cent bus fare, Bob declined the offer. He strongly believed that a college degree would increase his earning power after his athletic career ended. He had enjoyed teaching baseball and basketball at a summer camp, and wanted to become a physical education instructor and perhaps someday a basketball coach.[35]

Mesmerized by Bob's Madison Square Garden performance, boys in the New York metropolitan area tried to imitate his behind-the-back dribble. In a Newark, New Jersey, gymnasium, a coach watched future Seton Hall All-American and NBA player Richie Regan's bumbling attempt and told him to knock it off. "Bob Davies does it all the time," protested Richie. "You ain't Bob Davies," responded the coach.[36]

Some voters for All-American teams ignored or underrated Bob, probably because Seton Hall played a comparatively weak schedule, and his widely publicized NIT breakout game occurred at the tail end of the season. The Los Angeles-based Helms Foundation did not select him. However, *Collyer's Eye and Baseball Weekly* (not the better-known *Collier's* magazine) chose him as an All-American First Team member, and stated that he could play either guard or forward, and excelled on defense. Converse Rubber Company, the basketball shoe manufacturer, named him a forward on its All American Third Team.[37]

SUMMER BASEBALL

During the summer following his junior year, Bob again played for the Burlington Cardinals. In an exhibition game against the Triple-A International League Montreal Royals that raised $3,000 ($49,800 today) for British refugee children from German bombing attacks, Bob belted four hits, including a home run, in five trips to the plate and singled and then scored the tying run in the tenth inning. Reporters selected him as a second baseman in the Northern League All-Star Game. Thanks to Bob's generosity, his parents and siblings were able to drive to Burlington, stay in a cottage on Lake Champlain, and watch him play baseball. It was the Davies family's one and only vacation together.[38]

That summer, Honey Russell umpired Northern League games and kept a wary eye on Bennington Generals' first baseman Chuck Connors (later of TV's *Rifleman* fame). The Brooklyn Dodgers had tried to arrange a Seton Hall baseball scholarship for Chuck, but one was not available, so he received a basketball scholarship. When Honey learned of this arrangement, he insisted that the 6' 6", 205-pound

Connors, who had played high school basketball, join the Pirates basketball team. Russell had good cause to worry about irrepressible daredevil Chuck. For example, Chuck had bet his college teammates that he could walk around a hotel on a one-foot-wide seventh-story ledge, performed the stunt, and collected his winnings. [39]

From Chuck's point of view, Russell's nickname, Honey, constituted a misnomer. "With his big hawk face and his hook nose," Connors said, "he would rant and scream about defense, always defense. He wanted to play a slowdown, grind-it-out offense, but he couldn't control Davies, who was nothing less than an offensive genius."[40]

SENIOR SEASON AGONY

In the Wonder Five's senior season home opener on December 10, 1941, East Stroudsburg (PA) State Teachers College upset them, 40–37. Coach Russell thought that Teachers player Pete Pasko, juggling a toothpick in his mouth, distracted his players more than the Japanese bombing of Pearl Harbor three days earlier and the United States' declaration of war on Japan two days earlier. "They watched the toothpick instead of the ball," moaned Honey. In their seventh game, the Pirates, with Bob Davies scoring only five points, fell 43–42, to a taller Dartmouth College team that later lost in the NCAA tournament championship game.[41]

Interviewed after these disappointing losses, Bob remained humble: "No matter how good a player may seem, he's only as good as the team. And the team is made by the coach. If we fellows will only learn and heed what Coach Russell tells us, we'll give a good account of ourselves. He gives us a little every day, and each day we learn more and more. There's an awful lot to basketball."[42]

The Wonder Five even lost practice scrimmages, one by 35 points, to the more-talented Seton Hall freshman squad led by two future NBA players, Robert Francis "Bobby" Wanzer and John "Whitey" Macknowski. Always generous and helpful, Bob Davies worked with freshman players on set shooting, faking, and passing. After their preliminary games, the frosh cagers hurriedly showered and dressed, so that they could watch Bob dazzle the crowd in the varsity contests. "I idolized Bob," said John Macknowski, "we all did. He could do more with a basketball than anybody else, including Cousy, until Pete Maravich came along." Pistol Pete, a spectacular showman, opened up the game in the 1970s with circus shots and passes that many NBA observers considered outrageous.[43]

Two months before the publication of the Liberty magazine "Li'l Abner" story, Newsweek, the nation's second leading news magazine (450,259 circulation), had brought Bob's basketball showmanship to the nation's attention. The January 1942 Newsweek article, entitled "Court Magician," praised Bob as the year's outstanding collegiate ball handler and playmaker, and included a four-frame picture sequence illustrating his "rare" behind-the-back dribble that made fans swoon like bobby-soxers at a Frank Sinatra concert. [44]

Some teammates, however, were jealous of the publicity showered on Bob. Coach Russell spoke to them and defended his modest and even-tempered star: "You other fellows might as well realize that without Davies you wouldn't have gone anyplace. You never would have gone through last year undefeated, never would have made Madison Square Garden. You're just ordinary ballplayers who have hooked up with one great player to make a pretty fair team. You can go along being a pretty fair team, only if you cut out this jealousy business."[45]

In his most sensational collegiate performance, Bob lived up to his press notices in a 55–33 trouncing of the Providence (RI) College Friars. A pre-game story picture caption warned that "Seton's 'William Tell'[46] of the Courts… Strikes Terror in Hearts of Enemy Forces." The "blonde blitzkrieg" dribbled the length of the court and, dribbling behind his back, tied four Providence players in knots. Forced to the sideline, he tossed in an over-the-head shot. The ovation lasted five minutes. "My vision of him in that performance will never leave my mind," said Whitey Macknowski half a century later. "I loved the guy, not only as a ball player, but as a star player, he was not showy or discourteous."[47]

In a highly anticipated rematch, Seton Hall College and Long Island University, each with two losses, met on February 16, 1942, before 17,611 Madison Square Garden spectators. Early in the game, Blackbird Howie Rader administered Bob a verbal "barbering" worthy of a major league baseball team bench jockey. Bob stayed calm, ignored his tormentor, and concentrated on playmaking, but Rader's profane tirade angered and upset the other Pirates. *Newark Evening News* staff correspondent Harry Nash sharply criticized Rader for his abusive language, and columnist Hy Goldberg advocated that college basketball authorities adopt a rule prohibiting profanity. The Blackbirds double-teamed Bob and deployed a three-man zone defense against his teammates. Bob played his heart out, scoring 7 of Seton Hall's 13 first half points, but made just one foul shot in the second half and lost the ball twice attempting to dribble behind his back. Howie Rader left the game to the sound of a "luscious razz berry." Bob left to "thunderous cheers" that shook the building for five minutes. Dejected, Bob sat on the bench, head bowed, again fighting back tears, as the Blackbirds finished wiping out the Pirates, 51–30.[48]

"It was, in truth, fitting tribute to a grand boy and a stellar athlete," wrote a columnist. "I left the Garden knowing that I had witnessed something immortal. Seton Hall had lost to Long Island University but Davies had proved himself as good a loser as I have ever seen and also stood as a prodigious exception to a long standing rule. Invariably, if the champion lost his crown, his conqueror and not he received the applause. However, this champion came out of the battle with his toga still about him and his crown still in place."[49]

After reading newspaper stories reporting that two LIU players had cursed Bob, Coach Bee wrote him a letter asking whether the allegations were true. "If they had," replied Bob, "I didn't hear it." Bee never forgot Bob's act of sportsmanship.[50]

Bowing out in his last collegiate game on March 3, 1942, in the sold-out Walsh Gymnasium, Bob led the Pirates with 14 points in a thrilling 40–37 victory over LaSalle College. When the "Blond Bullet" left the floor with 15 seconds remaining, the crowd rose as one and cheered him almost ten minutes. "Tell 'em all thanks for me," Bob said to the public address announcer. Speaking later for the team, Bob was so emotional that he became virtually inarticulate. "That night Davies left as the champion he was," wrote a student reporter. "A smile washed with tears."[51]

In three seasons, Bob Davies led the Seton Hall Pirates varsity to 55 victories against five losses. He averaged 11.8 points per game as a sophomore (half the season on the second unit), 10.2 as a junior, and 11.8 as a senior for an 11.2 overall average. Contemporary collegiate backcourt aces John Wooden (Purdue University), Red Holzman (CCNY), and Andy Phillip (University of Illinois) averaged 9.9, 11.6, and 12.0 points per game respectively over their college careers. Official assists, steals, or turnover records were not kept, but a Seton Hall yearbook writer stated that Davies' assists exceeded his field goals. Bob was selected for the 1941–42 NCAA Consensus All-American First Team and 1942 Converse, *PIC* magazine, and Madison Square Garden All-American Second Teams.[52]

COLLEGE BASKETBALL'S STUDENT/ATHLETE ROLE MODEL

National fame as an athlete did not spoil Bob Davies. His strong character prevailed, and he never became overly impressed with himself. Seton Hall faculty, students, and prep school boys quickly recognized him as an exceptional role model.

First in his family to attend college, Bob graduated *cum laude* with a bachelor of science degree in physical education. A Seton Hall faculty committee elected him to the student honor society, the Order of the Cross and Crescent, which required an 85 percent or higher academic average, participation in extracurricular activities, gentlemanly conduct, and a pleasing manner and appearance reflecting credit on the college. [53]

The Seton Hall College yearbook editors extolled Bob, nicknamed Abbie, "Outstanding athlete, honor student, staunch friend. His personal qualities will live longer in our hearts than his nation wide basketball fame." The well-rounded young man's extracurricular activities included French Club, Rifle Club, Hi-S Club, and Knights of Setonia, a religious organization promoting spiritual devotion, student accomplishment, and gentleman-like behavior. New Jersey sports writers honored Bob as the state's outstanding collegiate athlete based on both character and performance. A fitting tribute, his picture hung on the Newark Central High School gymnasium bulletin board as an inspiration for the school's athletes.[54]

In a weekly inspirational bulletin distributed to 620 Seton Hall

Preparatory School boys, Father James Carey praised Bob as the gold standard for sports-hero role models:

> During the past few years we have written many bulletins on athletes and we have held them up before you so that we might have you follow their example. We have purposely delayed giving to you, the greatest example of them all and one of your own, Bob Davies. It is most fitting that we pay tribute to him now that he is nearing the end of his basketball career as well as his athletic career as a representative of Seton Hall College. All of you know him but probably because you see him so often you have never appreciated him. He has always been mild of manners; a possessor of fine poise; a most modest boy and a perfect gentleman. You all know how much personal publicity he has received the past few years and you know too that it has not bothered him nor added one iota to his stature. You probably do not know that he had to work hard for all that he ever attained. And even though he has been on the campus with you we would wager that many of you do not know that Bob is not a Catholic, but a true religious Lutheran.
>
> There are hundreds of things that we could write about him. We might tell you how courageous he has always been; how gentle and mild; how thoughtful and sincere but it might be well to leave most of those things unwritten because we feel that is the way Bob would want it. What we cannot leave unwritten, however, is his devotion to his mother and dad and his little brothers and sister. We have never in all our time found a boy who has had the sincere love and solicitude for his family that this boy had had, and for that we admire him most.
>
> We have noticed hundreds of boys here on the campus on your own court and hundreds of boys from other schools on their courts canter up and down the court trying to do Bob's "behind the back dribble." What we would have you do now is to adopt some of those fine qualities that have made him a grand Setonian and a perfect gentleman. If all through your lives you have the balance, the poise, and the modesty of Bob

Davies, you can be assured that you will be a success in life and a credit to Seton Hall.[55]

"Bob Davies certainly was a great role model," said former Seton Hall Prep School student Jack McDermott. After the Prep School Knights of Setonia members attended a weekly morning Mass, Bob and other college athletes served them coffee and donuts in the cafeteria. "Bob was a real nice fellow," remembered McDermott. "He always said hello. He gave me two donuts all the time."[56]

"Bob Davies was a role model for every young guy who went into Seton Hall Prep School," remembered Jim Lacey, a prep school freshman and fencer during Bob's college senior year. Lacey practiced in the Walsh Gymnasium fencing room while Bob worked out on the basketball court. "He always treated me with respect you wouldn't expect from an older, big sports hero. He never passed by without saying 'Hi' and my name even though we were never formally introduced. He really liked to encourage young fellows coming up poor through sports."[57]

But now it was time for young American men like Bob Davies to play a different role.

NOTES

1   Mary Davies, telephone conversations with author, Jan. 18, 2007, and Jan. 22, 2009; "Bob Davies Praised As Athlete At Seton Hall," BDSHOF; Tim Cohane, "The [Star] of the Week: Bob Davies," *N Y World-Telegram*, March 22, 1941; "a modest": Jack Dempsey, "Basketball's Li'l Abner," *Liberty*, March 21, 1942, 30–31; *N.W. Ayer & Son's Directory of Newspapers and Periodicals* (1942): 664.

2   *Seton Hall College Catalogue* (1938–1939): 14, 17; *Seton Hall University Charter Day Program, Feb. 28, 2003*, n.p.; Thomas W. Cunningham, *The Summit of a century: the centennial story of Seton Hall University, 1856–1956*, 65–66; Msgr. J.F. Kelley, *Memoirs of Msgr. ("Doc") J. F. Kelley*, 199, 205–8; Ted Vincent, *Mudville's Revenge: The Rise and Fall of American Sport*, 266; http://www.hoophall.com/halloffamers/RussellJ.htm.

3   "At the Criterion, Campus Confession," *New York Times Film Reviews*,

September 23, 1938; Grantland Rice, *The Tumult and the Shouting: My Life in Sport*, 265; Marty Glickman with Stan Isaacs, *The Fastest Kid on the Block: The Marty Glickman Story*, 71–72 (describes Luisetti as his era's Michael Jordan without the media and advertising buzz); John D. McCallum, *College Basketball, USA. Since 1892*, 49–61 (begins modern basketball section with a chapter entitled "Hank Luisetti: A Star is Born"); Jack Orr, "Hank Luisetti, Basketball Revolutionary," *Sport* (March 1962), reprinted by permission of Sports Media Enterprises, Inc., in Ken Shouler, Bob Ryan, Sam Smith, Leonard Koppett, and Bob Bellotti, *Total Basketball: The Ultimate Basketball Encyclopedia*, 55–58.

4   "We were": James A. Michener, *Sports in America*, 445–46.

5   Philip Pallette (author of *The Game Changer: How Hank Luisetti Revolutionized America's Great Indoor Game*), e-mail to author, Oct. 22, 2012 (Stanford teammate Dick Lyon recalled Luisetti dribbling behind his back in a University of Southern California game); "Stanford's Hank Luisetti is the player of the year," *Life*, Jan. 31, 1938, 27–28.

6   Fred B. Green, "Seton Hall's Crack Basketeer Can Dribble Behind His Back Without Changing His Stride," *PM*, Feb. 23, 1941, 23; "Studied Luisetti's Style," circa March 1941 (author's possession); Tim Cohane, "Star of the Week: Bob Davies," *N.Y. World-Telegram*, March 22, 1941; "Spotlight on Davies," circa March 1941 (author's possession); "If it": Mary Davies, telephone conversation with author, Jan. 19, 2007.

7   "0:01 Back Story," *ESPN Magazine*, March 19, 2001, 124 [behind-the-back dribble film clip sequence]; Dick Davies, telephone conversation with author, Jan. 29, 2009.

8   Salzberg, *Set Shot*, 47; Harold Weissman, "Coach Thought It Gag When Davies Reported For Seton Hall Team," *Daily Mirror*, BDSHOF; Garry Brown, "The Morning Line: Honey and Bob," *Springfield (MA) Sunday Republican*, April 12, 1970.

9   Ronald A. Smith and Jay W. Helman, A History Of Eligibility Rules Among Big-Time Athletic Institutions, 6–9, 20–30; Mikan and Oberle, *Unstoppable*, 27–28, 51, 61; Michael Schumacher, *Mr. Basketball: George Mikan, the Minneapolis Lakers, and the Birth of the NBA*, 11–12, 52; Jim Enright, *Ray Meyer: America's #1 Basketball Coach*, 72 (opines Mikan's fifth season "may have cost" DePaul a 1945–46 season tournament bid).

10   "Bob began": Bus Funk, "Cruising Around," *Harrisburg Patriot*, Jan. 5, 1939.

11   Salzberg, *Set Shot*, 47–48, 53; Jack Barry, "Davies' Dreams Came True Thanks to Hard Practice," BDSHOF.

12   Howard A. Hobson, *Scientific Basketball for Coaches, Players, Officials and Sportswriters*, 231, 233 and *Basketball Illustrated*, 36–37; Bob Davies as told to Al C. Weber, "How to Play Basketball: Best Scoring Weapon Is Basketball's Set Shot," *T-U*, Dec. 8, 1951; "Make Basketball Playing Fun—Have Confidence in Your Shots," BDSHOF; Bill Sharman, *Sharman on Basketball Shooting*, 67–72.

13   "Bob could": Dick Davies, telephone conversation with author, Jan. 27, 2012; Walt Frazier and Ira Berkow, *A Guide to Basketball & Cool: Rockin' Steady*, 74; Bob Wanzer, telephone conversation with author, Sept. 20, 2013; Wolff, *100 Years*, 20–21.

14   John Russell, *Honey Russell: Between Games Between Halves*, 115–16; John Macknowski, telephone conversation with author, Aug. 20, 2010.

15   Salzberg, *Set Shot*, 47–48; Harry Nash, "Accent on Setonia Youth As Senior Five Bows Out," *Newark Evening News*, March 4, 1942; Jay A. See, Jr., "Setonians Primed For Final Court Tilts In Village Gym This Weekend: Scranton, Baltimore Teams To Oppose Village Five," *South Orange (NJ) Record*, Feb. 28, 1941.

16   Dempsey, "Li'l Abner," *Liberty*, March 21, 1942, 31; Mike Douchant, *Inside Sports: Encyclopedia of College Basketball*, 36; "High Praise for Court Play Given Davies at Seton" and "Bob Davies Praised As Athlete At Seton Hall,", BDSHOF.

17   "Davies Joins Baseball Club," BDSHOF; Dominick Denaro, *A Centennial Field Scrapbook: Memories of the minor league's oldest ballpark*, 19, 21; Jack Falla, *NCAA: The Voice of College Sports: A Diamond Anniversary History, 1906–1981*, 37–39; U.S. Dept. of Commerce: Bureau of Census, *Historical Statistics of U.S.*; Scott Derks, ed., *The Value of a Dollar: Prices and Incomes in the United States, 1860–1999*, 227–29; Measuring Worth; "Davies can": Walt Hickey, "From The Press Box," *Burlington (VT) Free Press*, June 14, 1940; Whitey Killick, "Commentaries," *Burlington Free Press*, Sept. 3, 1940; "Cards Picked For All-Star Game, Aug. 1" and "Davies Will Return to Keystone for Cardinals Here This Year", BDSHOF.

18   Alan Delozier, *Images of Sports: Seton Hall Pirates; A Basketball History*, 33–34; Measuring Worth; "The House," "O'REALLY!" by O'Reilly, BDSHOF; Bill Davies, telephone conversation with author, May 21,

2008; Mary Davies, telephone conversations with author, Oct. 3, 2007 and Oct. 6, 2008.

19 "Seton Hall Downs Villanova, 41–29, To Remain Unbeaten in 35 Games," *NYT*, Jan. 16, 1941; "what made": incomplete clipping without publication name, date, title or author under subheading "Studied Luisetti's Style," circa March 1941 (author's possession).

20 Reynolds, *Bob Cousy*, 30–31; "Bob Davies: Seton Hall Basketball Star Scores With Either Hand," BDSHOF; "uncommonly small": Bill Roeder, "Bob Davies—Royal Playmaker," *Sport*, Feb. 1948, 50; "He changed": Jerry Izenberg, "Davies recalled as best," *Harrisburg Patriot*, April 24, 1990; Tim Cohane, "Star of the Week: Bob Davies," *NY World-Telegram*, March 22, 1941; "Seton Hall Trounces Rhode Island State, 70–54, on Garden Court," *NY Herald-Tribune*, March 20, 1941; "was born": Jerry Izenberg, "Davies recalled as best," *Harrisburg Patriot*, April 24, 1990; "do everything": "They Help Lead Pirate Cage Foes Off Plank," BDSHOF.

21 "a real hero": "Bob Davies Ranked With Hank Luisetti," dateline S. Orange, NJ, Jan. 21, 1941, BDSHOF; "Special Shots of Davies on Proctor's Screen," BDSHOF; Charles Fountain, *Sportswriter: The Life and Times of Grantland Rice*, 197; Green, "Seton Hall's Crack Basketeer," *PM*, Feb. 23, 1941, 23; https://en.wikipedia.org/wiki/PM_; https://en.wikipedia.org/wiki/ Harold_Teen; "expounded": "Canisius, Seton Hall Fives Favored in Games Tonight," BDSHOF.

22 "I like" and "You know": "Spotlight on Davies," circa March 1941, (author's possession).
        Reserves included 6' 4", 200-pound Albert Edward "Al" Negratti, who later played in the National Basketball League (NBL) and Basketball Association of America (BAA), and 6' 2", 175-pound Benedict Michael "Ben" Scharnus who played in the BAA. Jan Hubbard, ed., *The Official NBA Encyclopedia*, 3rd ed., 667 (Negratti), 733 (Scharnus).

23 "Davies Sinks Winner in Last Seconds, Scranton Almost Topples Hallers," *Setonian*, March 7, 1941, 3.

24 "Davies Sinks Winner In Last Seconds: Cagers Swat Bees To Climax Season; Slate Kept Clean," *Setonian*, March 7, 1941; "Village Collegians Conclude Schedule With Perfect Mark: Bob Davies Is Hero As Seton Hall Overtakes Baltimore Basketeers In Thrilling Battle Before 5,000

Fans," *South Orange Record*, March 7, 1941; Russell, *Honey Russell*, 118–19; "That play": Dempsey, "Li'l Abner," *Liberty*, March 21, 1942, 31; Bob Davies, interview by Charles Salzberg, Coral Springs, FL, 1986, tape recording and Bob Davies-edited transcript, Joseph M. O'Brien Historical Resource Center, Naismith Memorial Basketball Hall of Fame, Springfield, MA.

25 "THE BEST": "Bob Davies" clipping, BDSHOF; McCallum, *College Basketball*, 72 (confirming that in the early 1940s many sports writers considered Davies the best all-around player since Luisetti).

26 Joe Cummiskey, "Seton Hall Runs Wild… LIU a Winner," *PM*, March 20, 1941; "Seton Hall on Its Way to a Basket in Game at the Garden," *NY Herald-Tribune*, March 20, 1941 [picture caption].

27 "Basketball's young Barnum": Tim Cohane, "The Star of the Week: Bob Davies," *NY World-Telegram*, March 22, 1941; "Tim Cohane, 76, Sports Editor at *Look*," *NYT*, Jan. 24, 1989; "the closest": Arthur Daley, "Seton Hall and LIU Fives Gain Semi-Finals at Garden," *NYT*, March 20, 1941; "to step down": Dan Parker, "Garden Goes All Out for Seton Hall and Davies," *N.Y. Daily Mirror*, March 22, 1941; https://en.wikipedia.org/wiki/New_York_Daily_Mirror.

28 The Helms Athletic Foundation was a Los Angeles organization that selected collegiate basketball and football national champions and All-American Teams.

29 John A. Garraty and Mark C. Carnes, gen. eds., *American National Biography*, s.v. "Bee, Clair Francis"; Charley Rosen, *Scandals of '51: How the Gamblers Almost Killed College Basketball*, 18–22; http://www.sports-reference.com/ebb/leaders/win-loss-pct-coach-career.html/; https://en.wikipedia.org/wiki/Helms_Athletic _Foundation.

30 "They're": Bruce Anderson, "His Career Still Reads Like a Novel," *Miami (FL) Herald*, April 6, 1980; "Hit him": Milton Gross (syndicated sports columnist), "Basketball: Perfect Timing is Davies Secret, Seton Hall Ace Has Rare Athletic Sense," *New York Post*, March 21, 1941.

31 "I told": McCallum, "A Hero," *Sports Illustrated*, Jan. 7, 1980, 58.

32 Joe Trimble, "LIU Routs Seton Hall, 49–26; City Beaten," *NY Daily News*, March 23, 1941; "18,357 See Ohio U Set Back CCNY At Garden, 45 to 43… LIU Stops Seton Hall," *NYT*, March 23, 1941; Mokray, comp. and ed., *Ronald*, 1–8; Joe Goldstein, "Davies dribbles his way into history,"

http://espn.go.com/classic/s/goldstein_behind_the_back.html.

33 NCAA, *Official 2007 NCAA Men's Basketball Records Book,* 53; Arthur
    Daley, "LIU Halts Ohio U Five in Garden: Blackbirds Rally For 56–42
    Triumph," *NYT,* March 25, 1941.

    Basketball historian Neil Isaacs has pointed out that Seton Hall and
    LIU actually each won 39 consecutive inter-collegiate games because
    they were both erroneously credited with four victories against non-
    collegiate opponents including their alumni. If the NCAA corrected
    its records, Seton Hall and LIU would be tied for the seventh longest
    winning streak with Marquette University. Neil D. Isaacs, *All the Moves:
    A History of College Basketball,* 197; NCAA, *Official 2007 NCAA Men's
    Basketball Records Book,* 53.

34 Boris Kaplan, Talent Department, Paramount Pictures, Inc., to Mr. Bob
    Davies, March 21, 1941, in possession of Mary Davies, Longwood, FL;
    Dick Davies, telephone conversation with author, March 21, 2011.

35 Dempsey, "Li'l Abner," *Liberty,* March 21, 1942, 31; clipping, "Best I've
    seen - Russell," circa March 1941 (author's possession); Mary Davies,
    telephone conversation with author, Oct. 6, 2008; Jim Lacey, telephone
    conversation with author, July 5, 2013.

36 "Bob Davies does": Jerry Izenberg, "Davies recalled as best," *Harrisburg
    Patriot,* April 24, 1990.

37 "Davies, Harrisburg Court Player, All-American" and "All-American
    Net-Team Is Selected By Collyer's Eye," BDSHOF; "1941 All American
    College Basketball Teams," *Converse Basketball Year Book 1941,* 2–3.

38 Lloyd McGowan, "Royals Overlook Selves Aiding Vermont Fund,"
    BDSHOF; Measuring Worth; "Senators Shine As Northern All-Stars
    Win Classic, 5–2," *Montpelier (VT) Evening Argus,* Aug. 2, 1941; Bill
    Davies, telephone conversation with author, July 17, 2013; Dick Davies,
    telephone conversation with author, Oct. 19, 2009.

39 David Fury, *Chuck Connors: "The Man Behind the Rifle,"* 26–27; John
    Macknowski, telephone conversation with author, Aug. 20, 2010.

40 "With his": Charley Rosen, *The First Tip-Off: The Incredible Story of the
    Birth of the NBA,* 43.

41 "Pirates Upset: E. Stroudsburg Registers 40–37 Triumph," BDSHOF;
    "They watched": "Gripes Of Wrath" by Harold Parrott of *Brooklyn
    Eagle,* Athletic Collection, Monsignor William Noe Field Archives and

Special Collections Center, Seton Hall University, South Orange, NJ (hereafter cited as (SHUAC); "Dartmouth Downs Seton Hall, 43–42," *NYT*, Jan. 4, 1942.

42 "No matter": Dempsey, "Li'l Abner," *Liberty*, March 21, 1942, 31.

43 "I idolized" and "He could": Macknowski, telephone conversations with author Aug. 20, 2010 and May 14, 2011; http:// www.nba.com/history/ players/maravich_summary.html.

44 "Court Magician," *Newsweek*, Jan. 19, 1942, 50–51; *N. W. Ayer Directory* (1942): 669.

45 "You other": Tim Cohane column quoted in Russell, *Honey Russell*, 119–20.

46 "Seton's 'William Tell' ..." [caption] and "'Stops' Show: Fans Cheer Play, Halt Game for Five Minutes," BDSHOF.
      William Tell was a Swiss 14th-century folk hero noted for his skill as an archer, who allegedly shot an apple off his son's head.

47 "My vision": Macknowski, telephone conversation with author, Aug. 20, 2010.

48 "Official Program: LIU vs. Seton Hall—Brooklyn vs. Westminster," Madison Square Garden, Feb. 16, 1942, Harry Nash, "LIU Outclasses Seton Hall Five, Davies Shackled, Held to 8 Points," *Newark Evening News*, Feb. 17, 1942; SHUAC; "barbering": Everett B. Morris, "17,611 See Local Fives Score, Taking Both Ends of Twin Bill," *NY Herald-Tribune*, Feb. 17, 1942; Hy Goldberg, "Sports in the News," *Newark Evening News*, Feb. 18, 1942; "Seton Hall Cage Star Again Foiled," BDSHOF.

49 "It was": "O'REALLY!" by O'Reilly, BDSHOF.

50 "If they had": Joe Gergen, "Of Showtime And the Real Chip Hilton," *Newsday*, April 26, 1990.

51 "Seton Hall Victor, 40–37: Finishing Campaign by Defeating LaSalle Five—Davies Stars," *NYT*, March 4, 1942; Harry Nash, "Accent on Setonia Youth As Senior Five Bows Out," *Newark Evening News*, March 4, 1942; "Tell 'em": Frank Casale, "Morning View," BDSHOF; "That night": Frank H. McNally, "Coach Davies Will Try To Crack Record He Set As Player," *Setonian*, Nov. 25, 1946, 7.

52 File SHU 0031, Seton Hall University Office of Intercollegiate Athletics Records, Men's Basketball—Individual Statistics Files, 1939–1949, SHUAC; Tom Schott, Purdue Athletic Dept., e-mail message to

author, Dec. 19, 2011; Red Holzman and Harvey Frommer, *Red on Red*, 195; http://www.fightingillini.com/sports/m-baskbl/records/career-histcarr.html#INDALL. FCA; William G. Mokray, comp. and ed., *Ronald Encyclopedia Of Basketball*, 6–3, 6–9; Edwin C. Caudle, *Collegiate Basketball: Facts And Figures On The Cage Sport*, 1959 ed., 87; Mike Douchant, *Inside Sports: Encyclopedia of College Basketball*, 542; *Converse Basketball Yearbook 1942:* 2 and *1946:* 11; "PIC Magazine 1942 All-America Basketball Team," *PIC*, April 13, 1943, 44–45.

53   Robert Edris Davies Transcript of Record, Sept. 17, 1938–June 13, 1942, Seton Hall College, Registrar Office, Seton Hall University, S. Orange, NJ; *Seton Hall College Catalogue (1938–1939):* 24; *Seton Hall College Bulletin of Information, 1949–50:* 35–36.

54   "Abbie": Seton Hall *White and Blue* (1942): 70; ibid., 173; "Davies Gains Sports Award," *Harrisburg Patriot*, Jan. 9, 1942; "Sports Shorts," BDSHOF.

55   "During the": "Knights of Setonia Seton Hall Prep" bulletin, Feb. 20, 1942, SHUAC; *Official Catholic Directory* (1942), *s.v.* "Seton Hall Prep School"; *Seton Hall Prep School Tower* (1942): 58.

56   "Bob Davies certainly": Jack McDermott, telephone conversation with author, Aug. 21, 2013.

57   "Bob Davies was": Jim Lacey, telephone conversation with author, July 5, 2013.

DUTY TO COUNTRY

"TANKER TORPEDOED 60 MILES OFF LONG ISLAND," BLARED THE January 15, 1942, *New York Times* front page headline. Six weeks later, off New Jersey's Cape May, German submarines sank a tanker and torpedoed a U.S. Navy destroyer. By the time Bob Davies had played his last Seton Hall basketball game on March 3, German and Japanese submarines had sunk at least 27 ships off U.S. coasts. Bob inquired about employment with the Federal Bureau of Investigation, which was hunting saboteurs that German U-boats had dropped on U.S. shores. He attended classes arranged for seniors three extra hours a day so that they could complete their degree requirements early and join the armed forces. Four weeks after his last basketball game, Bob voluntarily enlisted in the United States Navy Reserve. Three days later, awaiting active duty orders, he returned to Seton Hall and participated in graduation exercises.[1]

GREAT LAKES NAVAL TRAINING STATION
After completing five weeks of basic training at Great Lakes Naval Training Station (GLNTS) in Chicago, Illinois, 22-year-old Third Class Petty Officer Robert E. Davies, dressed in Navy blue, married pretty 20-year-old Mary Helfrich in Harrisburg's Memorial Lutheran Church on August 8, 1942. Tom Davies, wearing a U.S. Army Air Corps corporal uniform, served as his brother's best man. [2]

Four years earlier, Mary's sister and Tom Davies had persuaded Mary to drive them to a baseball game and watch Bob play. His errant

Third Class Petty Officer Robert E. Davies married his lifelong sweetheart Mary Helfrich in Harrisburg's Memorial Lutheran Church. (Aug. 8, 1942, Courtesy of Mary Davies)

throw struck Mary standing along the first base line. After the game, Bob apologized and shyly asked her out. Mary remembered that they dated almost six months before he kissed her. The newlyweds traveled in a train to Chicago and moved into an apartment.[3]

During World War II, sports played a significant role in boosting American morale at home and overseas. Believing that Major League Baseball (MLB) would distract civilians from their war worries, President Franklin Delano Roosevelt authorized its continuation for the duration of the hostilities. "Athletics promote three requisites," maintained GLNTS Commanding Officer Rear Admiral John Downes, "clean living, sportsmanship and team play—most essential in molding good Sailors in wartime and good citizens in time of peace." Armed Forces bases sponsored basketball, baseball, and football teams that competed at a collegiate, and, in some cases, professional, level. The teams fostered pride in their branches of the armed services and provided entertainment for servicemen restricted to their bases. The GLNTS "Bluejackets" basketball team, resplendent in snappy winter dress blue uniforms, assisted in recruiting and in raising funds for the Navy Relief Society, which cared for Navy men's widows and orphans. [4]

Base commanders assigned sports team members like Bob Davies to "shadow" recruit company commanders or assistant commanders and learn their duties. After completing this indoctrination process, First Class Petty Officer Robert E. Davies commanded ("babysat") 120 recruits. Starting at 7:30 a.m. and finishing at 4 p.m., he marched them to and from the mess hall and classrooms, directed them in drills and calisthenics, posted watches, and supervised barracks discipline. When comedian Jack Benny performed for Chicago-area armed services personnel, Bob accompanied his enlisted charges. "I went to the show with my boss and sat with the officers," remembered spunky Mary, who worked as a secretary on the base. "Bob wasn't too happy about that."[5]

When the 1942–43 basketball season commenced, Bob's primary duties switched from the drill hall to the hardwood floor. Bluejackets coach Lieutenant Paul D. "Tony" Hinkle, the "Dean of Indiana College Basketball Coaches," had led Butler University (Indianapolis) to two Helms Athletic Foundation National Championships. Blessed at GLNTS with a roster of former college stars, Hinkle employed a two-platoon system. Forwards John Hiller (Notre Dame University) and Wilbur Schumacher (Butler University), center Dick Klein (Northwestern University), and guards George Sobek (Notre Dame University) and Gilbert Huffman (University of Tennessee) made up the starting lineup most of the season.[6]

Although an All-American basketball player, Bob Davies did not complain about playing guard on the fast-break-oriented, higher-scoring "mop-up" crew that usually entered games midway through the first quarter. 6' 5", 215-pound University of North Carolina All-American and two-time Helms Athletic Foundation Player of the Year George "The Blind Bomber" Glamack anchored this unit at center. Hampered by poor vision in one eye, George claimed that he shot his deadly hooks with either hand as far as 15 feet from the basket by gauging his position in relationship to the basket rim from the lines on the floor and a shadowy outline of the backboard. Forwards Eddie Riska (Notre Dame University) and Forrest Anderson (Stanford University) and guard George Hamburg (University of Colorado) completed the "mop-up" crew lineup. Future University of California (Berkeley) coach and Hall of Famer Pete Newell was a reserve guard.[7]

Taking a brief furlough, First Class Petty Officer Bob Davies played in the third annual College All-Star Basketball Game on November 27, 1942, before 12,000 spectators in Chicago Stadium (later the NBA Chicago Bulls home court). The *Chicago Herald-American* newspaper sponsored this contest between the best recently graduated white college players and the winner of the Chicago World Professional Tournament, which invited the nation's best white or black professional, semi-professional, company-sponsored, and Amateur Athletic Union (AAU) teams.[8]

The Chicago press stated that Davies came "out of the East with all-American rating at Seton Hall and enough press clippings to make even a super-showman like Bill Veeck [MLB team owner who used clever antics to promote his teams] take notice. The middle west only knew about the dandy Davies by remote control when he was picked for the 1942 College All-Stars. Here he was in person to challenge the topflight feats of native sons right in their own back yard."[9]

Highlighting the pregame ceremony, "Miss Victory of Chicago Defense Plants" Mary Hoffman led a huge "V" formation of Allied flags held by a native of each country dressed in indigenous costume.[10]

But a "package of dynamite answering to the name of Bob Davies stole the show with his magnificent floor work, passing and generalship." With the collegians trailing by one point at the beginning of the fourth quarter, Bob scored the go-ahead basket and then made two sensational buckets when the NBL champion Oshkosh (WI) All-Stars pulled within a point. In a 61–55 victory, Bob led the collegians in scoring with 12 points and was named the game MVP. [11]

"That set me up as far as the pros were concerned," said Bob. He had been a smashing success in the nation's two major media markets, New York City and Chicago, and in two of its largest basketball arenas, Madison Square Garden and Chicago Stadium.[12]

The 1942–43 Great Lakes Naval Training Station Bluejackets led by Bob Davies (top row, center) have been rated the best all-time (1941–69) Armed Services basketball team. (c. 1943, Great Lakes Naval Training Station)

In their seventh game, the undefeated Bluejackets, still becoming accustomed to one another's style of play and without star center George Glamack, met the taller, undefeated Big Ten Conference defending champion University of Illinois "Whiz Kids." Sparked by 6' 3", 195-pound All-American forward Andrew Michael "Andy" Phillip, this Fighting Illini quintet, one of college basketball's greatest teams, employed a fast break and a tenacious defense that were ahead of their time. At intermission, the Whiz Kids led, 37–32. Bob Davies, the most spectacular player on the floor with his behind-the-back dribbling and clever passing, sparked a rally to tie the game at 39–39. But

the Whiz Kids scored nine points in the last four minutes and overcame a four-point deficit to prevail, 57–53.[13]

Traveling over the Christmas holidays to New Orleans, the
Bluejackets competed in the eighth annual Sugar Bowl Cage Classic
held in conjunction with the New Year's Day Sugar Bowl Football Game.
"Blond Torpedo" Bob Davies scored 22 points as the sailors crushed
defending NCAA Tournament champion Stanford University, 57–41,
in the championship game. "The officers back at Great Lakes Naval
Training Station need not worry about gunnery practice for Coxswain
Bob Davies, blond torpedo from Seton Hall who certainly earned the
Croix de something for marksmanship," wrote New Orleans scribe
Hap Glaudi. Calling Bob the greatest player ever to perform in the
Classic and perhaps in any basketball game in New Orleans, Glaudi
continued the "Mon [sic] on the Flying Trapeze" smashed "the exist-
ing high and broad jump records a half dozen times as he soared into
space after roaring down the floor, remained suspended there for seconds (so it seemed) and then either shot the ball to a Bluejacket past the
bewildered Indians or dumped it in the basket." Bob also demoralized
Stanford on defense. Each time he left the game, the crowd erupted in
applause. Tournament officials awarded him the game ball.[14]

Sixteen years later, New Orleans sports reporters still remembered
Bob's legendary performance in the 1942 Cage Classic. Following
younger brother Dick Davies' 29-point scoring outburst for Louisiana
State University (LSU) against Loyola University (New Orleans),
Bayou City sports reporter Bob Roesler wrote under the headline
"Recall Bob Davies?": "Hoop stars will come and go in the Sugar
tourney each Christmas time and leave legendary performances in
their wake. But none will capture the imagination of New Orleans
sportsdom like Bob Davies did back in 1942." During the interven-
ing decade and a half, future Hall of Famers such as University of
Kentucky's Alex Groza and Ralph Beard, Saint Louis University's Ed
Macauley, Holy Cross College's Bob Cousy, and local favorite, LSU's
Bob Pettit, had played in the Classic.[15]

Led by Petty Officer Robert E. Davies, the Bluejackets compiled
the best 1942–43 season armed services basketball team record, winning 34 games and losing three. From the point of view of the GLNTS

command, this accomplishment almost equaled a fleet sinking 34 enemy vessels and losing only three, i.e., almost total victory. The Bluejackets split games with Northwestern University and overtime encounters with fifth-ranked Notre Dame University and won 24 consecutive games, including 13 in 27 days. Bob Davies led the team, which averaged 59.3 points per game, in individual scoring with 269 points (7.3 points per game). He was later selected one of the 40 best all-time armed services basketball players along with Paul Arizin (Quantico Marines), Bob Feerick and Red Holzman (Norfolk Naval Station), Hank Luisetti (St. Mary's Pre-Flight), Andy Phillip (Fleet Marines), Jim Pollard (Alameda Coast Guard/Hawaiian Command), Blackie Towery (71st Division), and George Yardley (Los Alamitos Navy).[16]

"I've never seen a better basketball team—professional or amateur—than the Great Lakes club," said future Hall of Famer Adolph Rupp, who had coached the University of Kentucky cagers 13 years and whose Wildcats lost to the Bluejackets, 53–39.[17]

Authors Seymour Smith, Jack Rimer, and Dick Triptow, in *A Tribute to Armed Forces Basketball,* rank the 1942–43 Great Lakes aggregation as the best all-time (1941–69) United States Armed Services basketball team. The Dunkel Rating System, which determined national basketball tournament seedings, rated Great Lakes first among 1942–43 season armed services teams and second among all college, armed forces, and AAU teams. The Big Ten champion University of Illinois Whiz Kids ranked number one on land, sea, and in the air.[18]

Before leaving Great Lakes Naval Training Station, Bob Davies made a decision about his future in athletics. Graduating with a .321 collegiate career batting average, he had given up his senior baseball season of eligibility and an opportunity for a Boston Red Sox spring training tryout. Pirates baseball coach Al Mamaux predicted that Bob would play in the major leagues within a few years as a second baseman. But Bob had studied the Bluejackets baseball team's six major league pitchers and concluded that he would need several seasons in the minor leagues before he could hit big league pitching. Although professional basketball was not well-established, Bob decided that his future lay on the court rather than on the diamond. "I don't agree with Bob," said his Seton Hall baseball teammate and ex-major league pitcher Steve Nagy. "He could have made it to the major leagues. Second basemen then didn't have to hit that much. Teams were built with defense down the middle."[19]

SUB CHASER TRAINING CENTER

After completing 16 weeks of Naval Reserve Officers Training at Fort Schuyler (New York City), Ensign Robert E. Davies reported to the U.S. Navy Submarine Chaser Training Center (SCTC) in Miami, Florida. Like other new arrivals, he heard the pep talk of a lifetime. SCTC Commanding Officer Eugene F. "Blood and Guts" McDaniel had served on a destroyer that responded to distress signals from a torpedoed British ship. What McDaniel observed made him a confirmed Nazi hater.[20] Pointing to a demonstration lifeboat riddled with fake bullet holes and doused with red paint simulating blood, Commander McDaniel yelled: "See what they do? Deliberately and callously machine-gun defenseless sailors as they float in their lifeboat. The Nazis are nothing but inhumane, ruthless murderers, and you and I will put a stop to it." [21]

During the grueling six-week SCTC program, Ensign Davies developed skills necessary for commanding a sub chaser. He mastered navigation, seamanship, docking, engineering, communications, radar and sonar, gunnery, anti-submarine warfare, and first aid and water life-saving techniques. As Mary tanned on Miami beaches, Bob trained day and night, using his minimal free time to star on the undefeated SCTC Sub Chasers basketball team. A Harrisburg sports writer noted that Bob's performances on Miami basketball courts proved to southeastern states reporters that he deserved his plaudits from their New York City, Chicago, and New Orleans brethren. To the detriment of his national fame, however, Bob Davies never played basketball in the continental United States west of the Rocky Mountains.[22]

OPERATION ANVIL-DRAGOON

Surviving the SCTC weeding-out process, Ensign Davies on May 3, 1944, reported to Sub Chaser (SC) 978, moored at Bizerte, Tunisia, on the Mediterranean Sea. As third and lowest-ranking officer on the ship, he assumed responsibility for engineering, communication, supply, and medical functions. The Axis submarine threat to U.S. coastal shipping had been eliminated, so sub chasers were being employed in patrol, escort, communication, and rescue operations. The 110-foot long and 18-foot wide, wooden-hulled, shallow-draft vessels were "the dwarf mutants among warships, the ragtag kid brothers with the hand-me-down design left over from World War I, the lowest of low in the navy's pecking order." Typically armed with a dual-purpose (anti-aircraft and surface) three-inch barrel cannon and twin 50-caliber machine guns, sub chasers chugged along at 12 knots cruising and 21 knots top speed (13.8 and 24.2 miles per hour). Officers shared a tiny wardroom with three bunk beds and a small fold-out writing desk. Sixteen enlisted men crammed into an 18-by-10-foot forward compartment and eight more into aft quarters that doubled as the mess area. There were no bathing or washing facilities. Superstar Bob Davies would never complain about dressing in a dingy NBA locker room.[23]

Although proud that he had served his country and especially that he had volunteered as an enlisted man and earned an officer's commission, Bob Davies never said much about his military experiences. He did mention to his brothers an admonishment because he played cards with crew members, in violation of the military prohibition against officers fraternizing with enlisted men. Pierre Salinger, the most famous officer to serve in the 438 sub chaser "Donald Duck Navy," and later President John F. Kennedy's press secretary, remembered "a kind of disciplined informality and camaraderie not found elsewhere in the Navy." When standing a four-hour watch with a crew member and without another officer within hearing range, Ensign Davies did not mind the enlisted man calling him Bob. "That doesn't surprise me," said brother Ed. "He was always like the neighbor next door."[24]

Ensign Davies liked, respected, and tried to help his men, including the only African American, mess attendant Teddy McKinney. He encouraged crew members to seek promotions and assisted them in preparing for examinations. "You couldn't ask for a better officer," said crewman James Thomas. "He treated everybody square. Nobody didn't like him. Bob was one of few people in my life who showed me compassion and understanding. He showed me how to respect myself. If Bob had told me to go through hell, I would have gone through hell with him."[25]

The SC-978, converted into a mine sweeper and outfitted with captured German sweeping equipment prior to Davies coming on board, operated from Sicilian, Corsican, and Italian harbors. The little vessel convoyed supply ships and landing craft, towed disabled vessels, patrolled harbor entrances, and conducted mine sweeping exercises. When Ensign Davies took shore leave, he visited historical and cultural sites such as Carthage, the ancient Roman city. "I never saw Bob on shore with any Red Cross babes like many other officers," said Seaman Thomas. "He was always faithful to his wife. He even thought he was having sympathy pains when she was pregnant. He worried about her all the time."[26]

Two months after American, British, and Canadian troops in Operation Overlord stormed the Normandy beaches in northwestern France, SC-978 participated in Operation Anvil-Dragoon, the Allied invasion of German-held southern France. Before dawn on August 15, 1944, 1,300 bombers with fighter escorts pounded the Saint-Tropez peninsula on the French Riviera coast. Three thousand war ships and smaller craft also participated in the action. Ten miles offshore, on HMS *Kimberley*, British Prime Minister Winston Churchill watched the unfolding drama through binoculars.[27] "Our little ship had a front seat," recalled Bob, "so we missed very little. It was quite an impressive sight to watch the Forts [B-17s] and Liberators [B-24s] smother the beach with bombs and then look around and see battleships, cruisers and 'cans' [destroyers] throwing salvo after salvo at gun emplacements. The din was terrific."[28]

Under heavy and accurate German shore battery fire, SC-978, the second minesweeper to enter the Bay of Pampelonne, dropped channel marker buoys for following ships. Within 150 yards of Yellow Beach and under enemy machine-gun fire, SC-978 dragged 300-foot-long cables attached to buoys extending three feet under the surface and skim-swept shoal water for anti-personnel mines. None were located. Behind the minesweepers, rocket-firing vessels—one with future New York Yankee catcher Lawrence "Yogi" Berra on board—detonated on-shore mines.[29]

In his action report, SC-978 Commanding Officer Bennet H. Eskesen stated that the "officers and men under my command displayed great calmness and courage under fire, and never slacked in performance of duty under the most trying conditions." SC-978 was awarded a Presidential Unit Citation, and Lieutenant Eskesen received a Bronze Star for "fearlessly" operating his vessel, "frequently under repeated heavy and accurate gunfire from hostile shore batteries," and "effectively" clearing beach coastal and harbor approaches for landing craft and supply boats, "thereby making possible the timely launching of the assault and the early opening of vital ports to support the advance of the Allied Armies."[30]

At 8 a.m. on August 15, U.S. Third Infantry Division troops landed on Yellow Beach and, by nightfall, had cleared out all German resistance. Compared to 2,499 Americans killed in the Normandy landing, only 95 died on the French Riviera beaches. Within 48 hours, paratroopers reached all their inland objectives. Eminent World War II historian Samuel Eliot Morison evaluated Operation Anvil-Dragoon as an almost perfect amphibious operation.[31]

Nine days later, SC-978 helped secure Port du Buoc, 20 miles west of the key French Mediterranean port, Marseilles. At dawn on August 24, SC-978 and other mine sweepers, under heavy and accurate enemy shore battery fire, commenced operations behind smoke screens in the Golfe de Fos and, in three days, opened a channel to Port du Buoc, which became the principal facility for unloading, storing, and transferring petroleum products to the northward-advancing American army.[32]

When on shore leave, Bob worked out. He played basketball with enlisted men on a makeshift court in a Palermo, Sicily warehouse. "He practiced like he played," remembered James Thomas. "All out! I got some pretty good bruises from his elbows. Nobody could stay with him." Bob organized an SC-978 baseball team and played first base so that Thomas, a semi-pro caliber infielder, could play his customary shortstop position. African-American mess attendant Teddy McKinney handled the catching duties.[33]

In October 1944, Lieutenant (Junior Grade) Robert E. Davies, recently promoted to SC-978 executive officer, received a cablegram announcing the birth of his first son, Jimmy, named for life-long friend, 38 year-old Seton Hall Assistant Athletic Director Father James A. Carey. Celebrating this important family event, Davies and crew members drank 37 bottles of champagne liberated from an abandoned German ship and ate candy bars that he had saved for the occasion. "I was the happiest boy in Europe," he wrote home. Later, Father Carey, who had landed in the first wave of American troops invading Sicily, reciprocated the honor. He painted the nickname, *The Seton Hall Flash*, on his Jeep. "Bob named his baby after me," explained Father Carey, "so, I named my jeep after him."[34]

PACIFIC THEATER COMMAND

As the Allied armed forces tightened their noose around Nazi Germany, American fighting men in the Pacific Theater were thousands of miles and many island battles away from reaching Japan. In November 1944, Lieutenant (JG) Robert Davies returned home on a month's leave. It was heartbreaking to spend so short a time with his wife and infant son, brothers and sister, and parents, and then have to return to a combat theater. But, like most American military personnel transferred from the European to the Pacific Theater, Bob never complained that he had risked his life, done his part, and deserved to stay home. Father Carey requested a combat assignment in the Pacific Theater, landed with the first assault group on Okinawa, and was promoted to Lieutenant Colonel and XXIV Corps Staff Chaplain. The Greatest Generation shared a common mission. America was still at war, and duty to country required finishing the job of defeating the enemy.[35]

On February 18, 1945, Lieutenant (JG) Robert E. Davies reported aboard SC-736, operating from Hollandia on Dutch New Guinea Island north of Australia. Two weeks earlier, the U.S. Sixth Army had entered Manila, the Philippine capital. At the Hollandia rear base build-up area for the Philippine Islands mop-up campaign and expected invasion of Japan, sub chasers performed routine, boring tasks, mostly as pilot ships or harbor entrance patrol boats. When off duty, Lieutenant (JG) Davies played tag football with his men on a beach. On August 8, his third wedding anniversary, he assumed command of SC-736.

Left: Ensign Robert E. Davies (shown with brother Army Corporal Tom) missed three professional basketball seasons while serving his country during World War II. (c. 1944, Courtesy of Mary Davies)

Below: Bob's life-long friend, Seton Hall Athletic Director Father James Carey (left), served as a Catholic chaplain in both the European and Pacific Theaters and nicknamed his jeep after Bob. (c.1944, Courtesy of Mary Davies)

After the Japanese Fourteenth Army surrendered on Luzon, the main Philippine island, SC-736 and three other sub chasers convoyed 1,300 miles to a port on the Philippine island of Samar. [36]

Although he never played basketball in the continental United States west of the Rocky Mountains, "Baffling Bob Davies, sensational basketball artist" starred for the 3,960[th] Navy Samar League team against a Signal Service Battalion squad in a game played in Manila's shell-pocked Rizal Memorial Coliseum located 6,900 miles west of San Francisco, California. Two days before Lieutenant (JG) Davies had arrived in the Pacific Theater, 40 American soldiers had been killed and 315 wounded in bitter fighting to defeat 750 Japanese defenders, who fought to their deaths defending their Rizal Memorial Stadium and Coliseum stronghold. In the game, Bob scored the winning basket on a hook shot from the corner, but suffered his first serious basketball injury—a severe cut over his left eye. [37]

On November 17, 1945, Lieutenant (JG) Davies disembarked from SC-736 for the last time. He brought home only one impairment from his military service. Having experienced seasickness on sub chasers that rolled and pitched in heavy seas, he would never enjoy a merry-go-round ride with his kids. He was far luckier than many basketball contemporaries. Wonder Five teammate John Ruthenberg died flying a B-24 over Germany; African-American Syracuse University basketball star and Tuskegee Airman Wilmeth Sidat-Singh died on a training mission; and Long Island University co-captain Sy Lobello perished during the Battle of the Bulge. Although entitled to a deferment, the legendary Hank Luisetti enlisted in the Navy, contracted spinal meningitis, and was never able to play professional basketball.[38]

Returning World War II combat veterans like Lieutenant (JG) Robert E. Davies did not consider themselves heroes. The Easy Company soldiers immortalized in Stephen Ambrose's book and HBO miniseries *Band of Brothers*, who landed at Normandy and fought in the Battle of the Bulge and on to Hitler's Eagle's Nest, believed that the war's real heroes were the individuals who sacrificed their lives for their country. Asked by a grandson whether he was a hero, one of the Band of Brothers replied in the negative, but stated that he had "served in a company of heroes." Army corporal Leland V. "Lou"

Lieutenant Junior Grade Robert E. Davies commanded SC-736 operating from Hollandia, Dutch New Guinea in the Pacific Theater. (c. 1945, National Archives)

Although the legendary Bob Davies never played west of the Rocky Mountains in the continental U.S., three months after the Japanese surrender in World War II, he starred in an armed forces game in war-damaged Rizal Memorial Coliseum, Manila, Philippines. (National Archives)

Brissie Jr. survived a German artillery round that killed most of his squad members, received the Bronze Star for valor, underwent 23 surgeries, and pitched six MLB seasons with a heavy aluminum brace on his left leg. Asked by Columbia Pictures about making a movie of his life, Brissie declined, declaring, "I'm not a hero."[39]

"I can tell you without hesitation," says *VFW Magazine* Editor-in-Chief Richard K. Kolb, "that no self-respecting veteran of any war regards himself as a hero. Even the ones who are genuine heroes would be the last to describe themselves as such. Traditionally, serving in uniform was an obligation of citizenship. That certainly did not make one a hero."[40]

By serving his country three years and nine months, Bob Davies missed three professional basketball seasons. When on leave, he played five games for Honey Russell's New York Westchesters in the New York/Philadelphia metropolitan area American Basketball League (ABL). He also played two games for Russell's Brooklyn Jewels against the African-American New York Rens, scoring 14 points in a 62–54 loss, and 17 points in a roughly played 60–58 win.[41]

Flying home from the Philippines, Lieutenant (JG) Davies arrived too late to attend the College All-Star Game testimonial dinner in Chicago and receive his miniature silver basketball MVP award. He obtained his honorable discharge from the Officers Separation Center in Philadelphia. His personnel record included a Letter of Commendation from Admiral Alfred H. Richards, who had commanded the mine-sweeping group during the invasion of southern France, and a letter of thanks from Secretary of the Navy James Forrestal. He received the World War II Victory Medal, American Theater Ribbon, European Theater Ribbon with star, and Asiatic-Pacific Theater Ribbon. He had served overseas a total of 18 months.[42]

As Lieutenant (JG) Davies mustered out of the Navy, representatives from the NBL Sheboygan (WI) Redskins and Youngstown (OH) Bears contacted him. During the war, the NBL had almost folded. In peacetime, team owners eagerly awaited the resumption of league play. And then Bob heard that somebody named Harrison, who did not mention a city or a team name, wanted to talk to him.[43]

NOTES

1   Cain Chamberlin, "Return To Cape May," *American Legion Magazine,*
Feb. 2012, 50–51; "Battle Of the Atlantic: Ducks & Men," *Time,* March 9,
1942, 23; "Seton Ace May Join U.S. Team: Bob Davies, Key Man of Seton
Hall's Cage Squad, May Soon Be Shooting Guns Instead of Baskets;
Mates Likely to Follow," *Newark Star-Ledger,* Jan. 22, 1942; Mary Davies,
telephone conversation with author, Aug. 18, 2009; "Seton Hall Star
Joins Navy," *NYT,* April 3, 1942.

2   Robert Edris Davies Notice of Separation from the U.S. Naval Service,
Jan. 5, 1946, National Personnel Records Center, St. Louis, MO
(hereafter cited as "Notice of Separation"); "Davies Completes Training;
Gets Camp Dewey Post," *Great Lakes Bulletin* (June 13, 1942): 7; "Miss
Helfrich Becomes Bride: Married to Robert E. Davies in Memorial
Lutheran Church," BDSHOF.

3   Mary Davies, interview by author, Coral Springs, FL, Dec. 3, 2007;
telephone conversations, May 22, 2009, and Sept. 8, 2011.

4   Roger S. Gogan, *Bluejackets of Summer: The History of the Great Lakes
Naval Baseball Team 1942–1945,* 16–17, 28–29; "Athletics promote": Roger
S. Gogan, *By Air, Ground And Sea: The History of Great Lakes Navy Football,*
53; Lt. Paul D. Hinkle, "'Basketball Is Best Sport for Morale' Says Paul
Hinkle, Great Lakes Coach," *Nevada State (Reno) Journal,* Jan. 3, 1943;
"An Editorial: Athletes Not War-Time Prima Donnas": *Great Lakes
Bulletin* (July 11, 1942): 2; Gogan, *By Air,* 33; "Editorial: Athletes Prove
Worth as Navy Leaders, Fighters in This War": *Great Lakes Bulletin* (Sept.
19, 1942): 2.

5   "Bob Davies Is Now An Ensign: Leaves Station," BDSHOF; Irv Kupcinet,
"Fast Pitches Around the Loop," *Chicago Daily Times,* Oct. 16, 1942; Lt.
Commander J. Russell Cook, "Basketball At Great Lakes," *Converse
Basketball Year Book 1942,* 27; "I went": Mary Davies, telephone
conversation with author, May 22, 2009.

6   http:// www.hoopball.com/halloffamers/bhof-paul-hinkle.html; Lt. Paul
D. Hinkle, "A Great Season At Great Lakes," *Converse Basketball Yearbook
1943,* 23.

7   "Sailors Risk Victory Streak Against Notre Dame," *Great Lakes Bulletin*
(Feb. 19, 1943): 7; Ken Rappoport, *Tar Heel: North Carolina Basketball,* 54,
56.

8   John Schleppi, *Chicago's Showcase Of Basketball: The World Tournament of Professional Basketball and the College All-Star Game,* 131, 137–38; https://en.wikipedia.org/wiki/Chicago_Stadium.

9   "out of the east": James E. Enright, "Royals Win All-Star Game," *Converse Basketball Yearbook 1952,* 37.

10   Harry D. Wilson, "College All-Star Championship Game," *Converse Basketball Year Book 1943,* 39.

11   "package": Leo Fischer, "All-Stars in Thrilling Cage Win, 61–55: Nip Oshkosh Pro Champs," *Chicago Herald-American,* Nov. 28, 1942; Howard Barry, "College All-Stars Rally To Beat Oshkosh, 61–55: Pro Quintet Weakens in Stadium Game," *Chicago Daily Tribune,* Nov. 28, 1942.

12   "That set": Salzberg, *Set Shot,* 49.

13   Champaign-Urbana News-Gazette, *Fighting Illini Basketball: A Hardwood History,* 7–13; "Illini Defeat Great Lakes, 57–53," *The News-Gazette (Champaign-Urbana, IL),* Dec. 20, 1942.

14   Wilfrid Smith, "Great Lakes And Stanford Fives To Clash Tonight," *Chicago Daily Tribune,* Dec. 30, 1942; "The officers": Hap Glaudi, "Navy's Scintillating Sailors Outclass Stanford, 57–41," *New Orleans Item,* Dec. 31, 1942; Pete Baird, "Davies Stars For All-Star Sailor Quint," *New Orleans Times-Picayune,* Dec. 31, 1942; Harry Martinez, "Sports From The Crow's Nest," BDSHOF.

15   "Hoop stars": Bob Roesler, "Recall Bob Davies? Now There's Dickie," *New Orleans Times-Picayune,* Dec. 22, 1958; http://www.allstatesugarbowl.org/site517.php.

16   Lt. Paul D. (Tony) Hinkle, "A Great Season At Great Lakes," *Converse Basketball Yearbook 1943,* 23; Gogan, *Bluejackets of Summer,* 16; Wilfrid Smith, "Sailors Beat Irish, 60 To 56, In Overtime," *Chicago Sunday Tribune,* Feb. 21, 1943; "Notre Dame Beats Great Lakes In Overtime," *Chicago Daily Tribune,* March 9, 1943; "Davies Winner Of Great Lakes Scoring Crown," BDSHOF.

17   "I've never seen": Joe Reister, "Lakes Best Team Rupp Has Seen," *Louisville (KY) Courier-Journal,* March 5, 1943; Tommy Fitzgerald, "UK Faces 2-Ocean Navy In Great Lakes" and "Great Lakes Tumbles Kentucky For 25th [*sic*] Consecutive Win 53–39," *Louisville Courier-Journal,* March 6 and 7, 1943.

18   Seymour Smith, Jack Rimer and Dick Triptow, *A Tribute To Armed*

Forces Basketball 1941–1969, 55–56, 85, 101, 103; "Final Dunkel Ratings For 1942–1943 Basketball Season," *Converse Basketball Yearbook 1943,* 10; Vincent, *Mudville's Revenge,* 272–74.

19   "Bob Davies Has Basketball Fans Agog," Seton Hall College Athletic Association Souvenir Program: Seton Hall College vs. Baltimore University, March 1, 1941, 12, SHUAC; Gogan, *Bluejackets of Summer,* 192; "I don't": Steve Nagy, telephone conversation with author, Oct. 28, 2008.

20   Notice of Separation; Sidney Shalett, "Our School of Death-to-U-Boats," *NYT Magazine,* Feb. 13, 1944, 11, 43–44.

21   "See what": Theodore R. Treadwell, *Splinter Fleet: The Wooden Subchasers of World War II,* 26–27.

22   Eric Purdon, *Black Company: The Story of Subchaser 1264,* 34–37, 44–45; Samuel Eliot Morrison, *History Of United States Naval Operations In World War II: 1 The Battle of the Atlantic September 1939–May 1943,* 231–33; Edward P. Stafford, *Subchaser,* 2–5; Mary Davies, telephone conversation with author, Oct. 1, 2007; "Sub-Chaser's Davies Lets Other Fellow Do Shooting," BDSHOF; "SCTC Hands Five By Five First Defeat," *Miami(FL) Daily News,* Jan. 14, 1944; Bert Collier, "Miami Sub Chasers Win 18 Straight; Best U.S. Service Five, Coach Says," *Miami Daily News,* Feb. 3, 1944; Seth Kantor, "Nuggets Wilt, Fall Before Royals, 81–65," *Rocky Mountain (Denver, CO) News,* Dec. 14, 1949.

23   USS SC-978 Deck Log, May 3, 1944, Records of the Office Bureau of Naval Personnel, RG 24, National Archives at College Park, MD (hereafter referred to as NACP); SC-978 War Diary, May 3, 1944, Records of Chief of Naval Operations, RG 38, NACP; "the dwarf": Treadwell, *Splinter Fleet,* 3; Ibid., 4–5, 20–24.

24   Dick Davies, telephone conversation with author, Dec. 30, 2011; "a kind": Treadwell, *Splinter Fleet,* x; Bill Davies, telephone conversation with author, May 21, 2008; "That doesn't": Ed Davies, telephone conversation with author, July 24, 2008.

25   "You couldn't ask": James Thomas, telephone conversation with author, Jan. 19, 2009; Thomas to author, Jan. 12, 2009 (author's possession).

26   Treadwell, *Splinter Fleet,* 74–75; Ted Treadwell notes on interview with Henry Serra, Northport, FL, Feb. 13, 1996, provided by Dan Treadwell, Tahoma Park, MD; SC-978 Deck Log, May 18 through June 19, 1944,

Records of the Office Bureau of Naval Personnel, RG 24, NACP; SC-978 War Diary, July 1, 1944, Records of Chief of Naval Operations, RG 38, NACP; "I never saw": Thomas, telephone conversation with author, Jan. 19, 2009.

27   William B. Breuer, *Operation Dragoon: The Allied Invasion of the South of France*, 44–45, 167, 174, 176, 236, 246–47, 249; Steven J. Zaloga, *Operation Dragoon 1944: France's other D-Day*, 37, 41–50, 89; William B. Breuer, *Feuding Allies: The Private Wars of the High Command*, 233.

28   "Our little": "Ensign Bob Davies Lauds Infantry In Invasion," BDSHOF.

29   SC-978 Deck Log, June 19, 1944, Records of the Office Bureau of Naval Personnel, RG 24, NACP; Gary Bloomfield, *Duty, Honor, Victory: America's Athletes in World War II*, 267–69.

30   "officers and men": USS SC-978 Action Report, Aug. 31, 1944, p. 4, Records of the Office Bureau of Naval Personnel, RG 24, NACP; "fearlessly": Lt. Bennet H. Eskesen Bronze Star Medal Citation, prepared Jan. 24, 1945, Records of the Chief of Naval Operations, Records of Awards and Decorations, RG 38, NACP.

31   Samuel Eliot Morison, *History Of United States Naval Operations In World War II: 11 The Invasion of France and Germany 1944–1945*, 225–27, 236–41, 248–49, 256–64, 275, 281–87, 291–92.

32   SC-978 Deck Log, Aug. 15–16 and 24–26, 1944, Records of the Office Bureau of Naval Personnel, RG 24, NACP.

33   "He practiced": Thomas, telephone conversation with author, Jan. 19, 2009.

34   "I was": "Good News Trebled," *Harrisburg Telegraph* (handwritten note dated Oct. 7, 1944), BDSHOF; "Silver Jubilee (1936–1961) of Rev. James Aloysius Carey," 2, SHUAC; "Bob named": "O'REALLY" by O'Reilly," BDSHOF.

35   "LT. Bob Davies Given Command," BDSHOF; Father Carey: "Silver Jubilee," 2, SHUAC.

36   SC-736 Deck Log, Feb. 18–Nov. 17, 1945, Records of the Office Bureau of Naval Personnel, RG 24, NACP; Daniel E. Barbey, *MacArthur's Amphibious Navy: Seventh Amphibious Force Operations, 1943–1945*, 179, 229–30, 233, 259; Samuel E. Morison, *History Of United States Naval Operations In World War II: 8 New Guinea and the Marianas March 1944– August 1944*, 35, 62, 80.

37 "Baffling Bob Davies": "Bob Davies Leads Navy To 50–48 Cage Win
    Over Signal Wildcats," BDSHOF; Robert Ross Smith, *United States Army
    In World War II: The War in the Pacific; Triumph in the Philippines*, 246–47,
    270, 275–79; 9, 431; Gogan, *By Air*, 308.

38 Mary Davies telephone conversations with author, Oct. 1, 2007, Sept.
    28, 2009; "What Became of Famous Five?" The *Setonian*, Oct. 21, 1946,
    7; Luke Cyphers, "The Lost Hero: Wilmeth Sidat-Singh, a two-sport
    star at Syracuse and a Renaissance Man," *New York Daily News*, Feb. 25,
    2001; Clair Bee dedication to *Championship Ball*; Gary L. Bloomfield, "Big
    Leagues Drained By Manpower Demands," *VFW Magazine*, Jan. 1999,
    31; Rob Newell, *From Playing Field to Battlefield: Great Athletes Who Served
    in World War II*, 8.

39 Maj. Dick Winters with Col. C. Kingseed, *Beyond Band of Brothers: The
    War Memoirs of Major Dick Winters*, 455–56; Stephen E. Ambrose, *Band
    of Brothers: E Company, 506th Regiment, 101st Airborne from Normandy to
    Hitler's Eagle's Nest*, 307; "I'm not": Richard K. Kolb, "World War II Vets
    Stood Out in Sports and War Alike," *VFW Magazine*, Nov./Dec. 2014, 36;
    Ibid., 32.

40 "I can tell": Richard Kolb e-mail to author, Oct. 23, 2014.

41 Notice of Separation; "Signed By Pro Court Team," *Harrisburg Telegraph*,
    Nov. 23, 1944; http://www.apbr.org/American Basketball League
    Statistics 1938–39 to 1952–53; Francis Feighery, "Renaissance Five
    Beats Brooklyn Jewels, 62–54" and Joseph Cassano, "Davies, Holzman
    Feature; Modzelewski Leads Whalers," BDSHOF.

42 Wilfrid Smith, "All-Stars Test Basket Champs: Collegians Meet Pros
    in Stadium Tonight," *Chicago Daily Tribune*, Nov. 30, 1945; Notice of
    Separation; James Forrestal, Secretary of the Navy, to "My dear Mr.
    Davies," Feb. 9, 1946, in possession of Dick Davies, Winchester, VA.

43 Salzberg, *Set Shot*, 49–50.

THE ROCHESTER ROYALS CINDERELLA SEASON

FORTY-ONE-YEAR-OLD LESTER "LES" HARRISON HAD DECIDED TO bring big-time hoops to his hometown, Rochester, New York. After graduating from high school, Les took over his father's horse and wagon grocery route and progressed to selling fruits and vegetables from the back of a truck. "I got my education in Public Market College," boasted Les, who had a proven track record promoting semi-professional basketball teams. His cagers initially played on the tiny Saint Stanislaus Church Hall court where, at one end, players leaped onto a stage after driving to the basket. As attendance improved, his teams upgraded to the East Main Street Armory and Columbus Civic Center. They won 133 games and lost 40, competing against the African-American Harlem Globetrotters and New York Rens, NBL Fort Wayne (IN) Zollner Pistons, Sheboygan Redskins and Oshkosh All-Stars, and AAU Akron (OH) Goodyears and Grumman Aircraft Company (Long Island) Flyers.[1]

After the austere war years, Rochester-area residents were looking forward to professional sports entertainment. Located on the Genesee River upstream from Lake Ontario, Rochester, with a population of about 325,000, was the nation's 23rd, and the Empire State's third, largest city. Eastman Kodak Company; Haloid (later Xerox); Bausch & Lomb (optical instruments); Stromberg-Carlson (telecommunications equipment); R.T. French Company (mustards and spices); Hickey-Freeman (men's clothing); Hickok Manufacturing Company (which awarded a belt with a jewel-studded solid gold buckle to the Professional Athlete of the Year), and several other profitable light industrial companies operated factories in the city. Newspaper magnate Frank Gannett published the morning *Democrat & Chronicle* and afternoon *Times-Union.* Residents attended Rochester Philharmonic Orchestra concerts and cheered for the Red Wings, the St. Louis Cardinals' top farm team.[2]

NATIONAL BASKETBALL LEAGUE FRANCHISE

Les Harrison and his brother Jack had pooled their assets, and Les had traveled to Chicago, Illinois, met with NBL Commissioner Ward "Piggy" Lambert, and purchased a franchise for $25,000 ($329,000 today). The eight-team NBL—the NBA's earliest precursor—was the nation's only professional basketball league with a paid commissioner, balanced schedule, and full-time players under contract. During the 1942–43 season, the league had been reduced to five teams, two of which had played African-Americans. [3]

The NBL in 1945 was a bush league compared to the modern NBA. Millionaire manufacturer Fred Zollner owned the only financially strong franchise, the Fort Wayne Zollner Pistons. A civic corporation, similar to today's NFL Green Bay Packers ownership group, operated the Sheboygan Redskins. A local traffic cop refereed some Oshkosh All-Stars home games. Indianapolis (IN) franchise owner Frank Kautsky sold game tickets over his grocery store counter. Although the New York Rens, Washington Bears, and Harlem Globetrotters had won three of the last five Chicago World Professional Basketball Tournament championships and over a million African Americans had served in the U.S. Armed Forces during World War II, not one African American played for an NBL team during the 1945–46 season.[4]

Now a bona fide franchise owner, "Lucky Les," as Rochester sportswriters nicknamed him, parked his produce truck for the last time and devoted his life to his basketball team. Operating from Jack's law office and aided by a secretary, Les functioned as principal owner, general manager, booking agent, player personnel director, scout, recruiter, travel coordinator, equipment manager, and, on a few occasions, janitor. Jack, assisted by Les, handled publicity, and they both played poker with reporters. Coaching chores were handled in a unique manner. Chief bench jockey Les sat next to calm and collected 34-year-old nominal coach Eddie Malanowicz, who some-times missed road games due to his responsibilities as a school prin-cipal in the Buffalo (NY) area. Eddie and Les, or Les by himself, made tactical decisions with input from their mature and experienced play-ers. Deservedly so, multi-tasking NBA pioneer Lester Harrison has been inducted into the Naismith Memorial Basketball Hall of Fame (Springfield, MA) as a Contributor.[5]

With the NBL opening game less than a month away, the Rochester franchise assets consisted of contracts with two journey-men semi-pro players, two used basketballs, and a lease for 4,200-seat Edgerton Park Sports Arena, a city-owned facility converted from a reform school drill hall. Les described the barn-like structure as "a glorified warehouse." There was a reason Les had not mentioned a team name when he left the message for Bob. The team did not have one. A teenager won a $100 Victory Bond Contest for selecting the team name. Rochester fans hoped that the "Royals" would soon bring a sports crown to their fair city.[6]

BUILDING A GREAT TEAM

"The team was put together by word of mouth," said Al "Digger" Cervi, a veteran of Harrison's pre-war semi-pro squads. And what an aggregation, especially for sports trivia buffs! The roster included two guards (Bob Davies and Al Cervi) and a future coach (Red Holzman) later inducted into the Naismith Memorial Basketball Hall of Fame, a Pro Football Hall of Fame quarterback (Cleveland Brown Otto Graham), a .500-hitting St. Louis Cardinal 1946 World Series baseball hero (Del Rice), and a future television and movie star (Chuck "The Rifleman" Connors)!

The word-of-mouth recruiting process had begun with a 1:30 a.m. phone call in late December 1944 to Coast Guardsman Andrew "Fuzzy" Levane, who was stationed in New York City. The caller iden-tified himself as Les Harrison and offered Fuzzy $150 ($2,020 today) for practicing on Saturday and playing in the Sunday game, as well as train fare to and from Rochester. When Fuzzy stepped outside the Rochester train station at 4:30 a.m. on Saturday, he could not believe his eyes. Les was waiting for him in a produce truck. [7]

Bob Davies played his entire professional career (1945–55) for the Rochester Royals in Edgerton Park Sports Arena, a city-owned facility converted from a reform school drill hall. (c. 1950, City of Rochester, NY Archives)

Savvy entrepreneur Les needed a Jewish player to keep his Jewish fan base happy. He mistakenly believed that Levane was Jewish. Finding out that Fuzzy was Italian, Harrison told him: "Get me a Jewish player. I don't care if he can play or not. Just make sure he's Jewish." Fuzzy recruited his Jewish friends, CCNY and St. John's University stars Red Holzman and Dutch Garfinkel.[8]

"There was one boy I didn't want to let get away from me," said Les. "I had seen him with Seton Hall and Great Lakes, and I knew he was the greatest offensive player in the business. I had to out-bid every pro club in the country for Davies, but I got him."[9]

After talking to Les on the phone, Bob checked out the Royals. Impressed by their six-win and no-loss NBL record, and their roster including several outstanding New York City area players, Bob decided to sign with the Royals.

*The Edgerton Park Sports Arena court was smaller than regulation
size and the end lines were close to walls. (c. 1954, Courtesy of the
General Mills Archives)*

Les called Bob back and asked how much money he wanted.
Bob had been earning $465 a month ($6,120 today) in combat pay as
a naval officer. Honey Russell had advised him that he could earn
$1,000 a month as a professional basketball player. Bob named that
figure. After a long pause, Les said that he needed to talk to Jack. The
Harrison brothers conferred and agreed to pay Bob $1,000 per month
($13,200 today) for the remainder of the basketball season.[10]

Thus was born one of the five early NBA franchises that sur-
vive today (now the Sacramento Kings via Kansas City Kings and
Cincinnati Royals).

Bob joined a cohesive group of mature men on the Royals roster.
"There was a closeness in those early days that we didn't really enjoy
later on," he remembered. "You can't forget that in the earlier days
the war had just ended and everybody was so happy that the war

was finally over. It was celebration time." On train trips, Les Harrison bought sandwiches and beer for everyone and played cards with his players. The teammates searched for restaurants serving large tasty portions at reasonable prices and ate together, met in bars after games, and shared hotel rooms. Sometimes Les joined them for dinner. [11]

Every Royal but one had served in the Armed Forces, and five had earned All-American honors, but Bob was the only ex-officer and only combat veteran. He fitted into the "speed boy" group with 6' 1", 195-pound Northwestern University All-American and Navy V-5 Flight School pivot man Otto Graham; 6' 2", 190-pound St. John's University and New York District Coast Guard forward/swingman Andrew "Fuzzy" Levane; 6', 190-pound St. John's University All-American and West Point Detachment guard Jack "Dutch" Garfinkel; and CCNY and Norfolk Naval Training Station guard Red Holzman. The other group included 5' 11", 185-pound high school dropout and Foster Field (Army Air Corps) guard Al Cervi; University of North Carolina All-American and Great Lakes Naval Training Station center George Glamack; 6' 8", 220-pound Georgetown College All-American and Wright Field center John E. "Long John" Mahnken; flatfooted 6' 2", 190-pound defense industry worker and semi-pro cager Del Rice (a baseball catcher with questionable speed who stole two bases in 17 major league seasons); and a fifth player, who varied throughout the season.[12]

REGULAR SEASON

A few hours after arriving in Rochester on December 15, 1945, Bob Davies played less than two minutes in a rough-and-tumble exhibition contest against the Chicago Colored Monarchs. He made his two field goal attempts, but, in a melee under a basket, suffered a cut, this time over his right eye, which required stitches.[13]

Three nights later, Bob Davies made an inauspicious NBL debut against the Sheboygan Redskins. His eye laceration unhealed, he played only a few minutes and failed to score. He needed time to adjust from military to civilian life, retool his basketball skills, and synchronize with his teammates. [14]

In his third NBL appearance, Bob showed flashes of brilliance as the Royals butchered the hapless Youngstown Bears, 70–27, before

3,800 Edgerton Park fans. "The darling of the pew holders, from the back bench of the bleachers [$1.44] to front row courtside center [$2.40]," gushed *Rochester Democrat & Chronicle* sports columnist Elliot Cushing, "was blond, blushing Bobby Davies, the rubber-legged kid. Blazing fast and apparently able to do everything with a basketball except swallow it, Bobby teamed with Otto Graham in some passing magic.... If it were the theater, the boys would be bedded today with injured vertebrae from answering curtain calls." *Rochester Times-Union* sports columnist Matt Jackson suggested that Harrison "copyright that Davies-Graham off-the-wrist pass which is about as close to the old shell game as we have ever seen on a basketball court." When Bob left the game, he received a tremendous ovation. In a post-game interview, he expressed dissatisfaction with his physical conditioning, feel for the ball, and familiarity with teammates. "I'll be ready in a week or so now," said Bob, "and then I hope to play well enough to earn my pay." [15]

"Bobby wasn't in top shape, naturally," said Les Harrison, "and his style is so different that about three-quarters of the season went by before the rest of the team learned to play with him. So there were times when he didn't look too good. In many a game we had to pull the guy. But finally he and the others meshed." Once Bob and his teammates became accustomed to each other, the Royals occasionally utilized a three-guard offense with Bob, the tallest, as swingman, along with Red Holzman and Al Cervi.[16]

Late in the season, Kevin "Chuck" Connors joined the Royals. During the war, Connors had played center for the Army West Point (NY) Detachment team and moonlighted a few times on weekend passes for Harrison's semi-pro squads. In locker rooms, train stations, and bars, free-spirited Chuck strained his Royals teammates' patience reciting, among other classics, "Casey at the Bat," "The Face on the Barroom Floor," and "The Charge of the Light Brigade." On the basketball court, Chuck mimicked referees and performed handstands. His basketball shooting, however, lacked his "Rifleman" TV show accuracy, and his 2.0 points per game scoring average wowed few spectators. Chuck's professional basketball moment of infamy occurred the next season when, as a Basketball Association of America

(BAA) Boston Celtic he attempted a dunk during warm-ups and shattered a Boston Garden glass backboard. [17]

"Bob Davies," said Connors, "was the first guy who could pass behind his neck, who could fake—he could dribble behind the back. He did the behind the back pass before anybody. A lot of players on that [Royals] team would get hit in the face because they weren't watching—he was like Magic Johnson—and if you weren't watching for that 'no-look' pass, you'd get hit in the face."[18]

As a professional basketball player, however, Bob Davies used only about 30 percent of his collegiate bag of tricks. He dribbled behind his back in three or four NBL games without gaining an advantage and stopped doing it. He did not have time to practice the trick on road trips and realized that he could not successfully execute it more than once against a savvy pro defender. And, most significantly, teammates, especially Red Holzman, as well as coach Les Harrison, frowned on showboating and intentionally embarrassing opponents. Consequently, Bob did not even dribble behind his back in pre-game warm-ups. He performed the dribble for a 1948–49 season film clip and a 1954 Wheaties TV commercial. "So I was limited in my style of play," said Bob. "And it did take a big part of my game away."[19]

"[Davies] was ahead of his time," pointed out Les Harrison. "I encouraged that. I thought it was the coming thing. Davies started the behind-the-back dribble. Davies started the fast break. He was way out of line because he was so far ahead of the game…. Sure he was different. But it was the modern basketball that he was leading us to."[20]

Despite a slow start and limitations on his ball-handling wizardry, Davies averaged nine points per game (PPG) for the season. George Glamack ranked third in NBL scoring with a 12.3 PPG average, and Red Holzman and Al Cervi followed at 10.7 PPG. Holzman garnered the Rookie of the Year award, and Holzman and Glamack All-NBL First Team, and Cervi All-NBL Second Team honors.[21]

NBL PLAYOFFS

The Royals finished second in the NBL eastern division behind the defending champion Zollner Pistons, and opened the 1945–46 playoffs in Fort Wayne (population 118,410) located in northeastern Indiana

Early NBA players traveling to Fort Wayne (IN) for games with the Zollner Pistons never forgot their chilly, predawn hikes from a railroad platform on the edge of a corn field to the Green Parrot Restaurant for a hearty breakfast. (Courtesy of William H. Willennar Genealogy Center, A Service of Eckhart (IN) Public Library)

13 miles south of the New York Central Railroad (NYCRR) east–west tracks. Taking a late night NYCRR train from Rochester, the Royals got off about 5:30 a.m. at an unscheduled stop—a wooden platform on the edge of an Indiana cornfield. Shivering in the bitter cold and carrying suitcases, they hustled a mile down a snow-covered, two-lane road into the hamlet of Waterloo. Someone in the group tossed pebbles against a second-story window of the Green Parrot Restaurant, and the owner and his wife arose, dressed, rushed downstairs, and served their tall customers hot coffee and a hearty breakfast. The vagabond cagers then snoozed through a cab ride to Fort Wayne, checked into the Hotel Van Orman, and slept until dinner time.[22]

The Zollner Pistons played in the Northside High School gymnasium, which seated 3,800 frenzied Hoosiers. Visiting players nicknamed the place the "The Snake Pit" or "The Bucket of Blood." Bob called it "The Lion's Den." A regulation-size basketball court was and still is 94 feet long and 50 feet wide; the Pit's floor measured just 80 feet long and 48 feet wide. An older woman, Ma Collins, walloped visiting players on the head with a big saddlebag purse as they ran onto the court. One night, Les Harrison, seated on the Royals bench, felt a sharp pain in the back of his head, jumped up, turned around, swung a roundhouse right, and gasped when the woman who had whacked him with her purse tumbled onto the floor in front of him. Fans behind a four-foot-high railing separating the front-row seats from the court pulled the leg hairs of visiting players trying to inbound the ball. A spectator leaned over a balcony railing and tossed a rolled tin foil ball that hit Royals coach Ed Malanowicz under the eye. Two BB pellets struck George Mikan in the leg, and a radiator regulator cap barely missed him. Fans sometimes jumped into fights between players. A Rochester newspaper published a cartoon entitled "Ft. Wayne Feudin" depicting Zollner Pistons fans holding placards reading "Censored" and "Ditto." "The place felt like you were in a bull ring, fighting bulls," said Boston Celtics coach Red Auerbach.[23]

Listening to the opening playoff game broadcast over a direct telephone line to radio station WHEC, Rochester fans suffered as Bob Davies missed all 14 field goal attempts and converted two of three foul shots. The cold Royals, shooting a pitiful 16 percent from the field, lost, 54–44. But, in the second contest, the Royals bounced back, winning 58–52, as Glamack netted 13 points and Davies and Holzman scored 11 each. In the third game, Bob "Mr. Kangaroo" Davies notched 23 points in a 70–54 Royals victory. "Davies, bouncing all over the floor on his 'rubber legs'," wrote a Rochester reporter, "raised havoc with the Zollners' offensive by leaping high into the air to drag down passes all through the final quarter." Al Cervi contributed mightily to the victory, holding Fort Wayne's great two-hand set shooter, Bobby McDermott, to five field goals in the four-game series.[24]

In the NBL Finals, the Royals swept three games from the Sheboygan Redskins. Sparked by Red Holzman's ten-point third period scoring outburst, they won the first game handily at home. In the Royals' second home game victory, "Rubber Legs" Davies netted 22 points. His fast break baskets, deadly set shots, ball hawking, and clever passing kept the Royals in the game in the first half, and his brilliant fast break leadership in a third quarter rally doomed the Redskins. During the third game in the Sheboygan Armory, 300 school kids, seated in court-end bleachers erected on a stage, bombarded the Royals, sitting in front of them, with chewing gum, folded newspapers, buttons, pebbles, tinfoil balls, and match boxes. Down on the 90-foot-long by 50-foot-wide court—the NBL's most spacious—Bob Davies, who scored 12 points, left the final game, a 66–48 rout, to thunderous applause. Displaying balanced scoring, Glamack, Davies, Holzman, and Cervi averaged 12.8, 12.3, 11.8, and 10.0 PPG, respectively, during the playoffs.[25]

"Les Harrison's All-Americans lived up to their laurels (there is no getting away from that)," wrote Sheboygan sports writer Harold Bogenhagen. "Those guys were a bunch of wildcats," said Nate Messinger, who refereed all three games. "I thought the Illinois Whiz Kids were fast, but Davies, Cervi, Holzman and Mahnken would have left those kids standing still. There is no offensive like the fast break when you have the men who can make it tick—and this Rochester bunch was tailored to order for the lightning break." [26]

"That 1945–1946 team was the best I ever played with," reflected Bob ten years later. "We had speed and drive. We ran our opponents into the ground."[27]

Lucky Les had brought the national professional basketball championship to his beloved hometown in only five months. It had been just four months since Bob Davies played in shell-pocked Rizal Coliseum in Manila, Philippines. "Here's your rags to riches story," rejoiced Al Cervi. "From St. Stanislaus Hall to the world's championship, Les, Eddie and I. Our dream has finally come true." The NBL awarded the Royals the Naismith Memorial Trophy symbolic of the national professional basketball championship.[28]

GLOBETROTTERS AND RENS

But the Royals' Cinderella season was not yet over. Prior to the NBL playoffs, Les Harrison had booked an exhibition game in Schenectady, New York. In addition to 34 league games, NBL teams, living hand to mouth, played exhibitions to help meet the payroll. Les provided deli sandwiches and drove with the players in two automobiles to nearby towns to play local teams. Before the opening whistle, he collected the Royals' share of the gate receipts and stashed the cash in a paper bag under his seat. He really liked the take in prosperous Schenectady, the home of General Electric Corporation. The promoters—the city police chief, county clerk, and a barber—guaranteed Les $1,000 ($13,200 today) per exhibition. And "Electric City" fans willingly paid "double" to see Bob Davies play.[29]

On March 26, 1946, the Royals played the first game between a present-day NBA franchise and the Harlem Globetrotters. Formed in 1926, the Trotters started barnstorming around the country the next year. To conserve their strength and to avoid alienating hometown fans, the Trotters clowned to hold down the pace of the game and the score differential. Owner-coach Abe Saperstein promoted his Globetrotters, the 1940 Chicago World Professional Basketball Tournament champion, as the world's best basketball team. [30]

Filling the Schenectady State Armory, 3,200 spectators eagerly looked forward to the matchup between the Globetrotters' Reece "Goose" Tatum, a.k.a. the "Crown Prince of Basketball," and the Royals' George Glamack, a.k.a. the "Blind Bomber." Bob Davies did not play because he had reported for work as the Seton Hall baseball coach. Uncertain of the NBL's long-term viability, he had hedged his bets and accepted a traditional job that fit his long-range career objective. After the Globetrotters performed their "Magic Circle" warm-up routine to the tune of "Sweet Georgia Brown," they played serious basketball. The *Schenectady Union-Star* headline told the story: "Royals, Minus Davies, Drop 57–55 Decision to Trotters." Glamack netted 23 and Tatum 20 points.[31]

Two weeks later, the Royals, this time with Bob Davies in uniform, met the New York Rens, the nation's other premier black professional basketball team, in the Schenectady Sports Club "All-American Basketball Invitation Tournament." In 1923, the Rens had started playing games in the Harlem Renaissance Casino. The 1939 Rens won the Chicago World Professional Basketball Tournament and are enshrined in the Naismith Memorial Basketball Hall of Fame as a team. Playing under the name "Schenectady Pros" and wearing uniforms emblazoned "Schd'ty," the Royals, in their 80th game of the season, defeated the Rens, 73–59, and claimed the All-American Basketball Invitation Tournament championship. Bringing down the curtain on the 1945–46 Cinderella season, Bob Davies, the "fair-haired boy of the Schenectady fans," captured the tournament "scoring toga" with an 18-point average and garnered Tournament Outstanding Player and All-Tournament First Team honors.[32]

NOTES

1   Donald M. Fisher, "Lester Harrison and the Rochester Royals, 1945–1957: A Jewish Entrepreneur in the NBA," 208–11, in *Sports and the American Jew,* ed. Steven A. Riess; "I got": Les Harrison, telephone conversation with author, Dec. 30, 1988; Jack Newcombe, "Old Pro From Syracuse," *Sport,* April 1952, 75; Roger Meyer, *Rochester Seagrams History 1936–1937 to 1944–1945,* 1–30.

2   Blake McKelvey, *Rochester: An Emerging Metropolis 1925–1961,* 156; Blake McKelvey, *Rochester on the Genesee: The Growth of a City,* 2nd ed., 209–12; Stanley Levey, "The Cities Of America: Rochester, NY," *Saturday Evening Post,* March 18, 1950, 38–39, 122–25; http://www.hickoksports.om/history/hickbelt.shtml.

3   Donald M. Fisher, "The Rochester Royals and the Transformation of Professional Basketball, 1945–57" in *International Journal of the History of Sport* 10, no. 1 (April 1993): 20–21; Measuring Worth; Murry R. Nelson, *The National Basketball League: A History, 1935–1949,* 1, 112–14, 142–44.

4   Robert W. Peterson, *Cages To Jump Shots: Pro Basketball's Early Years,* 132, 134; Todd Gould, *Pioneers of the Hardwood: Indiana and the Birth of Professional Basketball,* 112, 127; Elliot Cushing, "Sports Eye-View," *D&C,* March 10, 1947; Michael Clodfelter, *Warfare and Armed Conflicts: A Statistical Encyclopedia of Casualty and Other Figures, 1494–2007,* 561 (1,093,000).

5   Sam Goldaper, *Great Moments in Pro Basketball,* 29–30; Fisher, "Rochester Royals," 33; Jeff Marcus, *Biographical Directory of Professional Basketball Coaches, s.v.* "Malanowicz, Edmund E."; Roeder, "Bob Davies," *Sport,* Feb. 1948, 53; Hubbard, *NBA Encyclopedia,* 3rd ed., 111 (Harrison).

6   Elliot Cushing, "Sports Eye View," *D&C,* March 25, 1946; https://en.wikipedia.org/wiki/Edgerton_Park_Arena; "Schoolboy, 15, Names Pro Hoopmen 'Royals'," *D&C,* Nov. 9, 1945.

7   "The team": Al Cervi, telephone conversation with author, June 1, 2004; Fuzzy Levane, telephone conversation with author, Feb. 1, 2005; Meyer, *Rochester Seagrams History*, 29–30; Measuring Worth.

8   "Get me": Red Holzman and Harvey Frommer, *Red on Red*, 15; Neil D. Isaacs, *Vintage NBA Basketball: The Pioneer Era (1946–1956)*, 75–77.

9   "There was one": Roeder, "Bob Davies," *Sport*, Feb. 1948, 53.

10   "Davies Joins Royal Quint," *D&C*, Dec. 12, 1945; Salzberg, *Set Shot*, 50 (8–0 record incorrect); Bob Davies, interview with Charles Salzberg, Coral Springs, FL, 1986, transcription and Davies-edited transcript, Joseph M. O'Brien Historical Resource Center, Naismith Memorial Basketball Hall of Fame, Springfield, MA; E. Eastman Irvine, ed., *New York World-Telegram: The World Almanac And Book Of Facts For 1945*, 108–9; Measuring Worth.

11   "There was": Salzberg, *Set Shot*, 55.

12   "Speed boy" group: "Welcome To Rochester," *D&C*, Nov. 7, 1945; Bob Wanzer, telephone conversation with author, 2015; Smith, *Tribute*, 106, 114, 118; Roger Meyer, *Al "Digger" Cervi: Star Player, Great Coach, Hall Of Famer*, 5–6; "George Glamack Signs, Ex-Carolina Star Joins Pro Cagers," *D&C*, Nov. 13, 1945; "Al Cervi Returns; Royals Obtain Mahnken, Nagretti," *D&C*, Nov. 18, 1945; http://www.baseball-reference.com/players/r/ricede01.shtml.

13   George Beahon, "Monarchs Victim Of 7th Royal Win," *D&C*, Dec. 16, 1945.

14   Paul Pinckney, "Royals Drub Sheboygan: Levane Glitters In 61–49 Victory," *D&C*, Dec. 19, 1945.

15   George Beahon, "Royals Overwhelm Bears: Davies Sets Torrid Pace Before 3800," *D&C*, Jan. 6, 1946; "The darling" and "I'll be": Elliot Cushing, "Sports Eye View," *D&C*, Jan. 7, 1946; "$1.44" and "$2.40": "Basket Ball" (advertisement), *D&C*, Jan. 3, 1946; "copyright": Matt Jackson, "Flashy Frills," *T-U*, Jan. 7, 1946.

16   "Bobby wasn't": Roeder, "Bob Davies," *Sport*, Feb. 1948, 53; Isaacs, *Vintage NBA*, 81.

17   Red Holzman and Harvey Frommer, *Holzman on Hoops*, 89; Fury, *Chuck Connors*, 30–33, 35–38, 337.

18   "Bob Davies": Fury, *Chuck Connors*, 34.

19   Bob Ajemian, "Cousy Will Have to Drop Fancy Stuff If He Plays Pro, Says Rochester Ace," *Boston Evening American*, Feb. 18, 1950; Roeder,

"Bob Davies," *Sport,* Feb. 1948, 53, 87; Paul Pinckney, "Outclassed Royals Bow to Oshkosh Five, 58–50, Bob Feerick Leads Stars in Loop Win," *D&C,* Feb. 27, 1946 ("thrilled the court congregation on one occasion with his behind-the-back-dribbling."); film clip:"0:01 Back Story," *ESPN Magazine,* March 19, 2001, 124; "Champions are made, not born," General Mills Wheaties TV commercial W-118 (Oct. 1, 1954), courtesy of General Mills Archives, Minneapolis, MN; Bob Wanzer, telephone conversations with author, Feb. 8, 2011, Aug. 17, 2012, and June 4, 2014; "So I was": Salzberg, *Set Shot,* 52; Bob Davies, interview with Charles Salzberg, Coral Springs, FL, 1986, transcription and edited transcript, Joseph M. O'Brien Historical Resource Center, Naismith Memorial Basketball Hall of Fame, Springfield, MA.

Five seasons later, NBA rookie Bob Cousy immediately employed his behind-the back dribble and fancy passes, but not without repercussions. "He's making the spectacular play," complained Celtics coach Red Auerbach two months into the 1953–54 season with the Celtics in sixth-place in the nine-team league," but he's losing the ball too often. The opposition has been waiting for Cousy's behind-the-back dribble, and is jamming it down his throat. He's not going to keep throwing the ball away." George Beahon, "In This Corner," D&C, Dec. 31, 1953.

20 "[Davies] was ahead": Roland Lazenby, *The NBA Finals: A Fifty Year Celebration,* 44.

21 Hubbard, *NBA Encyclopedia,* 3rd ed., 460; Nelson, *NBL,* 241, 243.

22 Leonard Koppett, *The Essence Of The Game Is Deception: Thinking about Basketball,* 191–93; Glickman, *Fastest Kid,* 105–6; Work Projects Administration, *Indiana: A Guide To The Hoosier State,* 300, 414.

23 Leonard Koppett, *24 Seconds To Shoot: The Birth and Improbable Rise of the National Basketball Association,* 49; "The Snake Pit": Mikan and Oberle, *Unstoppable,* 87; "The Bucket of Blood": Holzman and Frommer, *Red on Red,* 19; "Lion's Den": Mary Davies, telephone conversation with author, May 30, 2011; "Official Rules," Craig Carter and John Hareas, eds., *Sporting News Official NBA Guide 2000–2001 Edition,* 702–3; "Difference to Lakers: Pistons Don't Like Their Court Either," *Minneapolis Tribune,* March 19, 1950; http://www.nba.com/encyclopedia/rochester_royals_1951.html; Elliot Cushing, "It's Rough on Officials, Too; There's

Limit to Abuse—Cervi," *D&C*, March 25, 1948; Mikan and Oberle, *Unstoppable*, 97, 99, and 100; Bill James, "Ft. Wayne Feudin'," *D&C*, March 29, 1948; "The place felt": Red Auerbach, telephone conversation with author, July 12, 1991.

24   Nelson, *NBL*, 152–54; WHEC advertisement, BDSHOF; Elliot Cushing, "Fort Wayne Clips Royals in Opener, 54–44: Sadowski Scores 21; Cervi Shines, Bags 17 Points," *D&C*, March 13, 1946; Elliot Cushing, "Royals Whip Zollners To Even Series, 58–52," *D&C*, March 14, 1946; "Davies bouncing": Elliot Cushing, "Glamack, Davies Spark Rout of Ft. Wayne Kings," *D&C*, March 17, 1946; Harry Wilson, "Rochester Royals," *Converse Basketball Yearbook 1946*, 45.

25   Elliot Cushing, "Holzman's 17 Points Lead Drive; Mahnken Sparkles," *D&C*, March 20, 1946; Elliot Cushing, "Royals Clip Sheboygan, 61–54, for 2–0 Lead: Davies Sinks 22 Counters In Glittering Performance," *D&C*, March 22, 1946; Elliot Cushing, "Royals Rip 'Skins' for League Title: Batter Western Champs for 6th Straight, 66–48," *D&C*, March 24, 1946; Elliot Cushing, "Sports Eye View," *D&C*, March 25, 1946; "Rochester Claims Pro Cage Honors 66 to 48: Royals Win at Armory," *Sheboygan Press*, March 25, 1946; https://en.wikipedia.org/wiki/Sheboygan_Red_Skins.

26   "Les Harrison's": Harold Bogenhagen, "Royals Tip Redskins In First Playoff Tilt," *Sheboygan Press*, March 20, 1946; "Those guys": Elliot Cushing, "Royals' Speed Lauded, Spirit Also Seen Factor In Title Win," *D&C*, March 25, 1946.

27   "That 1945–1946": Ralph Hyman, "The Davies Story: Bob Forsook Baseball for Cage Career," *T-U*, March 11, 1955.

28   "Here's your": Elliot Cushing, "Sports Eye View," *D&C*, March 25, 1946.

29   Holzman, *Red*, 18; Frank Keetz, "'We Really Liked To Play Basketball,' The Rochester Royals in Schenectady, NY, 1946–1949," 4; "double": Al DeSantis, "Time Out: Cage Great Drops In, Sch'dy Gives Davies 'Fondest Memories'," BDSHOF.

30   Chuck Menville, *The Harlem Globetrotters: Fifty Years of Fun and Games*, 7–40.

31   Hal Buell, "Royals, Minus Davies, Drop 57–55 Decision to Trotters Before 3200 at Armory Here," *Schenectady Union-Star*, March 27, 1946; "Player Sketches" (1948), SHUAC.

Usually the Minneapolis Lakers in 1948 are erroneously credited as the first present-day NBA franchise to play the Harlem Globetrotters. See John Christgau, *Tricksters in the Madhouse, Lakers vs. Globetrotters, 1948*.

32   Schenectady Sports Club, All-American Basketball Tournament Official Souvenir Program, 1, Ray LeBov Collection, Sacramento, CA; http://hoopedia.nba.com/index.php/Remembering_The_ Rens; Hal Buell, "Schenectady Wins Pro Cage Tournament: Clips Renaissance 73–59 Before 4,000 In Final At Armory," *Schenectady Union-Star*, April 12, 1946; "fair-haired": Al DeSantis, "Royals, Tired but Happy, Anxious to Get Home," *Schenectady Union-Star*, April 12, 1946; Keetz, "'We Really Liked,'" 1, 7–8, 10.

DOUBLE DUTY DAVIES

DURING THE 1946–47 BASKETBALL SEASON, BOB DAVIES ACCOM-
plished a remarkable feat that no NBA player will ever duplicate. He
earned MVP honors in the nation's premier professional basketball
league, the NBL, and coached a major college basketball team, the
Seton Hall Pirates, to an outstanding win-loss record. The brand-new
and weaker Basketball Association of America (BAA) did not choose
an MVP that season. Since NBL and BAA teams merged into the NBA
in 1948, only four small guards have been selected MVP—Boston
Celtic Bob Cousy, Philadelphia 76er Allen Iverson, Golden State
Warrior Stephen Curry, and, twice, Phoenix Sun Steve Nash. [1]

After returning from the South Pacific Theater and taking over as
Seton Hall athletic director, Father James A. Carey hired Bob Davies
as the Pirates' basketball and baseball coach. During the war, Honey
Russell had left the South Orange, New Jersey, campus when the
school dropped intercollegiate basketball. "The task confronting the
young mentor," observed the Seton Hall student newspaper, "is a
large one but observers are confident that the same drive, spirit and
determination that characterized his playing at the Hall will be witnessed in the players who will serve under him."[2]

When it did not interfere with his coaching responsibilities, the
Seton Hall administration granted Double Duty Davies brief leaves
of absence to play in Royals games, and Les Harrison paid his air-
plane and train fares. After pre-season workouts and exhibition
games in Walsh Gymnasium, Bob did not practice again with his

*The same season he was National Basketball League (NBL) Most Valuable
Player (MVP), Bob Davies (center) coached future Rochester Royals team-
mates Pep Saul (left) and Bob Wanzer (right) at Seton Hall. Here the three-
some is shown in a Toledo University dormitory room during 1949–50
NBA preseason training. (Oct. 14, 1949, Rochester Democrat & Chronicle/
Rochester Public Library)*

Royals teammates but occasionally scrimmaged with his college players. Weekdays he taught physical education, coaching theory, and
hygiene classes, and conducted basketball practices until 4 p.m. He
commuted 350 miles to Rochester, a two-and-a-half hour flight from
the Newark (NJ) Airport or a more than seven-hour train ride from
New York City's Grand Central Railroad Station. His jaunts were
longer in distance and time to other NBL cities except Syracuse, New
York. He also recruited high school prospects in Rochester and Fort
Wayne. A sports writer joked that Bob suffered from "an acute case
of housemaid's knee from climbing in and out of Pullman berths."[3]

Before the NBL season opened, the Royals took care of some unfinished business. On November 19, 1946, they again met the Harlem Globetrotters in the Schenectady State Armory. "This is the night, and we'll make the most of it," promised Les Harrison, simmering about Abe Saperstein's boast that the Globetrotters were the world's best basketball team. "The boys have been waiting to get even for a long time." The Trotters jumped to an early 11–5 lead, but at the end of the first quarter, the Royals knotted the score, 15–15. Bob Davies' fine floor game and four long set shots spurred the Royals to a 33–21 halftime lead. In a 60–49 win, he scored 13 points and proved the difference-maker in the first present-day NBA franchise victory over the Globetrotters.[4]

NBL FAN FAVORITE
Midway through the '46–47 season, Bob Davies turned in his best NBL performance. He scored 25 points, including three sensational one-handed flips, and distributed 14 assists, a personal and unofficial high, in a two-point loss to the Chicago American Gears. He "ran like a reindeer, dribbled expertly, leaped high into the air time and again to intercept enemy passes, stole balls, snatched loose balls that were on the verge of going out of bounds, raised havoc with the Chicago defense with his clever play-manipulating, and propelled perfectly timed passes into the hands of teammates who converted them into baskets." Highly partisan Chicago spectators loudly applauded his "Mr. Kangaroo Jack Armstrong antics" and miracle plays. Fifty fans waited for him outside the Royals locker room. "I've seen the best," said Harry Wilson, a founder of the Chicago World Professional Basketball Tournament and a basketball observer for a quarter century, "but Davies tops them all. He's from out of another world. And imagine how much sharper he would be—if such a thing is possible—were he not playing professional basketball on a part-time basis."[5]

Colorful Bob Davies was quickly becoming the NBL fans favorite player. On a Northside Chicago grammar school basketball court, ten-year-old Howard Blum drove for the winning bucket in a pickup game. His buddies complained that he illegally palmed (placed his hand under) the ball. "That's a Bob Davies move," insisted Howard.

"We all mimicked Bob Davies. Bob Davies was our hero and we all bragged about having his poster." Sheboygan and Oshkosh fans greeted Bob's sensational moves with "ohs" and "ahs." A bobby-soxer wrote him: "Oh Bobby! Oh Davies! If you only knew. That a certain young girl is just crazy for you." Six-year-old Vicki Stern, who had not seen Bob play but whose older sister had and constantly raved about him, wrote Bob: "I THINK ThAT You Are The best bAscet ball Player in The WURLD." He even received a fan letter from Spain.[6]

ROOKIE COACH

By late January 1947, the national media had started taking notice of the Davies-coached Seton Hall "Mighty Midgets" and their star players, 6', 170-pound former Marine Robert "Bobby" Wanzer; 6' 2", 185-pound Army veteran Franklin Benjamin "Pep" Saul Jr.; and 6' 1", 185-pound ex-sailor John Andrew "Whitey" Macknowski. A United Press (UP) headline announced: "Seton Hall Unbeaten as Kid Coach Clicks." An Associated Press (AP) story described the Pirates' 17–0 record as one of the most surprising among major teams. But the taller Loyola College of Maryland (Baltimore) Greyhounds in a one-point victory snapped Seton Hall's win streak at 18 games. Tacked onto the 1942–43 Pirates' season-ending 10 consecutive wins, Seton Hall had won 28 basketball games in a row. This combined streak ranks second for Seton Hall men's basketball teams after the Wonder Five's 43 games.[7]

After the Loyola College setback, the Pirates routed the Colored (now Central) Intercollegiate Athletic Association (CIAA) defending champion Lincoln University (Oxford, PA) Lions, 66–33. During the post-World-War-II years, white and black institutions of higher learning rarely scheduled athletic contests against each other. The Lincoln University yearbook stated that the Lions game with Seton Hall, as well as others with Brooklyn College and Albright College, "broke all precedents in inter-collegiate competition" and "can rightly be called the inauguration of interracial collegiate basketball." Lincoln University may have been the first African-American university or college to play three different white schools in the same basketball season.[8]

The paths of future NBA legends Bob Davies and Bob Cousy first crossed on February 8, 1947, in Seton Hall's Walsh Gymnasium.

Cousy played on the Holy Cross Crusaders' varsity all-freshman second unit. (Freshmen were eligible under special postwar rules.) A very-impressed Coach Davies remembered Cousy hardly glancing at the basket and sinking two difficult hook shots. After Bobby Wanzer left the game due to an ankle injury, and Pep Saul fouled out, the Crusaders rallied and eked out a 44–43 victory on their way to winning the NCAA Tournament. To the relief of Rochester Royals fans, the loss doomed Seton Hall's chance for an NIT bid and eliminated the possibility of any conflict between Double Duty Davies coaching in the NIT or participating in the NBL playoffs.[9]

The Pirates ended the season with an impressive 24 win and 3 loss record. The Metropolitan Basketball Writers Association (New York City) rated Bob Davies among the top ten for Coach of the Year honors. The Seton Hall student newspaper described his accomplishment as "one of the most brilliant, freshman coaching jobs in the nation," stamping him "as not only a topflight basketball player, but likewise a brilliant young coach." His win-loss record, with an assist from Bobby Wanzer (5–0 as unpaid acting coach in Davies' absences with the Royals), is ninth-best for a first-season coach in NCAA Division I history. The Converse-Dunkel Rating System, however, did not include Seton Hall among the nation's top 25 teams and ranked Holy Cross third behind Utah and Kentucky.[10]

ON THE COURT

In the NBL, the Royals posted the best regular-season record with 32 wins and 13 losses and averaged a league record of 62.9 points per game. The "Daviesless" Royals won 5 and lost 8 games (.387) but the Royals with Bob on the court won 27 and lost 5 (.844). Al Cervi led the league in total points (632). He and Bob Davies each averaged 14.4 points per game, which tied them for second in the league behind Chicago American Gear rookie center George Mikan's 16.5 PPG. Davies and Cervi garnered NBL All-Star First Team honors as forwards, and Red Holzman, who averaged 12.0 PPG, made the Second Team. On a negative note, Al Cervi and Fuzzy Levane criticized Bob's gambling defensive style. However, in the 13 games against 10 different teams in which Davies did not play, the Royals opponents averaged 60.2 points per game; and in the 30 games in which he played against them, they averaged 5 points less (55.2).[11]

MVP

Even though "playmaker deluxe and sharpshooter" Bob Davies missed almost a third of the season, managers and coaches, along with sports writers and radio sportscasters, voted him NBL MVP, the equivalent of today's NBA MVP. "The NBL had by far the best players, Mikan, Jim Pollard, Bobby McDermott, Davies, Wanzer, and Risen," said Al Cervi, later a successful BAA and NBA player-coach. "Compared to us, the BAA was like a high school league." After NBL and BAA teams combined, 11 of the 15 1948–49 All-BAA and 1949–50 and 1950–51 All-NBA First Team members were former NBL stars or from the new Indianapolis Olympians franchise composed of 1948 U.S. Olympic Basketball Team members. It can be said that of the two NBA tree roots, the deeper and stronger was the NBL and the shallower and weaker was the BAA. Five of the eight surviving mid-1950s NBA franchises originated in the NBL.[12]

Unfortunately, the national media did not provide much coverage about Bob Davies' outstanding season. Among major city newspapers, only Chicago's even minimally covered his MVP heroics. During the first three months of the season, Rochester's two newspapers did not publish due to a strike, so Royals fans heard about his exploits only through brief mentions on local radio news broadcast sports segments. Other newspapers in cities around the league, such as the Anderson (IN) *Herald*, Sheboygan *Press*, Toledo *Blade*, and Youngstown *Vindicator*, did not devote any special coverage to him. *The New York Times* and *Time* and *Newsweek* magazines did not even mention his MVP award.[13]

JUGGLING ROLES

A five-week interval between Seton Hall's last basketball and first baseball games allowed America's Number One Sports Commuter time to concentrate his efforts on the NBL playoffs. In the Royals' opening round first game victory over the Syracuse Nationals (now Philadelphia 76ers), "Minute Man" Davies scored six of the Royals' last eight points, as they overcame a six-point deficit with two minutes remaining, to tie the game in regulation and subsequently win in over-time. After the Royals lost the Wednesday night second game, Davies, switching roles, planned to take a Thursday noon plane to Newark and conduct a Seton Hall baseball practice, but returned to Rochester because the flight was delayed. On Saturday night, "Kangaroo Kid" Davies, scoring 15 points, led the Royals to victory in the third game. With the benefit of 14 hours sleep before the fourth and deciding game, he bounced "around the Arena boards like a battery-operated Jumping Jack, snatching balls out of the rafters and playing leap frog with chagrined Syracuse athletes," and again notched 15 points, as the Royals eliminated the Nationals.[14]

After ousting the Fort Wayne Zollners in the second playoff round, the Royals faced the Chicago American Gears in the Finals. Leading the Royals to an opening game victory, Bob scored 23 points and made 8 of 15 field goal attempts. "That Davies played one helluva game," commented American Gears player-coach Bobby McDermott. "We've got to stop him to win this thing. He's a great ballplayer." Bob, however, expressed dissatisfaction with his performance. "I had only a couple of assists," he said.[15]

With the NBL Finals tied at one game apiece, it appeared that Double Duty Davies might not be available for the critical third con-test. After overseeing an early afternoon baseball practice in South Orange, he boarded a plane and flew to Chicago, arriving just in time for the opening tip-off. He scored 19 points and fouled out in a devastating loss. He caught a plane back to Newark for the Pirate nine's season opener. When that game was rained out, he flew back to Chicago and, to everyone's surprise, arrived in time for the open-ing tip-off. He scored ten points, but the Royals lost and the American Gears won the playoff championship. However, the NBL owners had decided prior to the season that the team with the best regular season win-loss record would be declared league champion, and the Royals were again awarded the Naismith Memorial Trophy.[16]

Adding an extra flourish to an extraordinary basketball season, Bob Davies, in the next-to-last of 44 Royals exhibition games, drop-kicked a basket just before the final buzzer sounded on a victory over

The National Basketball League awarded the 1946–47 Rochester Royals the Naismith Memorial Trophy emblematic of the league championship. From left, top row: Harrison, Negratti, King, Glamack, Johnson, Beatty, Malanowicz; front row: Davies, Levane, Holzman, Cervi. (1947, Courtesy of Arvin J. Odegaard)

the Albion (NY) American Legion Post team. "Davies' feat," wrote a *Democrat & Chronicle* reporter, "and it was no small feat of footwork, evoked surprise not only from the overflow crowd and his opponents but also from his teammates and himself, as well. It was a dramatic way to end a season that otherwise had no kick against it."[17]

NOTES

1   http://www.nba.com/history/nba-mvp-award-winners/index.html.

2   "Davies Seton Hall Coach: Recently out of Navy, He gets Baseball and Basketball Jobs," *NYT*, Jan. 18, 1946; "The task": "Davies Assumes Reins March 15th: Davies Signed As College Coach," The *Setonian*, Feb. 20, 1946.

3   Mary Davies, telephone conversation with author, Jan. 18, 2007; "Pro

Tilt Tonight On Setonia Court," *Newark Evening News*, Oct. 29, 1947; Bob Wanzer, telephone conversation with author, Jan. 15, 2014; "NL Sees Davies Best in Basketball: Rochester Royals Star Here Thursday, Has Everything," *Schenectady Union-Star*, Dec. 9, 1946; The *Official Guide of the Airways* (March 1947): 12–13; *New York Central System Time Tables, The Scenic Water Level Route, Effective Sept. 29, 1946 — Form 1001*, 14–17; Elliot Cushing, "Sports Eye View," *D&C*, March 10, 1947; "Minster Cagers To Enter Seton Hall This Fall," BDSHOF; "an acute case": Elliot Cushing, "Sports Eye View," *D&C*, Feb. 21, 1947.

4 "This is": "Royals Get Long-Awaited Crack at Harlem Globetrotters Here Tonight," *Schenectady Union-Star*, Nov. 19, 1946; Hal Buell, "Royals Clip Trotters Before 3,500 Here, Oppose Rens Friday," *Schenectady Union-Star*, Nov. 20, 1946.

5 Elliot Cushing, "Gears Nip Royals, 57–56, Despite Brilliant 25-Point Exhibition by Bob Davies," *D&C*, Feb. 22, 1947; George Beahon, "Davies Sets Assist Record as Royals Win, 121–110: Old Pro Records 20, Plus 25 Points," *D&C*, Jan. 23, 1955; "ran like" and "I've seen": Elliot Cushing, "Sports Eye View," D&C, Feb. 23, 1947; Schleppi, *Chicago's Showcase*, 5 (Harry Wilson).

6 "That's a": Howard Z. Blum statement May 26, 2009 (author's possession); "Ohs": Elliot Cushing, "Sports Eye View," *D&C*, Feb. 22, 1947; "Oh Bobby": Unsigned to Bob, Oct. 14, 1948; "I THINK": Vicki Stern, letter to Bobby, and canceled envelope, n.d., BDSHOF.

7 "Davies Optimistic About Setonia" and Steve Snider, "Seton Hall Unbeaten As Kid Coach Clicks" (UP), dateline Jan. 21, 1947, BDSHOF; Ted Meier, "Seton Hall and Alabama Lead Only 10 Undefeated Quintets Left in Nation (AP)," *Syracuse (NY) Post-Standard*, Jan. 20, 1947; "Loyola Upsets Seton Hall, 54–53," *Syracuse Post-Standard*, Feb. 4, 1947; Alan Delozier, e-mail message to author, Oct. 1, 2007 (combined record).

8 G.A. Falzer, "Rout of Lincoln Quintet Shows Seton Hall Courtmen Back in Old Form: Saul's Return Aids Pirates," *Newark Evening News*, Feb. 5, 1947; "broke all": Lincoln University *The 1947 Lion*, 75.

The author has been able to identify only five basketball games between African-American and white institutions of higher learning prior to the three Lincoln University games. During the 1939–40 season, the Virginia (Richmond) Union Panthers won two of three games against Long Island University, and, the following season, defeated Brooklyn College. In a secret game played on Sunday, March 12, 1944, the African-American North Carolina College Eagles defeated an informal white Duke University Medical School team composed of former college players. Nelson George, *Elevating the Game: Black Men and Basketball*, 23–26; Ocania Chalk, *Black College Sport*, 128–29; Scott Ellsworth, "Jim Crow Loses: The Secret Game," *NYT*, March 31, 1996.

9   "Holy Cross Comeback Overtakes Seton Hall Near Game's End, 44–43," *Boston Globe*, Feb. 9, 1947; Jack Barry, "Celtics Clash With Indianapolis Jets at Garden Tonight," BDSHOF; Herbert Warren Wind, "Bob Cousy: The Man And The Game," pt. 2, *Sports Illustrated*, Jan. 16, 1956, 32; National Collegiate Athletic Association, *Official 2008 NCAA Men's Basketball Records Book*, 78; George Beahon, "Sports Eye View," *D&C*, Feb. 10, 1947.

10   Paul Horowitz, "Carnevale Cage 'Coach of the Year,'" BDSHOF; *Seton Hall Galleon 1947*, 92; "one of": "'46–'47 Hoop Team Called Seton's Best: Davies Men 24–3 Record One Of The Nation's Best," *The Setonian*, March 12, 1947: 7; Bob Wanzer, telephone conversation with author, July 21, 2007; National Collegiate Athletic Association, *Official 2008 NCAA Men's Basketball Records Book*, 154; "Utah Given First Place In Dunkel Rating," *Ft. Wayne (IN) Journal-Gazette*, March 31, 1947.

Norman Shepard posted the best first-year coaching record with his undefeated 1924 North Carolina Tar Heels and Jerry Tarkanian the eighth-best with his 1969 Long Beach State (CA) 49ers.

11   Keith Brehm, "Pro Basketball Takes On New Stature: National Basketball League," *Converse Yearbook 1947*, 22; "Daviesless": Elliot Cushing, "Sports Eye View," *D&C*, Feb. 10, 1947; NBL News Bureau, "NBL Scoring for 1946–47," RRSHOF 1946–1947 Season; Al Cervi, telephone conversation with author, Oct. 4, 2004; Fuzzy Levane, telephone conversation with author, Jan. 13, 2006.

12   "playmaker deluxe": "Davies Wins Double Honor, Cervi Makes All-Star Quint," *D&C*, March 26, 1947; "The NBL": Rosen, *First Tip-Off*, 233; Hubbard, *NBA Encyclopedia*, 3rd ed., 40–41, 198; Glenn Dickey, *The History Of Professional Basketball Since 1896*, 34; Alex Sachare, *Naismith Memorial Basketball Hall of Fame's 100 Greatest Basketball Moments of All Time*, 50 ("the NBL had the best pro basketball players of its day"); Jack H. Bender, *Basketball-Log*, 35 ("After a year of competition with the BAA,

the NBL still was the dominant professional team in 1947–48 ...."); Shouler et al., *Total Basketball*, 75, 78, 81, 96.

The five surviving originally NBL and mid-1950's NBA franchises are the Syracuse Nationals (Philadelphia 76ers), Fort Wayne Zollners (Detroit Pistons), Rochester Royals (Sacramento Kings), Minneapolis (Los Angeles) Lakers, and St. Louis (Atlanta) Hawks.

13 E-mail from Rochester and Monroe County Central Library Local History and Genealogy Division to author, Dec. 30, 2005 (newspaper strike from Nov. 9 to Dec. 31, 1947); The New York Times, *Index for the Published News of 1947*, passim; Newsweek, *Index to Vol. 29* (Jan. 6, 1947–June 30, 1947): 1–72; Time, *Index to Vol. 49* (Jan. 6, 1947–June 30, 1947): 1–66; Sarita Robinson, Bertha Joel and Mary Keyes, eds., *Readers' Guide To Periodical Literature* May 1945–April 1947: 181, 509, 1343, 1694.

14 Elliot Cushing, "Royals Edge Syracuse In Overtime: Tying Rally Led By Davies; Cervi Tally Wins, 66–64," *D&C*, March 19, 1947; Al C. Weber: "Royals' Comeback Fails, Bow to Syracuse: Lose Out In Closing Minute," *T-U*, March 20, 1947; Elliot Cushing, "Royals Subdue Nats, 54–48, for 2–1 Lead; Davies, Cervi Shine," *D&C*, March 23, 1947; "around the Arena": Elliot Cushing, "Sports Eye View," *D&C*, March 25, 1947; Bill Reddy, "Royals Eliminate Nationals by 62–57: NBL Champs Prove Class In Second Half," *Syracuse Post-Standard*, March 25, 1947.

15 Elliot Cushing, "Royals Down Gears For 1–0 Lead: Davies Nets 23 for Royals In 71–65 Win Over Gears," *D&C*, April 4, 1947; "That Davies": George Beahon, "McDermott Praises Davies As Mates Blow Off Steam About Horn-Tooting," *D&C*, April 4, 1947; "I had only": Elliot Cushing, "Sports Eye View," *D&C*, April 5, 1947.

16 Roeder, "Bob Davies," *Sport*, Feb. 1948, 50; Al C. Weber, "Royals 'Cornered', Rated Underdog to Chicago—Series Tied at One-All," *T-U*, April 7, 1947; Al C. Weber, "Royals Lose to Gears, 78–70, Face Elimination: Mikan Sparks Chicago" *T-U*, April 8, 1947; Al C. Weber, "Gears Rate Big Edge: Davies Missing For Tilt," *T-U*, April 9, 1947; Al C. Weber, "Gears Trip Royals, 79–68, Capture Playoff Title: Calihan, Glamack Stars," *T-U*, April 10, 1947.

17 "Davies' feat": "Royals Conquer Albion; Davies Sinks 'Dropkick'," *D&C*, April 15, 1947; "Royals Top Albion Post," *T-U*, April 15, 1947 ("Bobbie Davies added an extra flourish with a drop kick bucket.").

WIN IT FOR DOLLY!

DURING THE 1946–47 BASKETBALL SEASON, LES HARRISON, AS well as Bob Davies and the other Royals, played unique roles in a historically significant and little-known forward step in American race relations that has not received its deserved recognition. Six months before Jackie Robinson appeared in his first Major League Baseball (MLB) game, Les Harrison, without national media fanfare, signed an African-American player, Dolly King, to a Rochester Royals contract and helped reintegrate the NBL. Shortly before King signed, African-Americans Kenny Washington and Woody Strode for the Los Angeles Rams and Marion Motley and Bill Willis for the Cleveland Browns (quarterbacked by Otto Graham) had appeared in professional National Football League (NFL) and All-American Football Conference (AAFC) games. Although the Rochester Royals, now the Sacramento Kings, are one of eight surviving mid-1950s NBA franchises, the NBA credits the New York Knicks and Washington Capitols, respectively, as its first franchises to sign (Nat "Sweetwater" Clifton) and play (Earl Lloyd), an African-American, which occurred four years later.[1]

PIONEERING IN RACE RELATIONS
The Royals had won the 1945–46 NBL championship despite a critical weakness—not enough muscle in the battles for rebounds. Brutes like Fort Wayne's Ed "The Villain" Sadowski and Milo "Killer" Komenich, as well as Oshkosh's Leroy "Cowboy" Edwards, who initiated

Rochester Royals owners Les and Jack Harrison signed African-American Dolly King to a Rochester Royals contract before Jackie Robinson played for the Brooklyn Dodgers. (Oct. 15, 1946, Rochester Democrat & Chronicle/ Rochester Public Library)

George Mikan into pro basketball by knocking out four of his teeth, and Sheboygan's Ed Danker, the "NBL No. 1 Bad Boy," had battered the Royals lanky big men. [2]

Les Harrison knew a player who could bolster the Royals' back line. "If he can play, he can play," said Les, a Jewish entrepreneur, who had experienced anti-Semitism, was colorblind, and, basically, just wanted to win games and make money. Between 1937 and 1945, his semi-pro teams had won three games and lost one against the Harlem Globetrotters and won four and lost five against the New York Rens. Harrison had signed African-American Wilmeth Sidat-Singh to play for his Rochester semi-pro team in the 1940 Chicago World Professional Basketball Tournament. He had also paid Sidat-Singh's transportation costs from Washington, DC, to Rochester and back to play for a visiting team because Sidat-Singh attracted paying customers. Furthermore, Harrison had imported two other

African-Americans, three-time Chicago World Professional Basketball All-Tournament First Team member William "Dolly" King, a 6' 4", 217-pound center-forward, and two-time All-Tournament First Team member, William "Pop" Gates, a 6' 2", 205-pound forward, to play for his semi-pro squads in important games.[3]

At the end of the 1945–46 NBL season, Les called a team meeting, stated that he had played on integrated teams, and asked his players whether they would accept African-American teammates.

The Royals' response was a unanimous yes.

"It wouldn't bother us," said Fuzzy Levane. "We were almost all from the City [New York]. It was not uncommon to play with Negroes. If you were good enough in high school, you played no matter what your color."[4]

On October 14, 1946, Les and Jack Harrison signed 30-year-old Dolly King to a $7,000 NBL contract ($84,800 today) with a $500 signing bonus and an opportunity for an additional $1,500 in bonuses. It was reported that the NBL Buffalo Bisons signed Pop Gates at approximately the same time. Wendell Smith, sports editor of the *Pittsburgh Courier*, the largest-circulation African-American weekly newspaper, which was distributed nationwide through a network of International Brotherhood of Sleeping Car Porters, congratulated Harrison and the Royals "for signing a player without regard to race, creed, or color. It is another democratic step in the field of sports, and I am sure your liberal attitude will be appreciated by thousands of basketball fans throughout the country."[5]

The Harrisons paid Dolly King top dollar. MLB salaries averaged $7,000 in 1940 and $15,000 in 1949. Al Cervi, the NBL's seventh-highest scorer, was paid $6,500 for the 1945–46 season. Outstanding Royals swingman Fuzzy Levane earned $5,000. The Washington Capitols paid All-BAA First Team members Bob Feerick and Bones McKinney $9,000 and $7,000 respectively, and the New York Knicks paid their highest scorer, Sidney "Sonny" Hertzberg, $4,500 and a $1,500 season-end bonus.[6]

Dolly King, who came from an outstanding family, fit the profile for an ideal sports integrator. His brother John earned a Ph.D. from St. John's University and became a professor of education at Fordham

University. Another brother, Haldane, qualified for pilots' wings in the first Tuskegee Airmen class and retired from the U.S. Air Force as a lieutenant colonel. College-educated like Jackie Robinson, Dolly had starred on integrated Long Island University basketball, football, and baseball teams. He had even been co-captain of an otherwise all-white LIU Blackbirds basketball squad. He had dropped out of school his senior year to earn money, but would subsequently complete his B.A. studies at LIU and master's work at NYU. During World War II, Dolly had worked in the Grumman Aircraft Company plant on Long Island, and played on the integrated Grumman Flyers AAU basketball team. He had also starred for the Washington Bears, made up of former Rens, who won the 1943 Chicago World Professional Basketball Tournament.[7]

"A hell of a player, and a hell of a guy," remembered Red Holzman, "Dolly King hardly ever talked about racial issues. He just went about his business of playing basketball."[8]

ROCHESTER RACIAL RELATIONS

And overwhelmingly white-populated Rochester in the mid-1940s offered perhaps the best metropolitan environment in the nation for an African-American athlete to succeed on an integrated professional team. Jim Crowism had not poisoned a city whose white citizens felt no need for its malignant protection. "If you had to pick a town to play as a black without a lot of notoriety," said African-American NBA pioneer Earl Lloyd, "Rochester would be it. They were used to seeing whites play blacks. There were no problems for me in hotels or restaurants."[9]

Another African-American, William Warfield, later famous for his Broadway stage and screen singing roles in *Porgy and Bess* and *Show Boat*, grew up in Rochester at the same time as Bob Davies in Harrisburg. "I was lucky to be raised in Rochester, New York," Warfield (born January 20, 1920), wrote in his autobiography. "I wouldn't have traded my Rochester childhood for any other."[10]

Teachers in the integrated Rochester school system's exceptional music programs nurtured Warfield's extraordinary talent. He and his family participated in ecumenical exchanges between white and black

Powerfully-built Dolly King provided the Royals much needed strength in battles for rebounds. (1947, Courtesy of Mary Davies)

churches, attended the integrated Community Players amateur theatrical performances, and, in the Eastman Theater, heard world-class concert artists, such as Marian Anderson, who in 1955 became the first African-American to appear with the New York City Metropolitan Opera. Warfield's egalitarian Washington High School classmates elected him student body vice president, and staged a special performance to raise money for his travel expenses to compete in a national music contest. While he was an undergraduate student at the Eastman School of Music, however, the Phi Mu Alpha Symphonia music fraternity rejected him for membership, and many members resigned in protest. William Warfield did not really experience Jim Crowism until he left Rochester's sheltered and "friendly confines" and joined the army. [11]

When the Royals signed Dolly King in the fall of 1946, Rochester could be proud of its civil rights record. Overt organized racism did

not exist, and racial violence was virtually unknown.[12] Prior to the
Civil War, prominent black leader Frederick Douglass published his
North Star abolitionist newspaper in the city. Fugitive slaves made
their final Underground Railroad Station stop in Rochester before
escaping across Lake Ontario to Canada.[13] After the Civil War, the
Rochester "Unexpected" competed against other upstate New York
African-American baseball teams.[14] During the late 19th and early
20th century, suffragist leader Susan B. Anthony, a Rochester resi-
dent, championed African-American rights locally.[15] During the
1920s, the Ku Klux Klan (KKK), spewing anti-immigrant, -Italian,
-Catholic and -Jewish diatribes, held two organizational meetings in
the city, and 10,000 sympathizers and members from ten western
New York counties attended a Konvocation in a suburb. A ten-foot-
high cross burned one night in the 1930s on Pinnacle Hill.[16] During
World War II, Presidential Executive Order 8802 prohibited discrimination in defense industries, and five major Rochester companies, as
well as many smaller businesses, employed blacks.[17] Eastman Kodak
Company, the city's largest employer, recruited African-American
scientist Dr. William T. Knox Jr., but mainly hired blacks for janitorial
positions. [18] Training hospitals accepted black women in their nurs-
ing programs.[19] Prominent white civic leaders paternalistically sup-
ported the local National Association for the Advancement of Colored
People (NAACP) chapter. The Rochester superintendent of schools
removed the racially demeaning children's book *Little Black Sambo*
from the public school district reading list.[20] The Colgate Rochester
Theological Seminary and Eastman School of Music accepted blacks.
The private University of Rochester awarded George Washington
Carver, the distinguished African-American agricultural scientist, an honorary Doctor of Science degree.[21] After ecumenical pressure from local church leaders, the University of Rochester Medical
School admitted a highly qualified African-American student, Edwin
A. Robinson.[22] By 1946, a black freshman, I. Austin Jr., and a black
senior varsity soccer player, Mark Battle, added *de minims* diversity
to the university's undergraduate student body, but most of the city's
college-qualified black high school graduates matriculated at out-of-
town black institutions of higher learning. [23]

Approximately half of Rochester's 3,000 blacks (primarily from the West Indies and about one percent of the city population) lived in two blighted neighborhoods. Most blacks held menial, low-paying jobs or owned small, struggling businesses.[24] The city had only three physicians, two dentists, five trained nurses, one architect, one public school teacher, and one radio announcer who were black. The black community read their own weekly newspaper, the *Voice*; worshiped in their own Baptist, Methodist, and Episcopal churches; and joined their own Elks Lodge and Veterans of Foreign Wars (VFW) Post. The downtown YMCA and YWCA were minimally integrated and also operated branches in black neighborhoods. Most visiting blacks from out of town stayed at these branches or in two black-owned hotels.[25]

"During basketball season," Earl Lloyd said perceptively about racial civility in the Kodak City, "the weather was harsh. In the wintertime, nobody hated anybody. It's too cold to hate people. Whites and blacks would help push each other's cars out of snow banks. Then they'd go back to normal when the weather changed."[26]

In this social environment, the Rochester newspapers treated Dolly King no differently than his white teammates. A sports page cartoon depicted him as the "King," "The Royals' Negro Court Wizard," a "Tower of Strength on the Defense," a "clever ball handler," and an "important factor in the champions' offense." In a *Democrat & Chronicle* "Royal Court Tips" article series about basketball skills, Dolly discussed pivot play in which he stood near the foul circle key with his back to the basket and took a turn-around shot, or handed off or passed to a teammate cutting by or behind him. In the next article in the series, Bob Davies expounded on the two-hand underhand foul shot taken with the back straight and the ball between the knees held on the sides without palms touching it and swung upwards and released with a follow-through motion. A Royals exhibition game program contained an article about "powerful, classy" Dolly King, entitled "Star of First Magnitude," which pointed out his veteran presence had bolstered his former team, the Rens, with poise and steadiness, and evaluated his floor work as "beyond reproach."[27]

FIGHTING RACISM

In their season opener in Youngstown, Ohio, on November 11, 1946, the Royals easily defeated the Bears, 69–43. Used in a reserve role in order to lessen the pressure on him for immediate success as a representative of his race, Dolly performed inauspiciously, failing to score and committing three personal fouls. Two nights earlier, Pop Gates had appeared in the Buffalo Bisons (now the Atlanta Hawks via St. Louis, Milwaukee, and Tri-Cities from Buffalo) opening game, thus earning the distinction of the first African-American to play in a game for a present-day NBA franchise. Later in the season, blacks Bill Farrow and Willie King, respectively, joined the Youngstown Bears and Detroit Gems.[28]

Across the United States of America, an unwritten Jim Crow rule in the form of social custom prohibited white and black athletes from rooming together. St. Louis Cardinals manager Rogers Hornsby believed that major league baseball would never integrate because, in his and many other big leaguers' opinions, black and white ballplayers could not co-exist close together on road trips. The three blacks on the 1956 U.S. Olympic Basketball Team, Bill Russell, K.C. Jones, and Carl Cain, were treated as second-class citizens and forced to stay in segregated accommodations on a nationwide exhibition tour. During spring training in 1959, white hotels in Scottsdale, Arizona, denied African-American Boston Red Sox player Elijah "Pumpsie" Green a room, and during the season he interacted with his white teammates only in ballparks. Jim Bouton mentioned in his baseball classic, *Ball Four*, that a white and a black rooming together on the road was probably a unique situation as late as the 1969 MLB season. [29]

"The rule was not written in stone," said Fuzzy Levane. "It was never told to me."[30]

Defying prevailing American social mores, bachelors Fuzzy Levane, an Italian-American, and Red Holzman, a Jew, shared a room with Dolly King in the downtown Rochester Hotel Seneca, which advertised itself as in "the center of everything" and the place where "good fellows get together," but had never previously accommodated an African-American guest. Late at night, Les Harrison occasionally brought pastrami sandwiches to the threesome's room and joined them in a game of pinochle. Dolly amazed his roommates with his pre-breakfast routine, quaffing a small glass of sherry and a raw egg. "This drink builds up your muscles," said Dolly. "You guys should try it." Red and Fuzzy tested the concoction and vomited the rest of the morning.[31]

"It's gonna be tough," Les Harrison warned Dolly, "you're gonna be shunned in a lot of cities," a fact of life Dolly knew all too well from touring the country with the Rens.[32]

Concerned about potential racially motivated incidents involving Dolly in certain NBL cities, Bob Davies roomed with him on road trips. "Bob never had a prejudiced bone in his body," remembered his brother Dick. "He was far ahead of his time." Dolly impressed Bob with his fastidious personal habits, especially changing his silk underpants three times a day. Back in Rochester, Bob and Mary, without a second thought, invited another African American, Harlem Globetrotter Goose Tatum, to their apartment.[33]

Most racial incidents involving Dolly King occurred in Indiana, probably the most racist state outside the Deep South. Under the aegis of a strong Ku Klux Klan organization, Jim Crowism had dug its claws deep into the Hoosier state. Signs reading "Nigger, don't let the sun set on you here" blemished the edges of towns. In the capital, Indianapolis, blacks (15 percent of the population) lived in three contiguous, blighted neighborhoods. They usually held menial, low-paying jobs, attended their own churches, read their own weekly newspaper, and exercised at their own YMCA. The city code mandated segregated schools, public parks, swimming pools, and movie theaters. Blacks could get medical treatment in only one City Hospital ward. Blacks and whites sat separately in night clubs and basketball arenas. Most Indianapolis hotels and restaurants turned away people of color. Statewide, no black coached an integrated high school basketball team or had yet played basketball for Indiana University, and the Indiana Officials Association excluded black referees. [34]

The Royals rallied around Dolly on the road. "He was one of the guys," said Al Cervi. "You couldn't insult Dolly without insulting the rest of us." When the Claypool Hotel restaurant staff in Indianapolis refused to serve Dolly, his teammates ate with him in the kitchen, next to garbage cans and dirty laundry. After that experience, Red Holzman and Fuzzy Levane usually shared dinner with Dolly in a hotel room. In Fort Wayne, the best hotel denied accommodations to Dolly, so the Royals left and stayed in another hostelry, and, when a restaurant turned them away "because one of the most scholarly, gentlemanly and socially correct athletes in the party was a Negro," the entire team indignantly marched out of the establishment.[35]

During the hard-fought second playoff game in the "Snake Pit," Zollner players called Dolly racially discriminatory names that "threatened to cause trouble." Although Rochester WHAM radio station announcer Bob Turner apparently described the insults in some detail during a live broadcast, the exact language has not been preserved. It probably was not much different from the racial slurs directed at Boston Celtic Bill Russell ten years later: "Coon. Go back to Africa, you baboon. Watch out, [home team player's name], you'll get covered with chocolate. Black nigger. Big black gorilla. Black bastard."[36]

"Indianapolis was tough, Fort Wayne was tough," remembered Earl Lloyd. "St. Louis was tough. Boston was tough. Baltimore was tough. You heard it. You heard all the words you would expect. Boston was a big eastern city and you didn't expect it there at first, but then you got there and you heard it and you knew. You knew fast."[37]

Back in Rochester for the third playoff game, the Royals responded to the Pistons' racist attack on their teammate with a battle cry: "Win it for Dolly!" "Fired to oven temperature and bristling with determination and spirit," wrote *Rochester Democrat and Chronicle* Sports Editor Elliot Cushing, "the vengeful Royals completely vindicated their great Negro star and gentleman athlete, who was the target of a sulpherous and slanderous verbal attack from the Fort Wayne bench Sunday which was a disgrace in democratic America." In a 76–47 "triumph for American sportsmanship," the Royals eliminated the Pistons. Dolly scored ten points and more than held his own under the boards. In the locker room after the game, Dolly, overcome with emotion, wept tears of joy. "It's the happiest day of my life," he sobbed.[38]

During the final playoff round against the Chicago American Gears, Dolly drew the unenviable assignment of guarding six inches taller and 30 pounds heavier 6' 10", 245-pound George Mikan. In the

Royals' opening game victory, Dolly outscored "Mighty Mikan," 16 points to 14 and "protected the boards like a sentry at the US mint." But in the final game, which the Royals lost, Dolly, who scored 11 points, fouled out trying to stop "Rochester's Public Basketball Enemy No. 1." As Dolly left the court, Big George grabbed his arm and, waving bye-bye, escorted him to the Royals' bench. Dolly did not complain or try to push off Mikan. Upon reaching his seat, Dolly offered to shake hands with his giant adversary. Speechless at this demonstration of sportsmanship, Big George turned away. Earlier in the season, Mikan had complained to a referee that the Royals were calling him and his team mates uncomplimentary names. "You got your law degree, George," countered Dolly, "why don't you sue us?"[39]

"Dolly was a tough player, one of the best rebounders," said American Gears backcourt star Dick Triptow. "He was a class guy, held in high esteem by all the players." Dolly averaged 8.3 PPG in the 11 playoff games, double his regular season scoring average.[40]

HISTORIC DAY

On April 15, 1947, more than 600 Royals fans celebrated another memorable season at a sell-out testimonial dinner held in the Powers Hotel. The featured speaker, CCNY coach Nat Holman, attacked bigotry and racial discrimination in sports, and congratulated Les Harrison for signing Dolly. At the head table, Bob Davies dined next to Rev. Hugh Haffey, a Catholic high school teacher, and Dolly sat near Reverend Charles E. Boddie, pastor of the black Mt. Olivet Baptist Church. Only Bob and Dolly spoke on behalf of the players. Gentleman and sportsman Dolly, who the *Pittsburgh Courier* had recognized as the year's outstanding African-American basketball player, praised his teammates and Rochester fans. Commenting in the *Courier* about developments in race relations, Sports Editor Wendell Smith characterized 1946 as the greatest year for Negro athletes, especially professionals, dating back to track star Jesse Owens's Berlin Olympics gold medal performances in 1936 and heavyweight boxer Joe Louis's knockout of German Max Schmeling in 1938, which represented a triumph of democracy over totalitarianism.[41]

Earlier that day, Jackie Robinson, earning the MLB $5,000 ($53,000 in today's money) minimum salary, had made the first African-American appearance in a modern major-league baseball game. During spring training, Jackie and three other black Dodger prospects lived and ate separately from their white teammates. A few Dodgers threatened to strike rather than accept Jackie as a teammate. As dramatized in the movie *42*, shortstop Pee Wee Reese, the former marbles sharp-shooter, placed his hand on Jackie's shoulder, in a gesture of solidarity, publicly affirming that, at least on the diamond, the Dodgers accepted Jackie. Although no white Dodger roomed or dined with Jackie on road trips, bench jockeys taunted them for sleeping with him. Actually, Jackie, the loneliest man in sports, roomed with *Pittsburgh Courier* journalist Wendell Smith, whom the Dodgers had hired as a sort of chaperone to run interference for him. When a restaurant refused them service, Wendell found another place to eat. Later in the season, Jackie stayed in black-owned hotels with black pitcher Dan Bankhead and ate with him in black-owned restaurants or in friends' homes.[42]

DECISION TIME

After the Powers Hotel banquet, Bob and Mary returned to South Orange, New Jersey. He coached the Seton Hall baseball team one more season. His baseball teams over two seasons won 28 and lost 10 games. He took advantage of the G.I. Bill, which provided war veterans financial assistance for higher education, and, in three successive summer sessions at Columbia Teachers College (New York City), completed classes for a master's degree in physical education.[43]

America's Number One Sports Commuter faced a tough decision—whether to continue coaching college and playing professional basketball, just coach the Pirates, or just play for the Royals. Realizing that her husband could not maintain the back-breaking pace required to meet the demands of two jobs, Mary put her foot down. "He was never home on Saturday night," she lamented. Seton Hall Athletic Director Father Carey and Bob were close friends, but college coaches were poorly paid. On his part, Les Harrison wanted to avoid more anxious moments waiting for Bob's plane to arrive in blustery upstate New York snowstorms and to pay him the NBL's highest salary as a reward for his MVP season. Bob and Les shook hands on a four-year deal paying $100 per league and exhibition game, as well as a $2,000 bonus and covering Bob's income tax obligation. They estimated his base salary at $9,500 and the total pay package at about $15,000 ($159,000 today), which was higher than George Mikan's 1947–48 season $12,500 contract. By comparison, modern play-maker John Stockton, the NBA total career assists and steals record holder, earned $7,875,000 his final 2002–2003 NBA season and two-time NBA MVP Steve Nash was paid $9,701,000 the 2014–15 season.[44]

Dolly King did not return to the Royals the next season because the team no longer needed his services. He had averaged 4.0 points per game during the regular season, and second-year power forward Arnie Johnson, three and a half years younger and similar in size and ability, had averaged 6.2 PPG. During the 1947–48 season, Dolly appeared in one game for the NBL Dayton Rens and scored 11 points. Subsequently, he worked as a New York City housing project recreation program director, college and high school basketball game referee, and Manhattan Community College basketball coach. Dolly died too young, from a heart attack in 1969 at age 51.[45]

Before the 1947–48 season commenced, an NBL player personnel move sealed Bob Davies' and the Royals' fate for years to come. Minneapolis businessmen purchased the last-place Detroit Gems franchise for $15,000 ($159,000 today). After the Chicago American Gears' owner bolted the NBL and formed an independent league, which quickly folded, the NBL assigned the rights to "Rochester's Basketball Public Enemy No. 1" to the new Minneapolis Lakers franchise.[46]

NOTES

1   Alexander Wolff, "Lost History: The NFL's Jackie Robinson," *Sports Illustrated*, Oct. 12, 2009, 60–71; Kenneth Shouler, "The NBA's First African-Americans" in Shouler et al., *Total Basketball*, 140–43, and John Smallwood, "NBA Pioneers: The African-American Influence" in Hubbard, *NBA Encyclopedia*, 58–61.

   Actually, before the Knicks, the Washington Capitols on April 26, 1950, signed an African-American player, Harold Hunter, but he did not make the team. The Knicks signed Clifton on May 24, 1950. The first African-American drafted was Chuck Cooper by the Boston Celtics. Ron Thomas, *They Cleared the Lane: The NBA's Black Pioneers*, 14–15.

2   Schumacher, *Mr. Basketball*, 68–70; "NBL No. 1": "Cagers Corner," *D&C*, Feb. 5, 1946.

3   Bob Matthews, "Harrison's court vision ignited today's NBA," *D&C*, Dec. 25, 1997; "If he can": Holzman, *Red on Red*, 20; Meyer, *Rochester Seagrams History*, 5, 7, 12, 14,15, 17, 20–21, 25, 26, 29, 30; Schleppi, *Chicago's Showplace*, 19; "Flash That Red Signal, Seagrams! — Here Are Speedy Reds," *D&C*, Jan. 24, 1940; "Plane to Bring Singh For Game at Armory," *D&C*, Jan. 25, 1940; http://hometown.aol.com/apbrhoops/tourney.html.

4   "It wouldn't": Fuzzy Levane, telephone conversation with author, Nov. 23, 2005.

5   Paul Pinckney, "Royals Sign King, Negro Cage Great," *D&C*, October 15, 1946; "Dolly King Joins Royals: Negro Ace Signed by Boss Harrison," *T-U*, Oct. 16, 1946; "Dolly King Signs $7,000 Contract," *Pittsburgh Courier*, Oct. 19, 1946 (mentions Gates signing); "Rochester Star" (picture caption), *Pittsburgh Courier*, Nov. 30, 1946; Measuring Worth; "for signing": Wendell Smith to Les Harrison quoted without date in Fisher, "Lester Harrison," 229–30; John Gunther, *Inside USA 50th anniversary edition.*, 626–27 (*Pittsburgh Courier* printed 13 editions totaling approximately 280,000 copies); Caponi-Tabery, *Jump For Joy*, 16; Kevin Begos (AP), "Museum puts Negro League on display in Pittsburgh," *New Mexican* (Santa Fe), March 24, 2014.

Harrison always said that he lined up both King and Gates and gave Gates's services to the Bisons because he did not need Gates, who was primarily a scorer, and the Buffalo owner had volunteered to share in bearing the burden of any problems arising from bringing African-American players into the NBL. Fisher, "Rochester Royals," 46n40; Thomas, *They Cleared*, 15.

6   Jonathan Fraser Light, *Cultural Encyclopedia of Baseball*, 642; Al Cervi, telephone conversation with author, June 1, 2004; Fuzzy Levane, telephone conversation with author, Jan. 13, 2006; Rosen, *First Tip-Off*, 199; Salzberg, *Set Shot*, 19.

7   "Dolly King, LIU Star Athlete And a College Coach, Dies at 51," *NYT*,

Jan. 30, 1969; "Long Island University National Invitation Tournament Winners" (picture caption identifying King as co-captain), A.S. Barnes & Co. *American Sports Library:* The *Official Basketball Guide, 1941–1942*: 96; "Lt. Col. Haldane King," *Columbus (Ohio) Dispatch*, July 19, 2013; http://www.luckyshow.org/basketball/Grumman.htm; Leo Fischer, "1943 World's Championship Tournament," *Converse Basketball Year Book 1943*, 45.

8   "A hell": Holzman, *On Hoops*, 34; Ibid., 33.

9   "If you had": Earl Lloyd, telephone conversation with author, July 19, 2008.

10   I was" and "I wouldn't": William Warfield, *William Warfield: My Music & My Life*, 15 and 16.

11   Ibid., 19, 39–40, 45–51, 53–54; John A. Garraty and Mark A. Carnes, *American National Biography*, s.v. "Anderson, Marian."

12   Ingrid Overacker, *The African American Church Community In Rochester, New York, 1900–1940*, 63, 117, 196–97.

13   Norman Coombs, "History of African Americans in Rochester, NY (unpublished paper), 1–2, http://people.rit.edu/nrcgsh/arts/rochester. htm.

14   Randall Brown, "Blood and Base Ball, Part 5," http://ourgame.mlblogs. com2011/12/02/blood-and-base-ball-part-5/.

15   Overacker, *African American Church Community*, 182–83.

16   Bill Beeney, "Conversation Pieces: Supporters of Klan — They Were Here!" *D&C*, March 26, 1964.

17   Caponi-Tabery, *Jump For Joy*, 170; McKelvey, *Rochester: An Emerging Metropolis,140.*

18   Adolph Dupree, "Rochester Roots/Routes, Part IV," *about... time*, Oct. 1984, 24; Daniel Beaumont, *Preachin' the Blues: The Life and Times of Son House*, 113.

19   Overacker, *African American Church Community*, 117.

20   *McKelvey*, Rochester: An Emerging Metropolis, 236, 272, 287.

21   Adolph Dupree, "Rochester Roots/Routes, Part IV," *about... time*, Oct. 1984, 14.

22   Overacker, *African American Church Community*, 136–37, 176.

23   University of Rochester, *The 1947 Interpres*, 83, 150.

24   McKelvey, *Rochester: An Emerging Metropolis*, 8; Overacker, *African American Church Community*, 62–63.

25   Howard W. Coles, comp., *City Directory of Negro Business and Progress,
     1939–1940,* 4, 5, 8, 10, 11, 12; Daniel Beaumont, *Preachin' the Blues: The
     Life and Times of Son House,* 114–15; Adolph Dupree, "Rochester Roots/
     Routes, Part IV," *about... time,* Oct. 1984, 26; Charles E. Boddie, "A Study
     of the Relation of an Urban Negro Church to its Community" (master's
     thesis, University of Rochester, 1949), 3, 22, 25–27.
26   "During basketball season": Earl Lloyd, telephone conversation with
     author, July 19, 2008.
27   James, "Dolly King" Cartoon: *D&C,* Feb. 15, 1947; "Royal Court Tips:
     Pivot Play," *D&C,* Feb. 27, 1947; "Royal Court Tips: Play Making—Foul
     Shooting," *D&C,* Feb. 28, 1947; "Star of First Magnitude," Hershey
     Sports Arena Basketball Club Season of 1947 Program (April 11, 1947): 7
     (author's possession).
28   Charles A. Landolph, "Rochester Defeats Youngstown, 69–43 in
     National Pro Cage Opener: Visitors Completely Outplay Locals; 2,500
     Fans See Tilt," *Youngstown (OH) Vindicator,* Nov. 12, 1946; Joe Alli,
     "Bison Cagers Top Syracuse Rivals, 50–39," *Buffalo Evening News,* Nov.
     10, 1946; "Bisons Beat Nationals: Syracuse Pros Drop 50 to 39 Game in
     Buffalo" *Syracuse Post-Standard,* Nov. 11, 1946 (Gates scored 11 points);
     "Royals Jar Bears, 67–53, Rochester Trips Local Passers Third Straight
     Time," *Youngstown Vindicator,* Jan. 19, 1947 (Farrow); "Davies Faces
     Detroit Quint In Arena Tilt," *D&C,* Feb. 14, 1947 (Willie King); Rosen,
     First Tip-Off, 99.
29   "Sport: Rookie of the Year," *Time,* Sept. 22, 1947, 70; Bill Russell, *Go Up
     For Glory,* 57–58; Scott Ostler, "Local Pioneer: First in Boston 50 years
     ago," *San Francisco (CA) Chronicle,* July 21, 2009; Jim Bouton, *Ball Four:
     My Life and Hard Times Throwing the Knuckleball in the Big Leagues,* 310.
30   "The rule": Levane, telephone conversation with author, Jan. 13, 2006.
31   "the center": Official Program Rochester Royals Basketball Club
     1946–1947 Season, n.p., Rochester Royals Program 1946–1950 File, Bx.
     4, Professional Men NBL Collection, Joseph M. O'Brien Historical
     Resource Center, Naismith Memorial Basketball Hall of Fame,
     Springfield, MA (hereafter cited as PMHOF); Ocania Chalk, *Pioneers Of
     Black Sport,* 105; Leonard Lewin, "Memories Of Dolly," *NY Post,* May 6,
     1986; "This drink": Holzman, *Red on Red,* 20.
32   "It's gonna": Roland Lazenby, "Years ago, they didn't do it for the
     money," Sports Server NBA Correspondent.

33 Mary Davies, telephone conversation with author, Dec. 3, 2007; "Bob never": Dick Davies, telephone conversation with author, Dec. 30, 2011; Bo Davies (son), telephone conversation with author, May 24, 2009.

34 "Nigger": George, *Elevating the Game*, 118; Ibid., 117; http://Census. Gov/; Richard B. Pierce, *Polite Protest: The Political Economy of Race in Indianapolis, 1920–1970*, 5, 11–12, 18, 62, 130n1; Tom Graham and Rachel Graham Cody, *Getting Open: The Unknown Story of Bill Garrett and the Integration of College Basketball*, 17, 44, 55–57, 92, 111–12, 116, 193; Chalk, *Pioneers Of Black Sport*, 105.

Future NBA superstar, ten-year-old Oscar "Big O" Robertson, was growing up in an Indianapolis black ghetto and honing his formidable basketball skills on an outdoor court known as the "Dust Bowl." Young Oscar silently complied with Jim Crow rules barring blacks from public facilities reserved for whites. He attended black schools and, for his own well-being, avoided white private establishments. His mother worked part time as a cook for a wealthy white family; she entered their house through the back door and ate meals on the back porch. Oscar Robertson, *The Big O: My Life, My Times, My Game*. 9–11, 14–15, 20–21, 25–26, 28, 33.

35 "He was": Jim Myers, "Black History: Royals signed black pioneer," *D&C*, Feb. 2, 1986; "because": Elliot Cushing, "Sports Eye View, *D&C*, April 3, 1947; Holzman and Frommer, *Holzman on Hoops*, 33.

36 "threatened": Al C. Weber, "Ft. Wayne 'Out Roughs' Royals, Ties Series at 1–1, Rubber Tilt Set Tomorrow," *T-U*, March 31, 1947; Myers, "Black History," *D&C*, Feb. 2, 1986; "Coon": Russell, *Go Up For Glory*, combined 120 and 155.

37 "Indianapolis was": Earl Lloyd and Sean Kirst, *Moonfixer: The Basketball Journey of Earl Lloyd*, 82.

38 "Win it" and "Fired": Elliot Cushing, "Vengeful Royals Wreck Fort Wayne: Royal Five Busts Way To Playoff Series Win," *D&C*, April 2, 1947; "It's the": Elliot Cushing, "Sports Eye View," *D&C*, April 3, 1947.

39 Hubbard, *NBA Encyclopedia*, 3rd ed., 649 (Mikan); "protected the boards": "Royals Down Gears For 1–0 Lead: Davies Nets 23 for Royals In 71–65 Win Over Gears," *D&C*, April 4, 1947; George Beahon, "Sporting Scene," *D&C*, April 9, 1947; "You got": Elliot Cushing, "Sports Eye View," *D&C*, Feb. 28, 1947.

40 "Dolly was": Dick Triptow, telephone conversation with author, Feb. 20, 2006, author's calculation from playoff game box scores.

41 "Royals Lure Turnaway Crowd Again," *D&C*, April 16, 1947; "A 'Royal' Time Was Had by All as Fans Honor National Loop Cage Kings: City Fetes Royals," *T-U*, April 16, 1947; Testimonial Dinner In Honor of 'Les' Harrison and his Rochester Royals National Basketball League Champions 1945–1946 … 1946–1947 Program, Rochester Royals Testimonial Dinner Program, April 15, 1947 File, Bx. 4, PMHOF; Wendell Smith, "The Sports Beat: '46 Greatest Year for Negro Athletes," *Pittsburgh Courier*, Jan. 4, 1947; Caponi-Tabery, *Jump For Joy*, 125–27; Wendell Smith, "Brooklyn Prospect Tops Courier Poll," *Pittsburgh Courier*, Jan. 4, 1947.

42 Arnold Rampersad, *Jackie Robinson: A Biography*, 163–64, 167, 169, 171, 175–78; Jonathan Eig, *Opening Day: The Story Of Jackie Robinson's First Season*, 137, 172–73, 226; Measuring Worth.

43 Don Kerr, "Sports Diary," The *Setonian*, May 23, 1946; Seton Hall 1947 Season Baseball Record—Coach Bob Davies, SHUAC; Al C. Weber, "Bobby Davies Signs with Rochester Royals," *T-U*, Aug. 4, 1948.

44 "He was never": Mary Davies, telephone conversation with author, Jan. 18, 2007; Salzberg, *Set Shot*, 50–51; Measuring Worth; Mikan and Oberle, *Unstoppable*, 84–85; "2002–2003 NBA salaries—Western Conference," *USA Today*, March 18, 2003; "Highest-Paid Canadians in Major League Sports in 2014–15," *Maclean's*, Sept. 29, 2014, 27.

45 NBL News Bureau, "NBL Scoring for 1946–47," RRSHOF 1946–1947 Season; "Dolly King, LIU Star Athlete And a College Coach, Dies at 51," *NYT*, Jan. 30, 1969.

46 Roland Lazenby, *The Lakers: A Basketball Journey*, 64–66, 74–75; Nelson, *NBL*, 180; Measuring Worth.

THE MOST PERFECT TEAM

DURING THE LATE 1940S AND EARLY 1950S, THE ROCHESTER Royals reigned as one of the two best professional basketball teams in the world. The Royals (1945–1952) and Minneapolis Lakers (1947–1954) are two of only four NBL-BAA-NBA teams to win the playoff championship or finish or tie for first in their division or conference (the NBA changed from divisions to conferences in 1970–71) for five consecutive seasons. The other teams that have accomplished this feat were the Boston Celtics (1956–68) and St. Louis Hawks (1956–61). Even the Chicago Bulls with Michael Jordan and the Miami Heat with LeBron James did not match this standard of consistent excellence.[1]

Pre-eminent NBA historian Leonard Koppett described the Rochester Royals as "the most perfect" team of their era. According to former NBA Commissioner Walter Kennedy, nobody was better qualified than Koppett to make this judgment. Reporting successively for the *New York Herald-Tribune*, *New York Post*, and *The New York Times*, Koppett covered the NBA's first quarter century more thoroughly than any other sports writer. Koppett praised the Royals for their balanced style of play and evenly distributed scoring, as well as court sense, constant movement, alertness to openings, unselfishness, and polished ball handling.[2]

"There weren't any egos on the team," remembered the late Royals Hall of Fame guard Bobby Wanzer. "We respected one another and we all wanted to win. The team came first. We were evenly balanced and everybody did his job very competently. You never knew who would

The Rochester Royals were "the most perfect team" of their era. From left to right Top Row: Bill Calhoun, Arnie Johnson, Mike Nowak, Arnie Risen, Jack Coleman, Andy Duncan; Front Row: Bob Davies, Bobby Wanzer, Fran Curran, Red Holzman, Pep Saul (1950, Sacramento Kings)

be the high scorer. We moved the ball to whoever had a good shot and was hot. We protected the ball because there was no 24-second rule[3] and we might not get the ball back right away. Winning was everything. The only way we could make extra money was to get in the playoffs and keep winning."[4]

Wanzer made a striking comparison between the Rochester Royals and the 2014 NBA playoff champion San Antonio Spurs whom the sports media have lionized for their exceptional team play. "The San Antonio Spurs are the only team today that plays like we did," said Wanzer (before the emergence of the San Francisco Warriors). "They have discipline and patience. But they are just one team of 32. Most modern players don't have the mentality to pass the ball."[5]

*"Mr. Basketball" 6'10"
Minneapolis Laker
George Mikan guard-
ing "lithe, blond
whippet" 6'1 1/2"
Rochester Royal Bob
Davies were the early
NBA's best tall and
short players. (April 7,
1952, AP Photo)*

GEORGE MIKAN

Unfortunately for the Royals, George "Mr. Basketball" Mikan tipped the scales of the Royals–Lakers rivalry in favor of the Lakers. The Associated Press named Mikan the best basketball player of the first half of the 20th century. He led the Chicago American Gears and Minneapolis Lakers to seven playoff championships, won the scoring title six consecutive seasons, captured the rebounding title once, and earned All-League First Team honors seven times. Unfortunately, Big George staged many of his best performances against the Royals.[6]

"Mikan was a great player," said Les Harrison. "He made the rest of them. There was nothing we could do to stop him." And Les left no stone unturned trying. He even signed Mikan's brother Ed, at 6' 8", 230-pounds, for part of a season to try to stymie his monster big brother. [7]

"Mikan is 60 percent of the Lakers' strength," said Bob Davies.

"Besides being a great scorer and rebounder, Mikan is an immovable obstacle under the basket. He's big and he takes up space under there. He gets in your way when you try to work in."[8]

Hall of Fame New York Knicks coach Red Holzman believed that the Royals might have become a dynasty if Mikan had not been a Laker.[9]

BOB DAVIES

"If Mikan was pro basketball's first big-man hero," noted Dr. Peter C. Bjarkman in the *Encyclopedia of Pro Basketball Team Histories*, "then Rochester's Bob Davies was the sport's first true backcourt hero. A decade before Cousy it was Bob Davies who was displaying dazzling backcourt artistry and entertaining small if enthusiastic pro basketball crowds with his scoring and wizard-like ball handling."[10]

"Bob Davies was the team leader," emphasized Les Harrison. "He played hard all the time. He moved the ball. He was on top of everything." According to NBA historian Roland Lazenby, "Davies turned the wheel of the offense." His teammates knew that Bob would pass the ball to them if they broke open for a good shot.[11]

At the NBA quarter-century mark, Leonard Koppett chose Bob Davies as one of the NBA's 25 best players, and placed guards Bob Cousy, Oscar Robertson, and NBA logo figure Jerry West (Los Angeles Lakers) on a greatest-players "super-nine." Koppett stated that he would have included Davies in this group except that he played only the last half of his professional career in the NBA, and played some of his greatest seasons in the NBL, not to mention three seasons lost in the Navy.[12]

BOBBY WANZER

Their backcourt aces steered the Royals to their phenomenal success. Hall of Famers Bob Davies and Bobby Wanzer, in the words of Red Holzman, formed "the first famous backcourt duo in pro basketball history." *New York Times* basketball correspondent and NBA historian Sam Goldaper called Davies and Wanzer the top NBA pre-24-second clock era guard combination. Basketball historian Jack Clary and Boston Celtic Hall of Fame guard Bill Sharman, with Bob Cousy one-half of the second-in-terms of when they played NBA great backcourt

Rochester Royals Hall of Famers Bob Davies and Bob Wanzer formed the first great NBA backcourt combination. (Rochester Radio-Press Club)

duos, also recognized the Royals' "Bobbys" as the best early NBA backcourt combo.[13]

Born June 4, 1921, in New York City, Robert Francis "Bobby" Wanzer honed his basketball skills on an outdoor playground dirt court and on an indoor settlement house small-sized court. He was a New York City All-Scholastic First Team selection, and the only white starter on a Benjamin Franklin High School team that twice won the city championship. After his sophomore season at Seton Hall, Wanzer joined the Marine Corps, participated in the occupation and defense of Guam, played on the Miramar-Pendleton Marines (Oceanside, CA) basketball team, and was honorably discharged as a corporal. Wanzer has been inducted into the Marine Corps Sports Hall of Fame in Quantico, Virginia. [14]

Before Bill Sharman joined the Boston Celtics, Bobby Wanzer

stood out as the NBA's best backcourt marksman. During the 1948–49, 1949–50, and 1951–52 seasons, Bobby, nicknamed "Pinky" because his face reddened when he exerted himself, had the highest field goal made (FGM) percentage of any guard. Wanzer shot the most accurate and Davies the quickest set shots of their era. "Hooks" Wanzer also took his defender into the pivot. "Wanzer actually insults the big boys of the game by out-doing many of them on their 'money' shot, the hook," stated a *Minneapolis Laker News* writer. Three times Wanzer ranked in the NBA top ten in assists. An exceptionally able defender, always assigned to the opponent's best little man, Wanzer, a "clean player," committed the third fewest fouls among all starters and the fewest by a guard during the 1953–54 NBA season. [15]

"Wanzer," said Red Holzman, "is the ballplayer's ballplayer. If a young kid asks me how to learn by watching the pros, I tell him to watch Wanzer, especially when he doesn't have possession of the ball. He does things that people don't notice, but they are things that help you win."[16]

With the addition of Bobby Wanzer during the 1947–48 season, the Royals' on-court basketball brain trust included one former college coach, Bob Davies, and four future NBA coaches— Al Cervi (Syracuse Nationals 1954–55 NBA champions), Red Holzman (Milwaukee Hawks and New York Knicks 1969–70 and 1972–73 NBA champions), Fuzzy Levane (Milwaukee/St. Louis Hawks and New York Knicks), and Wanzer (Rochester and Cincinnati Royals).[17]

ARNIE RISEN

Trying to cope with Mighty Mikan, the Royals, in January 1948, purchased 23-year-old, 6' 9", 200-pound blue chip center Arnold "Big Slim" Risen's contract from the Indianapolis Kautskys for $25,000 (the cost of the original franchise and the highest-priced player transaction to that time, amounting to $246,000 in today's currency). It turned out to be money well spent.[18]

Born October 9, 1924, in Williamstown, Kentucky, in the state's northern Grant County (population 9,876), gentle, soft-spoken Arnie Risen grew up in a three-room, one-story farm house and attended a one-room school. He and his two brothers and sister started playing basketball by shooting a sponge-like rubber ball at a metal can bottom ring nailed to the side of their house. Arnie's high school senior class included only five boys, but the basketball team lost only one regular season game and the regional tournament's final game. Arnie starred for Eastern Kentucky State Teachers College (Richmond) and Ohio State University, but never graduated. He was classified 4-F for the draft because of his height and an asthmatic condition. During the 1946–47 season, he had finished third in NBL scoring and earned All-Star Second Team honors. Risen shot deadly hooks with either hand, passed smoothly from the pivot, and defended well and rebounded strongly despite his slight frame. [19]

During the Mikan era (1946–54), basketball pundits disagreed about which future Hall of Famer, Arnie Risen or Boston Celtic Charles Edward "Easy Ed" Macauley Jr., was the second-best center. Leonard Koppett stated that Risen "was second only to Mikan in the respect he generated around the league." Mikan named Risen to his All-Opponent Team and considered him the most difficult opposing center to defend. In their head-to-head duels, however, Mikan's 45-pound weight advantage took its toll on Risen. After the Royals cleared the defensive boards, the more mobile Arnie tried to sprint down court to get open for a pass before lumbering Big George caught up with him.[20]

ARNIE JOHNSON

The Royals' other Arnie, easygoing power forward 6' 7", 240-pound Arnitz "Arnie" Johnson, jousted with 6' 7", 230-pound Lakers Hall of Famer Arild Verner "Vern" Mikkelsen.

Born May 17, 1920, in the northwestern Minnesota farming community of Gonvick (population 250), Arnie excelled in high school basketball, football, baseball, and track and field. He worked in wheat fields and on highway construction projects to pay his way through Bemidji State Teachers College (enrollment 400) in Bemidji, Minnesota. He was a three-time basketball and two-time football All-Northern Teacher's College Conference First Team selection and a 1941 Converse All-American College Basketball team honorable mention. He threw the shot put and discus and ran on the "Beavers" 220-yard relay team.

Arnie "Big Louie" Johnson drove to the basket like a Sherman tank and provided muscle under the backboards. (Courtesy of Arvin J. Odegaard)

After graduating with a Bachelor of Science degree in physical education, Arnie taught high school P.E. for six months, and then joined the Army Air Corps. On leave, he joined Bob Davies on the 1942 College All-Star Game roster. He served 30 months at Buckley Air Force Base (Aurora, CO) as a physical training (calisthenics) instructor and played for the base's basketball team, nicknamed the Gunners.[21]

Converse Rubber Company representative Chuck Taylor, whose signature graces the classic basketball sneakers, spotted Johnson playing for the AAU Continental Airways team and recommended that Harrison take a look at him. Les sent Arnie travel money for a tryout. Worried that he might not make the team, Arnie hitchhiked in midwinter on a cattle truck 660 miles from Gonvick, Minnesota, to Chicago, Illinois, so that he would have the money, if needed, for transportation back home. Arnie passed muster, and Harrison signed him.[22]

Johnson rebounded strongly and made putbacks of missed shots, passed unselfishly, ran the court with surprising speed for a big man, defended aggressively, fired 15-foot one-hand push shots, and set formidable screens for the Royals' outside shooters. "It's just like shooting in practice with Arnie in front of you," said Bob Davies. When Johnson retired from the NBA, Les Harrison called him "the most unselfish player" he had ever seen.[23]

Teenage Royals fan and poetess Jody Cronau Low immortalized Arnie Johnson in this verse:

> Our Big Louie, the Sherman Tank,
> With his gears no-shift, his engine no-crank,
> Driving in for his famous layup,
> Had much to do with the post-season payup.[24]

JACK COLEMAN

Prior to the 1949–50 season, the Royals signed 25-year-old, 6' 7", 230-pound University of Louisville forward Jack Coleman. Born May 23, 1924, in Burgin (population 900) in central Kentucky, Jack enjoyed participating in sports with his three older brothers and developed into an outstanding all-around athlete. As a rangy 6' 4", 190-pound fullback, he led the Burgin High School Bulldogs to the Kentucky state six-man football championship. In a preview of the 1986 hit movie *Hoosiers,* in which Hickory High School from a small town, Milan, defeats a big city high school for the Indiana state championship, the 60-student-body Burgin High School team, led by MVP Jack, beat John Marshall High School (Richmond, VA), Greenville (SC) Senior High School, and Durham (NC) High School and won the 1942 Southern High School Invitational Basketball Tournament held in the Duke University gym. Jack was Kentucky team captain and game co-high scorer in the fourth annual Kentucky–Indiana High School All-Star Game. After completing his sophomore year at Duke University, he enlisted in the Navy. He played on the 1943–44 Great Lakes Naval Training Station Bluejackets basketball team that won 34 and lost 3 games and has been ranked as the second-best all-time armed forces service basketball team. He also starred as a pass-catching end on the GLNTS football team. After leaving Great Lakes, he graduated from the Bainbridge Naval Training Station Petty Officer School in Maryland.[25]

Jack Coleman, a gifted 6'7", 230-pound forward, utilized the two-hand overhead set shot as his outside offensive weapon. (Courtesy of Jack L. Coleman II)

Coleman served nine months in the Pacific Theater on the USS *Gilbert Islands,* an escort-type carrier whose two Marine Corps fighter squadrons provided close air support to American troops fighting on Okinawa, and attacked Japanese kamikaze aircraft bases on nearby islands. The ship's Corsair and Hellcat pilots also furnished air cover for Australian forces landing in Borneo. As World War II wound down, the *Gilbert Islands* lay off the coast of Japan as part of a build-up for a dreaded invasion. Jack liked to reminisce about the ship's undefeated basketball team practicing on the flight deck. He joked about using Kentucky windage for his long shots and chasing the ball to keep it from rolling off the deck. Whenever the *Gilbert Islands* arrived in a port, a signalman sent out messages, found a team, and set up a game. [26]

Upon his discharge from the Navy, the Cleveland Browns football team and a St. Louis Cardinals Class D minor-league baseball team tried to sign Coleman, but he decided to complete his education at the University of Louisville. He married his high-school sweetheart, Janet

Powell, and they lived on her teacher's salary, his G.I. Bill of Rights stipend, and financial aid from the university. A three-sport letterman, Jack earned Little All-American Football and National Association of Intercollegiate Basketball (NAIB) All-Tournament First Team honors. Les Harrison sent Fuzzy Levane to scout Jack, and then selected him in the NBA draft. Fellow Kentuckian and friend Arnie Risen advised Jack on contract negotiations, and he signed a one-year deal for $6,500 ($64,500 today).[27]

An excellent two-hand overhead set shooter, rebounder, and passer, Jack Coleman proved a worthy antidote to the Lakers' great Hall of Fame forward, 6' 4", 190-pound James "Jumping Jim" Pollard, the first professional cager to play above the rim. With a running start, Pollard could dunk from the foul line, but BAA and early NBA players did not dunk in games because it was considered showboating, and opponents would knock them down and possibly injure them. Pollard handled the Lakers' dribbling chores in full-court press and stalling situations, drove to the basket when unimpeded by Mikan anchored in the post, swished one-hand push and jump shots, and excelled at tip-in baskets.[28]

"Jack Coleman is very underrated," says Bobby Wanzer. "He was a different type of player. He was very strong and had the best hands around the basket. He was a better shooter and rebounder than Pollard, but not as mobile." In their regular season NBA careers, Coleman made 41.6 percent of his field goal attempts, many overhead set shots from the sideline, and averaged 9.2 rebounds per game to Pollard's 36.1 percent and 7.8 rebounds.[29]

RED HOLZMAN

The other member of the Royals' gold-plate guard triumvirate, who also functioned as number one strategy advisor, Red Holzman, sat next to Les Harrison on the team bench and recommended substitutions and game tactics. Les called Red "the smartest basketball player in the game" and "Reddo" dubbed himself the "best paid substitute in basketball."[30]

Born August 10, 1920, William "Red" Holzman grew up in New York City watching Rens and Brooklyn Jewels basketball games.

Diminutive guard Red Holzman was "the smartest player in the game" and destined to become a great NBA coach for the New York Knicks. (Sacramento Kings)

Franklin K. Lane High School, which he attended, did not have a gym, so its basketball team practiced in the school yard (weather permitting) and played all games on opponents' courts. After graduating from high school, Red pushed a hand wagon through the New York City garment district for a year before the University of Baltimore granted him a scholarship. He later transferred to CCNY, and played his junior and senior years under Coach Nat Holman. In the summer of 1942, Holzman enlisted in the Navy and was assigned to the Norfolk Naval Training Station's (Virginia) "morale unit," which exercised and drilled recruits and maintained recreation facilities. He played for the 1942–43 (26–4) and 1943–44 (31–2) Norfolk Naval Training Station teams that have been ranked 17th and 6th all-time, respectively, among armed-services basketball teams. [31]

Iron Man Red missed no regular season games beginning in the 1945–46 NBL season and ending in the 1949–50 NBA season. Referees ejected him only once for arguing. Rochester sportswriter George Beahon characterized Red as a "complete gentleman on and off the court" and "a merciless marksman, an uncanny playmaker and deadly passer," as well as a flawless defender."[32]

CHAMPIONSHIP TEAM

"If you want a championship team," said master talent evaluator and team builder Les Harrison, "everybody has to fit in their parts. That's what I had." [33]

Contemporary basketball experts agreed with Harrison's evaluation. *New York Times* basketball correspondent Sam Goldaper labeled the Royals as "the top team of their time." Lakers coach John Kundla hailed them as "the team with the finest style in basketball." In Red Holzman's opinion, the 1950–51 Royals and his 1972–73 NBA champion Knicks "played the greatest brand of team basketball ever."[34] Incredibly, none of the Royals core six players utilized a conventional jump shot.

If the Royals had played when the three-point shot (23 feet 9 inches or more from the basket rim) rule was in effect, they would have been even more potent offensively. "Davies would have eaten up the three-point shot," said Les Harrison. "He made most of his shots outside the foul circle." Jack Coleman believed that he, Davies and Wanzer each would have made three to five three-point shots a game.[35]

CONTRASTING STYLES OF PLAY

But the rules without a 24-second shot requirement favored the rugged Lakers' slower, methodical style of play, and their physical strength wore down the Royals in playoff series with home and away games on successive nights. The Lakers controlled the defensive boards, grabbed more than their share of offensive rebounds and made put-backs, and managed game tempo. If 5' 10", 170-pound Hall of Fame guard Slater "Dugie" Martin could not take advantage of a fast-break opportunity, he waited for Mikan to establish his position in the pivot. Using an elbow as a battering ram to protect the ball and clear out the victim guarding him, Mikan, who fractured his elbows several times and wore elbow pads toward the end of his career, scored on hook shots with either hand from both sides of the six-foot-wide foul lane. "The joke around the league," said former Syracuse National John Macknowski, "was that if you happened to be in his way when he whirled for the basket, they'd pick you up with a blotter."[36]

Defending the 47-foot-wide (rather than regulation 50 feet)

Minneapolis Auditorium court and six-foot-wide (expanded to 12 feet in 1952) foul lane, the Lakers deployed two brutes and a finesse artist. Even though more games are played in a modern season, Vern Mikkelsen's 127 career disqualifications for personal fouls is the all-time, as well as longest-standing, NBA record. Mikkelsen and Mikan set individual records for most seasons (3) and consecutive seasons (3) leading the NBA in personal fouls. Mikan holds the record for most personal fouls committed in a five-game playoff series (27), and Mikkelsen is tied for second-most personal fouls in a seven-game series (36). On the other hand, Jim Pollard, who could out-jump Mikan and Mikkelsen, was known as the NBA's cleanest player and averaged about two personal fouls per game. "They used to say that when Mikan, Mikkelsen, and Pollard stretched their arms across that narrow court," recalled Al Cervi, "nobody could get through." The Lakers' guards tightly defended the Royals' set shooters and forced them to drive into the Lakers' formidable back line. [37]

EDGERTON PARK SPORTS ARENA

The Royals' even smaller Edgerton Park Sports Arena 85-foot-long (rather than regulation 94 feet) and 46-foot-wide court also worked to the Lakers' advantage defensively and, in Red Holzman's opinion, to the Royals' disadvantage offensively. Holzman believed that the speedy and constantly-moving Royals scored more points on regulation size courts.[38]

Visiting players complained about how close the Edgerton Park Sports Arena walls and front row seats were to the court end lines and sidelines. New York Knicks broadcaster Marty Glickman remembered the walls as being within five feet of the end lines. There was room for a row of folding chairs at one end where three sets of double doors opened into a passageway from the concession area. On occasion, a player, unable to stop, burst through one of the doors and collided with a fan holding a hot dog and soda. At the other end, the doors opened outside. One night Bob Davies' momentum carried him under the backboard and through a door into a snow bank. The door slammed shut and the Royals competed a man short until someone noticed that Bob was missing-in-action and opened the door for him.[39]

In George Mikan's opinion, the Royals–Lakers rivalry ranked as one of the greatest in NBA history. Between 1948 and 1954, the Lakers won one more regular season game than the Royals (267 to 266), and the Royals finished with better regular-season records three times and tied the Lakers once. Amazingly, one season the Royals and Lakers scored exactly the same total points against all their opponents. But the Lakers won five playoff championships and the Royals only one. The Lakers' four Hall of Famers missed very few games during their run for the championships; Mikan and Martin each sat out two regular-season games and Mikkelsen five. The Royals were not so fortunate in the injury department.[40]

"Mikan would always beat us," remembered Bob Davies. "If they needed two points, he got them." [41]

"It was like every year we were a bridesmaid, but never the bride," Bobby Wanzer said.[42]

NOTES

1   Neft and Cohen, *Sports Encyclopedia: Pro Basketball*, 5th ed., 43–44, 58, 67–68; http://www.basketball-reference.com/leagues/NBA(year).html.

2   "the most perfect": Koppett, *24 Seconds*, 72–73; Walter Kennedy, NBA Commissioner, foreword to *Championship NBA—Official 25th Anniversary* by Leonard Koppett.

The Rens faded into oblivion and the Globetrotters evolved into international entertainers. In the Chicago World Professional Basketball Tournament, the Rens lost in the 1946 second round to the Oshkosh All-Stars, in the 1947 first round to the woeful Toledo Jeeps, and in the 1948 championship round to the Lakers. After the BAA rejected their application for a franchise, the Rens entered the NBL as the Dayton Rens and finished the 1947–48 season in last place. After the two 1946 encounters in Schenectady, the Royals never again played the Globetrotters. In February 1948 and February 1949, the Trotters defeated the Lakers. Yes, Mighty Mikan lost his first two encounters with Goose Tatum. But then the Lakers won five consecutive games between March 1949 and January 1952. Schleppi, *Chicago's Showcase*, 88, 103, 115; Nelson, *NBL*, 206–19, 238; "Dayton Rens": http://www.ohiohistorycentral.org;

http://stewthornley.net/mplslakers_trotters.html.

3   In 1954, the NBA adopted a rule that forced a team to shoot the ball within 24 seconds or lose possession of it. Read more about the 24-second shot rule in Chapter 12.

4   "There weren't": combined from telephone conversations between Bobby Wanzer and the author, July 11 and August 22, 2014.

5   "The San Antonio": Bobby Wanzer, telephone conversation with author, July 11, 2014.

6   Schumacher, *Mr. Basketball*, 167; Dan Barreiro, "George Mikan: The First Icon" in Hubbard, *NBA Encyclopedia*, 3rd ed., 26–29.

7   "Mikan was": Les Harrison, telephone conversation with author, March 10, 1990; Hubbard, *NBA Encyclopedia*, 3rd ed., 649 (Edward Anton Mikan).

8   "Mikan is": Joe Hendrickson, "Sports Opinions: Royal Flush? That's What It'd Be If You Dealt Mikan Out, Says Foe," *Minneapolis Tribune*, April 14, 1948.

9   Scott Pitoniak, "NBA champion Royals get another day in spotlight," *D&C*, Feb. 4, 1990.

10   "If Mikan was": Peter C. Bjarkman, Ph.D., *Encyclopedia of Pro Basketball Team Histories*, 202.

11   "Bob Davies was": Les Harrison, telephone conversation with author, March 10, 1990; "Davies turned": Roland Lazenby, *The NBA Finals: The Official Illustrated History*, 40.

12   Koppett, *Championship NBA — Official 25th Anniversary*, 191, 207.

13   "the first famous": Holzman, *Red on Red*, 17; Sam Goldaper, *Great Moments in Pro Basketball*, 39; Jack Clary, *Basketball's Great Moments*, 40; Sharman, *Sharman on Basketball Shooting*, 69–70.

14   Bob Wanzer, telephone conversation with author, July 11, 2014; Isaacs, *Vintage NBA*, 137; http://www.usmc-mccs.org/sports/hof/2007-wanzer. cfm.

15   Shouler et al., *Total Basketball*, 76, 79, 85; Salzberg, *Set Shot*, 53; "Wanzer actually": "Wanzer Outshines Giants With Deadly Hook Shot," *Minneapolis Laker News 1952–1953* (#5896), 52; "Pollard 'Cleanest' Player In NBA," *Minneapolis Laker News: Philadelphia vs. Minneapolis* (1954–55), 25, LeBov Collection, Sacramento, CA.

16   "Wanzer is": George Beahon, "In This Corner," RRSHOF 1953–54 Season.

17   Jeff Marcus, *Biographical Directory of Professional Basketball Coaches*, 73–74, 171–73, 226–27, and 411–12.

18   George Beahon, "Harrison pushing Risen for the Hall," *T-U*, July 30, 1991; Measuring Worth.

19   John Erardi, "Second Tristater to enter Basketball Hall of Fame," *Cincinnati (OH) Enquirer*, Sept. 27, 1998; Jim Sargent, "Arnie Risen: Remembering the 3-Time Champion Pivotman," *Ragtyme Sports*, May 1996, 38–45.

20   "was second": Koppett, *Essence Of The Game Is Deception*, 141; George Beahon, "Harrison pushing Risen for the Hall," *T-U*, July 30, 1991.

21   Dr. Don L. Danielson, Myra Ness Edevold, and Darlene Clemenson-Sawyer, *A Window To The Past: A History of the Gonvick Area*, 107–8; "1941 All American College Basketball Teams," *Converse Basketball Yearbook 1941*, 2; "Meet The Gunners," Arnie Johnson Scrapbook in possession of Arvin Odegaard, Fairport, NY.

22   http://www.chucksconnection.com/articles/ConverseArt49.html; "This And That About Rochester Royals," *Knickerbockers vs. Rochester, Baltimore vs. Sheboygan, Madison Square Garden January 22, 1950*, program, 15, SHUAC; Harry D. Wilson, College All-Star Championship Game," *Converse Basketball Yearbook 1943*, 39.

23   Arnie Johnson "Royal Court Tips: Push Shot," *D&C*, Feb. 23, 1947; "It's just": Elliot Cushing, "Sports Eye View," *D&C*, Feb. 17, 1949; "the most": Bob Matthews, "Former Royals forward 'Arnie' Johnson dies at 80," *D&C*, June 8, 2000; "Royals Board Ace: Johnson Night Listed Sunday for Vet Star," *D&C*, March 13, 1951; Wanzer, telephone conversation with author, Sept. 20, 2013.

24   "Our Big Louie": Jody Cronau Low, "The Rochester Royals of '51" File, Bx. 4, PMHOF.

25   Jim Sargent, "An NBA Rebounding Giant: Jack Coleman," *Sports Collectors Digest*, Nov. 1, 1996, 152–54; "Burgin's 34–16 Win Nets Six-Man Title," "Burgin, Ky. Trims Durham To Capture Cage Crown," "Kentucky Outfit Upsets Bulldogs," and "Hoosiers Come from Behind to Win, 41–40," Jack Coleman Scrapbook in possession of Jack L. Coleman II, Harrodsburg, KY; Smith et al., *Tribute*, 101.

26   Sargent, "NBA Rebounding Giant," 152–54.

27   Ibid., 153; Measuring Worth.

28   Lazenby, *Lakers*, 68; Grundman, *Pollard*, passim.

29   "Jack Coleman is": Bob Wanzer, telephone conversation with author, July 11, 2014; Hubbard, *NBA Encyclopedia*, 3rd ed., 444 (Coleman) and 697 (Pollard).

   Recently, Jack Coleman has been recognized as perhaps the first obviously deserving player snubbed in the selection process for an NBA All-Star Game. During the 1951– 52 season, Jack ranked fourth in field goal percentage, tenth in rebounds and 18th in assists. Chris Ballard, "Scorecard: Take Your Pick," Sports Illustrated, Feb. 9, 2015, 15–16.

30   "the smartest" and "best paid": George Beahon, "In This Corner," *D&C*, Dec. 16, 1950.

31   Holzman and Frommer, *Red on Red*, 6–14; Smith et al., *Tribute To Armed Forces Basketball 1941–1969*, 62, 101, 106.

32   "complete gentleman": George Beahon, "Marksman, Playmaker, Passer— That's Holzman, Royals' 5-Year Veteran of Pro Cage Warfare," *D&C*, March 5, 1950.

33   "If you want": Harrison, telephone conversation with author, March 3, 1990.

34   "the top": Goldaper, *Great Moments*, 39; "the team": Elliot Cushing, "Sports Eye View," *D&C*, Jan. 27, 1948; "played the": Lewin, "Memories Of Dolly," *NY Post*, May 6, 1986.

   It should be pointed out that the great UCLA coach John Wooden believed that the 1939 Rens played the best-ever brand of team basketball. "They had great athletes," remembered Wooden, "but they weren't as impressive as their team play. The way they handled and passed the ball was just amazing to me then, and I believe it would be today." http://hoopedia.nba.com/index.php/Remembering_the_Rens.

35   "Davies would": Harrison, telephone conversation with author, Oct. 8, 1989; Sargent, "Rebounding Giant," *Sports Collectors Digest*, Nov. 1, 1996, 153.

36   Mikan and Oberle, *Unstoppable*, 129–31, 166–68; "The joke": Johnny "Mack" Macknowski, *Dynamics of Basketball*, 63.

37   "NBA Timeline" in Hubbard, *NBA Encyclopedia*, 3rd ed., 883; Shouler et al., *Total Basketball*, 544, 548; "Yearly Leaders and Records for Personal Fouls," http://www.basketball-reference.com/leaders/pf_yearly.html; Craig Carter and John Hareas, eds., *Sporting News: Official NBA Guide*

2000–2001 Edition, 257; "Pollard 'Cleanest' Player In NBA," *Minneapolis Laker News, Philadelphia vs. Minneapolis,* 25, LeBov Collection; "They used to say": Hubbard, *NBA Encyclopedia,* 197.

38   "Difference to Lakers: Pistons Don't Like Their Court Either," *Minneapolis Tribune,* March 19, 1950; Louis Effrat, "Royals Turn Back Knicks Five, 92–65, in First Test: Rochester Takes First Game in Final Play-off Series for Pro League Title," *NYT,* April 8, 1951(Edgerton Park court measurements); George Beahon, "In This Corner," RRSHOF 1953–54 Season.

39   Leonard Lewin, "Royals Thump Knicks, 92–65, In First Test," *New York Post,* April 8, 1951 ("three feet shorter than the Garden floor and four feet narrower"); Glickman, *Fastest Kid,* 105; Holzman, *Red on Red,* 19.

40   Mikan and Oberle, *Unstoppable,* 142; Schumacher, *Mr. Basketball,* 87; Hubbard, *NBA Encyclopedia,* 3rd ed., 193–98, 630 (Martin), 649 (Mikkelsen), 697 (Pollard missed 39 games).

41   "Mikan would": Bob Davies, interview by Charles Salzberg, Coral Springs, FL, 1986, tape recording and Bob Davies-edited transcript, Joseph M. O'Brien Historical Resource Center, Naismith Memorial Basketball Hall of Fame, Springfield, MA.

42   "It was like": http://ewww.nba.com/encyclopedia/rochester_ royals_1951.html.

ADULATION AND FRUSTRATION

AS THE LAKERS JUGGERNAUT REPEATEDLY FRUSTRATED THE
Royals' championship ambitions, the Davies Comet soared across
the professional basketball horizon. Bob Davies, George Mikan, and
Philadelphia Warrior Joe Fulks emerged as the first NBA "superstars"
(a word not then coined). Compared to recent NBA icons, Bob Davies
would rank in terms of popularity with the Cleveland Cavaliers'
LeBron James, Golden State Warriors' Stephen Curry, and Oklahoma
City Thunder's Kevin Durant. According to Hall of Famer and New
York Knicks coach Joe Lapchick, Bob Davies contributed the most,
after George Mikan and Joe Fulks, the revolutionary jump shooter,
to the survival of the early NBA. Boston sports writer Jack Barry considered Bob Davies and Jim Pollard the two best NBA players after
Mikan. Royals teammate Arnie Risen said that no player attracted
more fans through the turnstiles than Davies. And a *New York Daily
Mirror* sports writer warned his readers not to "waste a few bob betting that our Bob [Davies] isn't a bigger box office draw than the celebrated 'Mr. Basketball.'"[1]

Significantly, *SPORT*, the nation's leading sports magazine (circulation slightly over 400,000), immediately recognized Bob Davies'
prominence as a major star in the small world of professional basketball. The magazine's second article about a pro cager, following
one a month earlier about Joe Fulks, featured "BOB DAVIES—Royal
Playmaker." A year elapsed before *SPORT* published an article about
the bespectacled giant George Mikan. According to writer Bill Roeder,

Bob Davies' All-American-boy appearance appealed to "a considerable bobby-sox following" and "his court mannerisms, flashy deftness, and graceful mobility somehow set him apart from the run of players." He was "a performer with spectacular ability and corresponding crowd appeal" and "something almost extinct in the modern game: a showman."[2] The story mentioned that, when not traveling or practicing, Davies, the NBL's highest-paid player, worked at the Rochester Whiting-Buick dealership and rotated through its departments in order to learn the retail automobile business.[3]

1947–48 NBL SEASON

Early in the 1947–48 NBL season, Bob Davies and his Long Island University nemesis, Howie Rader, now a Buffalo Bison, renewed their pre-war acquaintanceship, and traded body blocks in Edgerton Park Sports Arena. Near the end of the first half, Bob attempted a floating jumper, and Howie knocked him on his back, fell on him, and ground an elbow into his ribs. Bruised but undaunted, Bob finished as the game's high scorer with 14 points, and the Royals prevailed, 78–57.[4]

Twelve games into the season, Davies, who ranked fourth among NBL scorers with a 14.5 PPG average, tore ligaments in his left knee. After a 16-day layoff, he appeared briefly in a game, drilled his only set shot, and limped off the court to a noisy ovation. The next game, he played only two minutes and failed to score. He lacked his "high octane pickup on fast breaks" and winced on quick stops and pivots, but, operating at about 40-percent efficiency, did his best for the team.[5]

Hard-nosed opponents showed vulnerable Bob no mercy. In late January 1948, during perhaps the first televised Royals game, a Laker "body-blocked" him "almost out of" the Minneapolis Auditorium. Badly shaken, Bob missed his first free throw attempt, and the Royals took the ball out of bounds rather than his attempting the second shot. He sustained two more shuddering body blows—so obviously fouls that the Lakers fans did not disagree with the calls, and another battering for which no foul was whistled. On another Minneapolis Auditorium visit, resourceful Les Harrison brought in an NFL Chicago Bears trainer, Jackie Goldie, to minister to the battered Royals.[6]

In a mid-February victory in Edgerton Park Sports Arena over the Tri-Cities (Moline and Rock Island, Illinois and Davenport, Iowa) Blackhawks – formerly the Buffalo Bisons - Bob Davies crashed to the floor in a melee under the basket, an opponent fell on him, and he sustained a fractured rib. He missed four games, and in his first game back converted only three foul shots. In the next-to-last regular season game, which clinched the eastern division championship, he returned to form, flashing down-court and "hitting teammates with spectacular scoring passes," contributed an exceptional defensive performance, and rained set shots through the hoop as he scored 15 points.[7]

At season-end the Royals led the NBL eastern division with a 44-win and 16-loss (.733) record, and the Lakers topped the western division with 43 wins and 17 losses. The Royals ranked first defensively, holding opponents to 56.0 points per game, and second offensively, scoring 64.7 points per game. Mikan, who set an NBL single game scoring record of 41 points against the Royals, led the league in scoring at 21.3 PPG. In the balanced Royals scoring attack, Risen ranked fifth in league scoring with 13.3 PPG, followed by Cervi with 13.1 PPG, and Holzman with 10.2 PPG. Despite his missing 12 games, playing sparingly in others, and his scoring average dropping to 9.9 PPG, the media and coaches selected Bob Davies for the NBL All-Star Second Team as a forward, and Lakers coach John Kundla named him to the Lakers All-Opponent First Team.[8]

After eliminating the "battering-ram" Fort Wayne Zollners, three rough-house games to one, in the opening playoff round, the Royals faced the Anderson (IN) Duffey Packers on their 70-foot-long (24 feet shorter than regulation) and 50-foot-wide "postage stamp" court. Frenzied partisans in the 3,500-seat "Wigwam" had outdone their Fort Wayne counterparts and earned Anderson (population about 42,000) the reputation as "the toughest" fan town for visiting teams. In a regular season encounter, Bob Davies, preparing to take a foul shot, had been struck with a paper clip that stuck in his hand. Nonetheless, "eagle-eyed" Davies led the Royals in scoring in the first and third playoff games, and they eliminated the Packers. Unfortunately, in the last game Anderson center Howard "Big Howie" Schultz swung an elbow and broke Arnie Risen's jaw.[9]

The media had been touting the upcoming Finals as a battle

between the two best NBL centers—George Mikan and Arnie Risen. In the previous season's Chicago American Gears–Indianapolis Kautsky playoff series, Mikan had totaled 96 and Risen 95 points. But Risen was hospitalized; Al Cervi, the Royals' second-leading scorer and best defender, was hobbling on a recalcitrant knee; Red Holzman, the third-highest scorer, was limping on a sprained ankle; and ace swingman Fuzzy Levane was ill. In the opening game loss, rookie Bobby Wanzer led the Royals with 16 points. Despite Bob Davies' valiant 23- and 20-point efforts in the second and final contests, the Lakers easily took the 1947–48 NBL championship playoff series from the Royals' "cripples," three games to one. "Some critics said that we wouldn't have won it if Risen had played," said Mikan, "but there's no way to know that."[10]

Although no longer employed as a Seton Hall coach, humanitarian Bob Davies did not miss an opportunity to help an athlete from a deprived economic background improve himself through an athletic scholarship, and at the same time strengthen the Pirates' basketball program. Bob dropped off a suit at a tailor's establishment in Rochester and chatted with the African-American lady waiting on him. Mrs. Dukes proudly described her son's high school hoop exploits. Impressed, Bob arranged for Walter to attend Seton Hall Prep School on an athletic scholarship. Walter and his grateful mother sent Bob a telegram stating that a "man may be great or he may be small but when he is a good man he is a friend to all." As a Seton Hall University Pirate, 7', 220-pound Walter Dukes set a NCAA Division-I single season rebounds record, earned Consensus NCAA All-American First Team recognition, and led his team to an NIT title.[11]

1948-49 BAA SEASON

Before the 1948–49 season commenced, the Rochester Royals, Minneapolis Lakers, Fort Wayne Pistons, and Indianapolis Jets joined the Baltimore Bullets, Boston Celtics, Chicago Stags, New York Knicks, Philadelphia Warriors, Providence Steam Rollers, St. Louis Bombers, and Washington Capitols in the 12-team BAA. With greater financial resources and larger arenas, the original BAA owners prevailed over the former NBL owners, and Commissioner Maurice Podoloff placed the Royals (geographically in the east) and Lakers, indisputably the two best teams, as well as the Pistons and Jets, in the western division, so that an original BAA team would be guaranteed an appearance in the playoff Finals. The Anderson Duffey Packers, Dayton Rens, Denver Nuggets, Oshkosh All-Stars, Sheboygan Redskins, Syracuse Nationals (with player-coach Al Cervi), and Tri-Cities Blackhawks remained in the NBL, which folded at the end of the season. "With George Mikan and Bob Davies and their teammates now in the circuit," pointed out basketball historians David Neft and Richard Cohen, "the BAA was certainly the best professional league in the country." [12]

MARQUEE ATTRACTION

The BAA moguls welcomed the Royals because Bob Davies, the "Blond Bomber" and "Kangaroo Kid," with his movie-star looks, All-American image, and flashy style of play, helped fill arena seats. Prior to the four NBL teams' switchover, BAA owners had coveted Bob Davies, Al Cervi, and 7', 250-pound Tri-Cities Blackhawk center Don Otten as the players they most wanted to lure from the rival league. "Davies was the BAA's top driving guard and a master at triggering the fast break," commented Neft and Cohen. *Baltimore Evening Sun* Sports Editor Paul Menton prognosticated that 28-year-old Court General Robert Davies might emulate 31-year-old player-manager Lou Boudreau, who had led the Cleveland Indians to the 1948 World Series baseball championship.[13]

Bob Davies immediately became a BAA marquee attraction. Before his Madison Square Garden professional debut, the *New York World-Telegram* printed a cartoon captioned "Magician Comes Back" showing Bob dribbling a basketball in front of his body with his right hand and holding another behind his back in his left hand. The Garden marquee from then on usually advertised: "KNICKS and ROYALS—BOB DAVIES." Prior to his first appearance in the Boston Garden, the *Boston Globe*, in a "Hoop Happy" cartoon, promoted slick Bob Davies and his sleight of hand with a mirage of a dozen basketballs disappearing from his extended right hand to behind his left hip. For his Chicago Stadium professional debut, the *Chicago Sun-Times* described Bob as "basketball's classiest playmaker" and "one of the best

HOOP HAPPY! . . . . . By Gene Mack

Newspapers in NBA cities, including the Boston Globe, *published cartoons illustrating Bob Davies' ball-handling wizardry. (Dec. 6, 1948, Gene Mack/Boston Globe/Getty Images)*

drawing cards in the game because of his ball-handling finesse." An AP cartoon portrayed "clever court ace" Davies as basketball's "most amazing dribbler." A Minneapolis Lakers game program included an article about Bob Davies, Arnie Risen, and Washington Capitol Bob Feerick entitled "These Stars Are Poison To The Lakers," as well as a full page "A Picture For Your Album" of Davies. "He [Davies] was what we called a 'fancy Dan'," said Hall of Famer Philadelphia Warriors owner/coach Eddie Gottlieb, "and it is meant in the most complimentary way. He was one of the first truly great guards to play what we call present-day basketball. He was an excellent shooter, an exceptional passer and team player."[14]

Early in the 1948–49 season, Davies had a hard time guarding 6' 2", 175-pound Providence Steamroller Howard "Howie" Shannon, who featured a new-fangled jump shot. Before the evolution of the jumper, backcourt defenders usually had to contend only with their opponents' two-hand set or one-hand push shot from the outside, and a drive to the basket. Jump shooters, however, started to drive, stopped on a dime, leapt, and released from the forehead or the top of the head an almost impossible-to-block one-hand shot. Davies realized that this weapon would add to his offensive repertoire, and he developed not a conventional vertical jump shot, but a horizontal floating jump shot, perhaps best-described as a "jumping radar-like one-hander," usually taken within ten feet of the basket.[15]

In late January 1949, Bob Davies scored his professional career high, 33 points, against the Indianapolis Jets. "He doesn't know how to take it easy on the court," glowed *Times-Union* scribe Al C. Weber. "Trying to stop him would be like checking Niagara Falls. Watch him bring the ball up court: give-and-go; float between two opponents; stop and set; and drive, drive, drive. He has perfect physical coordination, a feather touch and extraordinary basketball sense. He's a show within a show, and a favorite with the gallery all around the league."[16]

The next night, the Davies Comet bewildered the Bombers in St. Louis, Missouri, the BAA western outpost. *Saint Louis Post-Dispatch* reporter Bob Broeg described Bob's 26-point performance as the best long-distance shooting exhibition he had witnessed in three BAA seasons. Impressed by Bob's "fly-weight's footwork and quick hand action," Broeg dubbed him "the Royal Flush."[17]

Three weeks later, the Royals appeared in their second locally televised game. They defeated the defending BAA champion Bullets, 90–76, on the Baltimore Coliseum bandbox floor that doubled as a roller skating rink. Risen and Davies scored 27 and 25 points respectively. When Bob left the game, the Bullets' fans cheered him wildly.[18]

Extraordinary performance on the basketball court and the resulting public adulation exacted a price, however, in the rough-and-tumble pro ranks, and Bob Davies, after three seasons absorbing physical punishment, lost a bit of his Boy Scout luster. When physically abused, he no longer turned the other cheek. With ten games remaining in the 1948–49 season, he led the BAA in personal conduct fouls assessed for complaining to referees. "If Davies has a weakness," wrote *Philadelphia Inquirer* scribe Fred Byrod, "it's his temper. When affairs don't suit him, he explodes." *Democrat & Chronicle* sports editor Elliot Cushing chided Bob for letting loose "a volley of pet names" at referees and hurting the Royals' cause because the opposing team was awarded free throws. In an article published near the end of Davies' professional career, a Rochester sportswriter pointed out that Bob would have been "a cinch" to make a referees' "All-Squawkers" team and opined that Bob probably would have commented that "champion squawker" George Mikan had been voted the greatest player of all time. The other top box office draw, high-scoring Joe Fulks, who had an unstoppable jump shot and endured a nightly beating from frustrated defenders, also complained vociferously to officials, and many BAA observers considered him a prima donna due to his verbal outbursts.[19]

Bob Davies acknowledged his differences with referees. As verified by Hall of Fame contemporary Bill Sharman, Davies was the premier driver in the professional ranks. His speed and dexterity provided him an advantage over men guarding him, and he refused to let them abuse him and eliminate a key part of his game. "Basketball is a livelihood to the pro," said Bob, who had struggled through the Great Depression, fought for his country, and was supporting a growing family and assisting his parents financially, "and besides he cares about winning too much. I can remember getting fined for arguing and I knew I was going to get fined but I wanted to win so much I didn't care."[20]

Driving to the basket in the early NBA years through the six-foot-wide foul lane tested a player's courage. "Bob Davies took a beating because he went to the hoop," explained Syracuse Nationals enforcer Earl Lloyd, who played against him for four seasons and knew what he was talking about as the NBA leader in personal fouls and disqualifications the 1953–54 season. "He took hard fouls. I never heard him utter a cuss word. If he complained, it would be hard not to go along with him. I'm surprised the star he was that the referees didn't protect him." Officials protected George Mikan because fans paid to watch (and jeer) him, not his back-up.

"If a player kept driving the lane against your team," pointed out Lloyd, "you had no choice—you just knocked the guy down. Sometimes a player would drive to the basket and one of us would call out, 'I've got him.' Then we'd flatten the guy!"[21]

"If a player drove down the middle—especially a guard—," confirmed Syracuse Nationals center Johnny Kerr, "you didn't let the guy take a lay-up, you flattened him. You didn't even think twice—the guard drives, you kill.... We never thought about the blocked shot, we just went for the body block, instead."[22]

Super-competitive on the basketball court, Bob Davies definitely was a Christian gentleman in his private life. In Chicago for a Stags game, he visited his brothers Ed and Bill, who were students at Wheaton College located about 20 miles west of the Windy City. Bob accompanied them to a church service and heard prominent English Baptist evangelist Stephen Olford preach. Responding to the reverend's call, Bob walked down the aisle, accepted Jesus Christ as his savior, and became a devout Christian. "When we go out together on the basketball court," Bob believed, "we're all on God's team." [23]

Taking his religious conversion seriously, Bob read the Bible assiduously. Waiting in a train station, he noticed a Holy Book left on a bench. When the Bible owner returned, Bob started a conversation with him that continued after they boarded the train. At 3:30 a.m., Les Harrison suggested that Bob get some sleep. Before they parted, Bob and his new Christian friend knelt and prayed together.[24]

But Bob paid a price for his religious convictions. He had been joining his teammates for a post-game beer or two. Now, he stopped drinking, bought the other Royals a round, and endured their friendly teasing about carrying a Bible. He became a loner. "Bob was really popular at Seton Hall," remembered Bobby Wanzer. "With the Royals, it was not that he was not popular. He just didn't mingle." In his absence from barroom gossip, Davies believed that jealousy developed among other players about his higher salary.[25]

The Royals finished the season with the BAA's best record, 45 wins and 15 losses (.750), one game ahead of the Minneapolis Lakers in the western division. "Brains had beaten brawn," noted Leonard

Rochester Democrat & Chronicle *columnist Henry Clune described Bob Davies as "the consummate performer" and a "good spectator athlete." (Sacramento Kings)*

Koppett. Incredibly, both teams netted 5,042 points in 60 games and tied for the highest team-scoring average at 84.0 PPG. Mikan led the league in scoring with a 28.3 average, followed by fourth and seventh highest scorers Risen and Davies, with 16.6 and 15.1 averages respectively. Risen had the best field goal percentage of .423 followed by Mikan's .418 and Wanzer's sixth best .379. The Lakers ranked first in team defense, holding opponents to 76.7 PPG, and the Royals second at 77.4 PPG.[26]

In his first season that assists were recorded, Bob Davies led the BAA with 321 for a 5.4 per game average; Wanzer was tenth with 3.1 assists per game (APG). (Assists were defined as passes leading directly to field goals with no more than one dribble or step taken by the scorers, but not passes back out to open teammates.) Steals and turnovers were not tabulated. Davies joined Mikan, Fulks, Pollard, and 6' 2", 170-pound Chicago Stags two-hand set shot marksman Max Zaslofsky on the BAA All-Star First Team. Arnie Risen made the BAA All-Star Second Team. Abe Saperstein, whose Globetrotters often played a stooge opponent on BAA doubleheader cards, selected Davies for his personal all-star team along with Mikan, Fulks, Zaslofsky, and Feerick.[27]

The Royals swept the two-game western division opening round playoff series against the hapless St. Louis Bombers. Rochester newspaper columnist Henry W. Clune, self-admittedly not a basketball aficionado, observed Bob Davies scoring 23 points in the opener:

> I watched the yellow-thatched Mr. Davies with pleasure and delight, for he indeed is an athlete, and one who does things with the easy grace—the sang froid—of the consummate performer.... Mr. Davies has everything that makes a good spectator's athlete. He starts like a quarter horse, stops on a dime, and pirouettes like a ballet dancer. He had an uncanny cunning with the big leather apple..., plunking it from all angles of the floor through the hoop, clean as a children's story hour. He was "it" for tag, and the Bombers never caught him. They never came close. And he was so charmingly insouciant in his elusiveness. It was like a man playing with a child.[28]

Unfortunately, the Royals next faced Mikan and the Lakers in the western division final playoff series. This time it was Bob Davies who was *hors de combat*. Suffering from a severe case of influenza, he sat on the bench much of the first game as the Lakers, converting 23 of 24 foul shots, eked out an 80–79 victory. In the second and deciding game, won by the Lakers 67–55, the Royals did not score a field goal in the final quarter. Bob Davies, far from his effective self, scored only two points in the game. "Davies was sick," said Les Harrison, "shouldn't have been playing at all. This team can't afford to lose Davies anytime." The Royals divvied up $13,500 ($134,000 today) in "playoff swag." The Lakers defeated the Washington Capitols in the BAA Finals.[29]

1949–50 NBA SEASON

For the 1949–50 season, the BAA added five more NBL teams and renamed itself the National Basketball Association (NBA). The Anderson Duffey Packers, Denver Nuggets, Sheboygan Redskins, Tri-Cities Blackhawks, and Waterloo (IA) Hawks joined the new Indianapolis Olympians with their former University of Kentucky and 1948 U.S. Olympic Basketball Team members in the western division, and the Syracuse Nationals entered the eastern division. Rochester and "Mikanopolis" squared off in the central division.[30]

Before and after Thanksgiving Day, the Royals played back-to-back, away-and-home games against the Waterloo Hawks. They defeated the Hawks, 90–71, in their 7,500-seat Dairy Cattle Congress Hippodrome, despite occasional well-timed blasts from a huge, manually operated hot-air blower that caused their shots to wobble like knuckleballs. Then, in Edgerton Park Sports Arena, they clobbered the Hawks, 120–95. In this encounter, the Royals set team game records for total points and assists. Coleman contributed ten, Wanzer seven, and Davies six of the 39 feeds. "Brilliant" Bob Davies, who sat out the fourth quarter, made 12 of 17 field goal attempts and led the Royals in scoring with 26 points.[31]

The day after Christmas, in Madison Square Garden, before 16,000 fans, "blonde basketball magician" and "play-making and goal-making genius" Bob Davies staged his most spectacular NBA performance. In an 83–80 double overtime victory over the Knicks, "sharpshooting" Bob scored 32 points and contributed 14 assists, his assist high prior to the adoption of the 24-second shot rule. "My arms were tired because I never shot that much," recalled Bob. His incredible field goal with five seconds left in overtime is preserved on YouTube and is one of the best all-time NBA clips including those featuring dunks. Forced out of bounds and airborne, his left-handed, Frisbee-type throw won the game. *The New York Times* reported that Bob "dropped in a floating underhand lay-up that left the crowd gasping" and the *New York Daily News* deemed the flip "impossible." Defensively, Bob intercepted three passes, deflected three more, blocked a shot, and tied up a Knick for a jump ball. "Any basketball team with Bob Davies on it should be allowed only three other men," Leonard Koppett opened his *New York Herald-Tribune* game story describing this legendary performance. Probably more fans in the stands and watching on TV saw Bob in this New York metropolitan area televised game than any other in his career to date, and his sensational performance cemented his popularity in the Big Apple.[32]

The Davies Show marched on in New York City. "Bob Davies Night" took place on January 22, 1950, before a Madison Square Garden standing-room-only crowd. During pre-game ceremonies, a new two-door Buick Roadmaster hard-top automobile worth $3,200 ($31,500 today) was given to Bob by 54 New Jersey and 20 Rochester area admirers. As the ultimate tribute, Father James Carey retired Bob's Seton Hall jersey number 11. Playing refrigerated basketball in front of Sonja Henie Ice Show props stored at one end of the court and on a floor "rigged" over ice, Bob Davies, like many athletes honored on a special night, started ice-cold. He scored his first field goal three minutes before intermission and finished the game with 13 points, as the Knicks defrosted the Royals, 81–71.[33]

Ten nights later the John Harris High School–Edison Junior High School Boosters Club sponsored "Bob Davies Night" at the Philadelphia Arena. Three hundred Harrisburg residents, including Bob's parents, two brothers, and sister, as well as the high school and junior high school basketball squads, traveled 120 miles to the event. "We consider this night in your honor a small token of our appreciation in return for the aspirational hopes you have given to the youth of our city," said the Boosters Club president. The John Harris High School Outstanding Athlete Award was a lifelike statuette of Bob in a basketball uniform. Gentleman Bob shook hands with each boy. "He was an inspiration to them all," said Edison JHS coach Dick Hohenshelt. Climaxing the first half, Bob swished a beautiful basket, slipping as he released sort of a hook shot and, from a prone position, watching it drop through the hoop. He sat out most of the second half, finishing with 13 points, as the Royals defeated the Warriors, 82–68.[34]

During a bruising early March road victory over the Zollners, Davies badly sprained an ankle and missed the next four games. Rookie Frank "Pep" Saul, the former Seton Hall star, ably filled in for him. After 13 days out of action, Davies led the Royals in scoring with

12 points in a must-win over the Knicks. In their last games of the season, the Royals won and the Lakers lost. By winning 15 games in a row, the Royals set a still-existing NBA record for season-ending consecutive victories. Rochester and Minneapolis finished as central division co-leaders with identical 51 win and 17 loss (.750) records. The Royals' 33–1 home record remained the NBA best until the Boston Celtics' 40–1 in the 1985–86 season.[35]

A coin flip in the New York City Empire State Building NBA office provided the Royals the home-court advantage in an unprecedented sudden-death game to decide a NBA division title and determine opening round division playoff opponents. The Royals' chance for a victory looked promising because they had won all three home games against the Lakers, and the night before the critical encounter, the Lakers had played an exhibition game against the Harlem Globetrotters. However, with two minutes remaining in the sudden-death game and the score tied, the Lakers held the ball and stalled. As the clock ticked down, Jim Pollard and substitute Tony Jaros passed the ball back and forth, trying to find an opening to feed the ball to Mikan. With three seconds left and the Lakers' bench players screaming at him to shoot, Jaros, the Laker's second worst field goal shooter (29.4 percent), heaved a 40-footer that rippled through the net. In "the granddaddy of all heartbreakers," a 78–76 loss, Bob Davies scored 26 points on 10 of 17 shooting from the field and 6 of 6 from the foul line.[36]

Rather than face the weak Chicago Stags, the Royals opened the central division playoffs against the brawny Fort Wayne Zollners. Known as the NBA "Bad Boys," the Zollners, taking no prisoners that season, committed the most personal fouls (2,967), an average of 30 per game, and the clean team, the Royals, committed the fewest (1,586), an average of 23 per game. But the Royals were not soft, and ranked as the league's best defensive team, allowing an average of only 74.6 points per game Earlier in the season, the referees had called 45 personal fouls against the Zollners and 33 against the Royals in the roughest game ever played in Edgerton Park Sports Arena. [37]

In a best two out of three playoff series, the Royals lost at home by six points, and the next night in "The Snake Pit" by one point in overtime and were eliminated. Davies fouled out of the first game, accumulated five fouls in the second, and scored a total of only 15 points in the two very physical encounters. The Lakers, who had knocked off the Chicago Stags, out-muscled the Zollners for the central division playoff championship, defeated the western division playoff champion Anderson Duffey Packers, and, in the Finals, eliminated the Al Cervi-coached Syracuse Nationals.[38]

Bob Davies, who led the Royals in scoring with a 14.2 average (13th in the league) and in assists with 4.6 per game (third in the league), was named to the NBA All-Star First Team with Mikan, Pollard, Zaslofsky, and Indianapolis Olympian center Alex Groza. The United Press and popular *New York Daily News* sports columnist Jimmy Powers selected Davies for their All-National Basketball Association First Teams. Continuing the Royals' share-the-ball policy, Davies, Wanzer, and Holzman dished out 294, 214, and 200 assists, respectively.[39]

During the summer, Bob Davies stayed in shape playing semi-professional baseball for the Newark (New York) Bears in the Finger Lakes League. The Bobby Davies All-Stars lost to the Negro American League Philadelphia Stars, 8–5, in Rochester's Red Wing Stadium. Batting against the ageless African-American pitcher Satchel Paige, who had been released by the Cleveland Indians, Bob singled and struck out.[40]

NOTES

1   Bob Matthews, "Royals star Bob Davies was innovator," *T-U*, April 24, 1990; Jack Barry, "Davies Again Looms in Path of Celtics at Arena Tonight," *Boston Globe*, Feb. 17, 1950; Jack Slattery, "Highlighting Sports," *Syracuse Herald-Journal*, March 7, 1954; "waste": Weissman, "Coach Thought It Gag When Davies Reported for Seton Hall Team," BDSHOF.

2   https://en.wikipedia.org/wiki/Sport_magazine; *N.W. Ayer & Sons Directory* (1948): 698 (circ. 404,091); e-mail message, George Rugg, Curator, Dept. of Special Collections, Hesburgh Library, University of Notre Dame, to author, March 9, 2011; Herb Good, "Report On A Warrior," *Sport*, Jan. 1948, 37, 76–78; Francis J. Powers, "Mikan Makes All the Money," *Sport*, Jan. 1949, 48–50, 84–85; "a considerable" and "a performer": Bill Roeder, "Bob Davies—Royal Playmaker," *Sport*, Feb. 1948, 50.

3   Ibid., 53, 87.

4   "Buffalonian Al Cervi, Davies Lead Royals To Win Over Herd," *Buffalo Evening News*, Nov. 28, 1947; Mike Calandra, "Brilliant Bob Davies In Aud Basketball Farewell Next Week," BDSHOF.

5   "NBL Standings," BDSHOF; "Royals Face Jeeps: Bob Davies Injured, Out of Game," *T-U*, Dec. 6, 1947; "Injury Sidelines Davies As Royals Face Toledo," *D&C*, Dec. 6, 1947; Al C. Weber, "Royals Teamwork Smothers Indianapolis: All Hands Share in Scoring," *T-U*, Dec. 19, 1947; "Royals Whip Oshkosh for 11th in Row, 65–50," *D&C*, Dec. 22, 1947; "high octane": Elliot Cushing, "Sports Eye View," *D&C*, Dec. 24, 1947; Elliot Cushing, "Sports Eye View," *D&C*, Jan. 28, 1948.

6   Nelson, *NBL*, 190, 260n35; Elliot Cushing, "It's True, Folks: Royals 53, Minneapolis 50," *D&C*, Jan. 29, 1948; "body-blocked": Matt Jackson, "In Doghouse: Clutch Games Old Stuff To Royals, but They've Reached New High," *T-U*, Jan. 30, 1948; Elliot Cushing, "Minneapolis Offense Led By Jaros' 20," *D&C*, Jan. 27, 1948.

7   "Davies Lost to Royals For Contest at Flint," BDSHOF; "Royals Continue Spell Over Nats, Earn 64–52 Win," *Syracuse Post-Standard*, Feb. 29, 1948; "hitting": George Beahon, "Royals Blast Nats for East Toga, Davies Sparkles In 76–48 Victory," *D&C*, March 19, 1948.

8   Nelson, *NBL*, 237–38, 241 and 243; "Final Scoring in National Basketball League," RRSHOF 1947–48 Season.

9   Nelson, *NBL*, 196; Anderson High School Dedication Pamphlet (Nov.21, 1924): 2, Anderson Public Library, Anderson, IN; "Wigwam": Gould, *Pioneers of the Hardwood*, 134; "the toughest": untitled clipping, BDSHOF; Salzberg, *Set Shot*, 56; George Beahon, "Royals Subdue Anderson 71–66, to Capture Lead in Series,Davies Sparkles," *D&C*, April 1, 1948; Matt Jackson, "Royals Take Series Edge; Holzman Injured, 71–66, *T-U*, April 1, 1948; George Beahon, "Risen Sidelined By Broken Jaw In Title Clincher," *D&C*, April 4, 1948.

10 Richard F. Triptow, *The Dynasty That Never Was: Chicago's First Professional Basketball Champions; The American Gears*, 84–85; George Beahon, "Cervi, Holzman See Little Action, 'Cripples' Clipped," *D&C*, April 14, 1948; George Beahon, "Crippled Royals Again Bow To Late Laker Drive, 82–67," *D&C*, April 15, 1948; George Beahon, "Lakers Blast Royals For Title: Mikan Scores 27, Jim Pollard 19 in 75–65 Hoop Final,"

D&C, April 18, 1948; "Some critics": Mikan & Oberle, *Unstoppable*, 94.

11   Elliot Cushing, "Sports Eye View," *D&C*, Feb. 14, 1950; Herb Good, "Campus Chatter: Bob Davies' Visit to Tailor Sent Dukes to Seton Hall," *Philadelphia Inquirer*, Jan. 30, 1953; "man may": Walter Dukes's and his mother's telegram to Bobby Davies (date undecipherable), BDSHOF; Richard Goldstein, "Walter Dukes, 70, a Standout At Seton Hall and in the NBA," *NYT*, March 16, 2001.

12   Hubbard, *NBA Encyclopedia*, 3rd ed., 198; "BAA Grows Stronger: Addition of Four Clubs from National League Boosts Its Stock," *Sport Annual* (1948–49): 81; "With George Mikan": Neft and Cohen, *Sports Encyclopedia: Pro Basketball*, 5th ed., 79.

13   "Blond Bomber" and "Kangaroo Kid," Al C. Weber, "Bob Davies Signs With Rochester Royals," *T-U*, Aug. 4, 1948; "Davies was": Neft and Cohen, *Sports Encyclopedia: Pro Basketball*, 5th ed., 79; Paul Menton, Sports Editor, "It's All In The Viewpoint: Citation Is Simply Too Good For Field," *The Evening Sun (Baltimore, MD)*, Oct. 21, 1948; "Bob Davies," *Sport Pix*, Feb. 1949, 43.

14   "Magician Comes Back": *NY World-Telegram*, Dec. 1, 1948; George Beahon, "Rochester's championship season," *T-U*, May 22, 1982; "Hoop Happy! By Gene Mack," *Boston Globe*, Dec. 6, 1948; "basketball's classiest": Emil Stubits, "Stags take on Rochester, Bob Davies," *Chicago Sun-Times*, Dec. 14, 1948; "one of": Emil Stubits, "It's father-son day as Stags face Royals," *Chicago Sun-Times*, Jan. 9, 1949; "most amazing": "Royals! Robert" By Pap, copyright 1948, AP; Minneapolis Lakers News: Anderson vs. Minneapolis (#18149), 6, and Minneapolis Laker News: New York vs. Minneapolis (#11530), 24, LeBov Collection, Sacramento, CA; "He was what": Zander Hollander, ed., *The Pro Basketball Encyclopedia*, 198·

15   Salzberg, *Set Shot*, 52–53; Hubbard, *NBA Encyclopedia*, 3rd ed., 742 (Shannon); "jumping": "Davies, Wanzer Star in Victory," undated clipping, BDSHOF; Dick Davies, telephone conversation with author, April 15, 2008, Bob Wanzer, telephone conversation with author, June 13, 2008, Pep Saul, telephone conversation with author, Nov. 27, 2009 and John Macknowski, telephone conversation with author, Aug. 20, 2010.

16   "Royals Tackle Bombers, Defeat Jets: Royals Nip Jets In Chicago, 70–66: Bob Davies Sets Pace Scoring 33," *D&C*, Jan. 20, 1949; "He doesn't

know": Al C. Weber, "Popshots: Davies Having Best Season," BDSHOF.

17 "Royals Tie for Top as Davies Bombs Bombers: Bobby Scores 26 Points, *D&C*, Jan. 21, 1949; "fly-weight's footwork": Bob Broeg, "'Royal Flush' Davies Takes A Hand, Scoring 26 Points; Bomber Streak Ends at Three," *St. Louis (MO) Post-Dispatch*, Jan. 21, 1949.

18 George Beahon, "Royals Drop Bullets In Second Half, 90–76," *D&C*, Feb. 11, 1949; Elliot Cushing, "Sports Eye View" and "Bullets' Fans Cheer Davies," BDSHOF.

19 "If Davies": Fred Byrod of *Philadelphia Inquirer*, "That's No Hurricane, Son," BDSHOF; "a volley": Elliot Cushing, "Sports Eye View," *D&C*, Feb. 22, 1949; "would have been": "Bobby Bows Out: Fans Bid Farewell to Davies Saturday," BDSHOF; Salzberg, *Set Shot*, 57; Good, "Report On A Warrior," *Sport*, Jan. 1948, 78.

20 Sharman, *Sharman on Basketball Shooting*, 70; Dick Davies, telephone conversation with author, Oct. 19, 2009; "Basketball is": "Basketball Great Bob Davies Says: Too Many Deals Made," *Lancaster (PA) New Era*, July 6, 1961.

21 Hubbard, *NBA Encyclopedia*, 3rd ed., 883; "Bob Davies took" and "If a player kept": Lloyd, telephone conversation with author, July 19, 2008; Neft and Cohen, *Sports Encyclopedia: Pro Basketball*, 5th ed., 110; Schumacher, *Mr. Basketball*, 213, 226.

22 "If a player drove": Johnny Kerr and Terry Pluto, *Bull Session: An up-close look at MICHAEL JORDAN and courtside stories about the Chicago Bulls*, 233–34.

23 Bill Davies, telephone conversation with author, May 21, 2008; Ed Davies, telephone conversation with author, July 24, 2008; "A Memorial to Dr. Stephen F. Olford," http://www.olford.org; "When we go": Al C. Weber, "So You Want to be an Athlete: Credits Dad's 'Clean Living Formula' with Pro Sports Success" undated clipping, BDSHOF.

24 *Ashland (WI) Daily Press* undated clipping, BDSHOF.

25 Roeder, "Bob Davies," *Sport*, Feb. 1948, 52; "Bob was": Bob Wanzer, telephone conversation with author, Sept. 15, 2014; Salzberg, *Set Shot*, 56.

26 "Brains had": Koppett, *24 Seconds*, 38; Neft and Cohen, *Sports Encyclopedia: Pro Basketball*, 5th ed., 83.

27 Hubbard, *NBA Encyclopedia, 3rd ed.*, 198; "Royals, Lakers Finish Tied at 5,042 Points" and "Davies, Mikan, Pollard, Zaslofsky, Fulks Picked,"

BDSHOF; Gene Kessler, "Basketball's biggest card," *Chicago Sun-Times*, Feb. 25, 1949.

28   Charlie Wagner, "Royals Win, 93–64, Eye Playoff Clincher, *T-U*, March 23, 1949; "I watched": Henry W. Clune's "Seen and Heard: Play-Off," *D&C*, March 26, 1949; Darryl Arata, ed., *2006–07 Sacramento Kings Media Guide*, 137.

29   Charlie Wagner, "Rochester One Down After 80–79 Thriller," *T-U*, March 28, 1949; Matt Jackson, "Field Goal Famine In Fourth Period Gives Lakers Win," *T-U*, March 30, 1949; "Davies was": "Cousy Will Have to Drop Fancy Stuff If He Plays Pro, Says Rochester Ace," *Boston Evening American*, Feb. 18, 1950; Matt Jackson, "Royals Split Playoff $$, Make Off-Season Plans," BDSHOF; Measuring Worth.

30   Hubbard, *NBA Encyclopedia*, 3rd ed., 197.

31   Al Ney, "Hawks Facing Rough Weekend In East: Reserves Run Thin; Hawks Lose to Rochester, 90–71, After Tying 56–56 in Third," *Waterloo (IA) Courier*, Nov. 24, 1949; Nelson, *NBL*, 204; Glickman, *Fastest Kid*, 105; George Beahon, "Victors Score 30 or More Points In Each of 3 Periods—Both Teams Shoot Torridly," *D&C*, Nov. 26, 1949.

32   "blonde basketball magician": Hy Turkin, "Royals 83, Knicks 80 On Davies O'Time Goal," *NY Daily News*, Dec. 27, 1949; "My arms": Salzberg, *Set Shot*, 54; http://www.youtube.com/*Bob Davies (NBA Hall of Fame)*; "dropped in": Michael Strauss, "Rochester Snaps Knicks' Streak With 83–80 Triumph in Overtime: Davies, High Scorer With 32 Points, Sinks Shot in Last Five Seconds to End Local Five's Bid for 8th in Row at Home," *NYT*, Dec. 27, 1949; Game DVD (author's possession); "Any basketball team": Leonard Koppett, "Davies Leads Royals to Victory Over Knicks in Overtime, 83–80," *NY Herald-Tribune*, Dec. 27, 1949; Mario R. Sarmento, "The NBA On Network Television: A Historical Analysis" (Master's Thesis, Univ. of Florida, 1998), 16.

33   "Knicks And Royals In Garden Tonight," *NYT*, Jan. 22, 1950; "Seton Hall Honors Davies At Presentation in Garden," *D&C*, Jan. 23, 1950; "Look How Buicks Deliver! (advertised price)," *Sacramento Bee*, Jan. 9, 1950; Measuring Worth; Dick Davies, telephone conversation with author, Jan. 27, 2012; Paul Horowitz, "The Greatest: That's Rating Seton Hall Gives Bobby Davies," Knickerbockers vs. Rochester, Baltimore vs. Sheboygan, Madison Square Garden January 22, 1950, program, 3;

Michael Strauss, "Knicks Top Royal Five, Bullets Halt Redskins in Pro Twin Bill at the Garden: New York Checks Rochester, 81–71," *NYT*, Jan. 23, 1950; "Knicks Repulse Royals 81–71, 1st Time This Season in NBA before Sellout Garden Crowd," *D&C*, Jan. 23, 1950.

34 "Recognition as One of Game's Greatest Players Deserved by Local Star of Rochester Club," *Harrisburg Evening News*, Jan. 19, 1950; "We consider": "Gifts Given Former Local Court Star," BDSHOF; "He was": "Home-Town Support Helped Bob Davies, Court Star Reports," BDSHOF; "Davies' Dreams Came True Thanks to Hard Practice," BDSHOF; Fred Byrod, "Royals Top Warriors Five, 82–68, Stags Nip Celtics At Arena, 78–76," *Philadelphia Inquirer,* Feb. 2, 1950.

35 "Royals Outlast Fort Wayne, 65–60, Pick Up Full Game on Losing Lakers: Rochester Sweeps Weekend Series With Hoosiers," *D&C*, March 6, 1950; Al C. Weber, "Saul Sparkles as Royals Run Win Streak to 12," *T-U*, March 13, 1950; George Beahon, "Royals Nip Knickerbockers, 77–74, With Great Rally in 'Must' Contest: New York Five Sets Fast Scoring Pace In Arena Clash," *D&C*, March 19, 1950; George Beahon, "Rochester Draws Tie: Hot Royals Humble Baltimore Bullets, 97–68; Face Lakers Here Tomorrow in Division Tie," *D&C*, March 20, 1950; Neft and Cohen, *Sports Encyclopedia: Pro Basketball*, 5th ed., 89; Steve Aschburner, "Big finishes important, though the biggest ever went flop," http://NBA.com (posted March 18, 2010).

36 Al C. Weber, "Davies May Give Royals Edge: Title Game Here Tomorrow As Royals Tie Minneapolis," *T-U*, March 20, 1950; George Beahon, "Jaros' Set Shot with 3 Seconds Remaining Gives Lakers Tingling 78–76 Win over Royals: Obscure Minneapolis Substitute Thwarts Rochester Chance At Central Crown," *D&C*, March 22, 1950; Charlie Wagner, "They Told Me to Shoot, And I Shot'—Jaros," *T-U*, March 22, 1950.

37 Al C. Weber, "Hard-Hitting Pistons, Royals in Playoff: Ft. Wayne Leader in Personals," *T-U*, March 23, 1950; George Beahon, "Zollners Clip Royals, 92–84, Halt Arena Win String at 23 In Roughest Game in 5 Years," *D&C*, Feb. 12, 1950.

38 George Beahon, "Zollners Beat Royals, 90–84, A Late Rally Falls Short; Big Men Dominate," *D&C*, March 23, 1950; George Beahon, "Zollners Shade Royals in Overtime, Eliminate Harrisonmen from NBA Playoffs:

Thrilling Rally Knots Count, Johnson, Wanzer Shots Miss in Victory Bid," *D&C*, March 25, 1950.

39   Shouler et al., *Total Basketball*, 523; "Davies, Cervi, Mikan, Pollard, Braun Picked on UP All-Pro Club," BDSHOF; Jimmy Powers, "The Powerhouse," BDSHOF; Arata, ed., *2006–07 Sacramento Kings Media Guide*, 138.

40   Dave Warner, "Bobby Davies' Stars Lose, 8–5," BDSHOF.

NBA CHAMPIONSHIP GAME

THE 1950–51 NBA SEASON STANDS OUT AS THE HIGHLIGHT OF
Bob Davies' professional career, as well as a significant one in Royals
franchise and basketball history. The first great NBA little-man rivalry,
between 30-year-old Bob Davies and 22-year-old Bob Cousy, began.
African-American players reappeared in the pro ranks. Bob Davies
starred in the first NBA All-Star Game. The Royals finally defeated
the Lakers in the divisional playoffs. And, in the first-ever NBA Final
seventh game, Bob Davies swished clutch free throws to clinch the
Royals' long-awaited championship.

Six years after Bob Davies introduced the transition and penetration styles of play to the NBL, Bob Cousy entered the NBA. In the
defunct Chicago Stags' player dispersal draft, the New York Knicks
selected first and took the 1947–48 BAA scoring leader Max Zaslofsky,
the Philadelphia Warriors chose next and garnered outstanding playmaker Andy Phillip, and the Boston Celtics, by default, obtained the
rights to 6' 1 ½", 175-pound rookie Bob Cousy. According to New
York City sports columnist Jimmy Powers, the new Celtic's greatest
compliment as a collegian had been recognition as "the post-war Bob
Davies," the "most colorful and capable of pre-war players." Cousy
later identified Bob Davies and Bobby Wanzer as the veteran backcourt men that he most wanted to impress as an NBA rookie. [1]

Asked about Cousy's potential, Davies predicted that he would
be "a real good pro player." "One of Bob's [Cousy] first great admirers," noted the *Minneapolis Laker News* two seasons later, "was the

Boston Celtic Bob Cousy, guarding, and Bob Davies, releasing his famous two-hand set shot, were the two greatest guards in the early years of the NBA. (Oct. 12, 1953, Bangor Daily News)

very person who many felt would resent the Worcester magician—Bobby Davies. The Rochester wizard was all for Bob's stuff and one of the first players in the loop who thought the legerdemain of Cousy would go in the big show. Now these two stage some brilliant duels when the two teams meet, but both have a world of admiration for each other."[2]

Three and a half years after George Mikan, waving bye-bye, escorted Dolly King to the Royals bench, 6' 6", 220-pound African-American Earl Francis "Big Cat" Lloyd, without a murmur from the crowd, stepped onto the Edgerton Park Sports Arena court for the Washington Capitols in the season opener. Lloyd, who was paid $5,000 ($49,200 today), scored six points and grabbed ten rebounds, but the Royals won, 78–70.[3]

A month and a half into the season, the Royals and Lakers, riding five-game winning streaks and half a game apart in the western division race, met in the Minneapolis Auditorium. The Royals stalled in the second half and took only 16 shots. Bob Davies dribbled time off the clock, forcing the Lakers to chase him and try to steal the ball. The Lakers started to foul, hoping to trade a one-point foul shot attempt for a two-point field goal attempt. "What a game Davies played... as the Lakers threw most of their beef at him on drive-ins," reported the *Minneapolis Tribune*. Davies scored 28 points, half from the free-throw line. "He was driving like a Mack truck and getting hit with consistent regularity," noted the *Rochester Times-Union*. "It did get a little rough towards the end," said Bob, who was twice knocked into the seats. The Royals won, 82–72, despite Mikan's 43 points.[4]

Two days after Christmas, in the infamous Fort Wayne "Snake Pit," right-handed Bob Davies fractured his left little finger. Writhing in exasperation on the Royals bench in Edgerton Park Sports Arena ten nights later, he witnessed an ignominious affair that *Times-Union* Sports Editor Matt Jackson dubbed "The Thing." The Royals and Indianapolis Olympians ended regulation time tied, 65–65. During the five-minute overtime (OT) periods, both teams tried to work the ball for a high percentage shot or hold it for the last shot. In the first OT, each team notched a field goal. In the second, Indianapolis attempted the only shot and missed. In the third, each team scored two points. In the fourth, neither team took a shot. In the fifth OT, each team scored four points. In the sixth extra period, the Royals controlled the ball most of the last three and a half minutes and called a time-out to plan a play. With four seconds remaining, Arnie Risen tried a desperation shot and missed a put back. Olympian center Alex Groza slapped the ball to Paul "The Ghost" Walther, who threw a three-quarter court length pass to "mercury-footed" guard Ralph Beard, who scored a split second before the buzzer sounded.[5]

The Olympians had won the longest game (78 minutes) in NBA history, a marathon 75–73 snorer (the Olympians scored ten points and the Royals eight points in 30 minutes of overtime). The next night, only five Olympians reached the Tri-Cities court in time for the opening tip-off, and the Royals arrived 55 minutes late for their game in Minneapolis. A quarter-century later, basketball historian Sam Goldaper called this fiasco "one feat from pro basketball's dark ages probably destined to live forever." As an interesting aside, Red Holzman played 75 of the 78 minutes, and the Olympians shot nine and the Royals ten foul shots (total 19), apparently setting NBA regular season game records for most minutes played by a player and fewest foul shots taken by both teams.[6]

After missing five games, Bob Davies, with the fracture set and two fingers taped together so that he could grip a golf club, returned to action against the Baltimore Bullets and scored 15 points. Two weeks later, he scored 25 points and 7 of the Royals' 14 extra period points in a four-overtime victory over the New York Knicks. A week after that, the Blond Bomber scored 28 points, 13 in the final quarter, as the Royals defeated Baltimore, 95–90. Praising his seven brilliant assists, a Bullets staff person said, "that darned Davies had four eyes out there tonight." Next, Davies battled evenly against two other NBA Superstars, scoring 24 points to Cousy's 22 and 28 points to Mikan's 30.[7]

FIRST NBA ALL-STAR GAME

Broadcasters and newspaper reporters unanimously selected Bob Davies as a western division starter in the inaugural NBA All-Star Game. Many pundits predicted that the All-Stars would use the occasion to show off their individual skills, and that they would not play team basketball. Davies, however, believed that professional pride would prevail and make the contest an artistic success. "I'm sure," said Bob, "that most of the players will be trying just as hard to set up plays, pass off, and play smart defensive basketball, as well as score. When you play with an all-star team, you don't want just to convince the paying customers—you want to convince your teammates, the men you've been playing against most of the time—that you can do a real job." [8]

This first All-Star Game, staged before 10,094 fans on March 2, 1951, in Boston Garden, was not broadcast, even locally, on radio or TV. A month and a half late, the NBA presented 31-year-old Bob Davies, the oldest participant, with a birthday cake. The lone Royals representative on the West squad, Davies turned in the first of three outstanding performances in his four All-Star Game appearances. He

Thirty-one-year-old Bob Davies, the NBA's grand old man, was presented a birthday cake at the First NBA All-Star Game in honor of being its oldest participant. (March 2, 1951, Courtesy of Mary Davies)

connected on four of six field-goal attempts and all five free throws for 13 points, grabbed five rebounds, and dished out five assists, but Easy Ed Macauley outplayed Mikan and the East defeated the West, 111–94. Commissioner Maurice Podoloff complimented Bob, one of his "special favorites," for making "a very good contribution to the artistic success of the game." The NBA presented each All-Star a $100 war bond (worth $911 today).[9]

The editors of *Sports Album*, a short-lived Dell Publications magazine, selected the "lithe, blond whippet, one of the best crowd pleasers in either college or professional ranks," Bob Davies as best all-around, "short" professional basketball player, and "Mr. Basketball" George Mikan as best all-around, "tall" professional player, who "ranked far ahead of Davies or any other player." Les Harrison agreed. "If not for George Mikan," he said, "Bob would have to be classed as the greatest in 50 years."[10]

Spurting to ten wins in their last 12 games, the Royals finished second in the western division, three games behind the Lakers. Playing 63 of 68 games, and coping with a damaged left little finger in more than half of them, Bob finished second on the Royals in scoring average (15.2) and led the team in assists (287). Risen ranked tenth in the league with a 16.3 scoring average, Davies sixth in assists, Coleman fourth and Wanzer tenth in field goal percentage, and Risen and Coleman fourth and tenth in rebounds. [11]

Bob Davies joined Mikan on the All-NBA First Team with Boston Celtic Easy Ed Macauley and Indianapolis Olympians Alex Groza and Ralph Beard. Bob Cousy, who utilized his full bag of tricks, including the behind-the-back dribble, garnered Rookie of the Year honors. *People Today* magazine named guards Bob Davies and Bob Cousy, center George Mikan, and forwards Ed Macauley and Syracuse National Adolph "Dolph" Schayes to its "Pro Basketball All-Stars First Team." The Lakers selected "troublemaker" Bob Davies and "whirlwind" Ralph Beard as the guards on their all-opponent team; Jim Pollard voted for the Royals' only jump shooter, 6' 3", 180-pound William C. "Bill" Calhoun, a reserve and defensive specialist, who often shackled him, as a best opposing forward.[12]

PLAYOFFS

The Royals met the Zollners in the western division playoff opening round. Early in the first game, Bob Davies went wild. He blocked a break-away shot, stole the ball and scored on a left-handed lay-up, fed Arnie Risen for a basket, and then scored five more points to break open the contest. In the third quarter, Davies and Coleman combined for 15 points to clinch a 110–81 victory. "In six years he's never played a bad game against us," said Zollners executive Carl Bennett about Davies, who totaled 21 points, "but tonight he was simply from another world." After losing 83–78 in Fort Wayne, the Royals, sparked by Bobby Wanzer with 20 points followed by Risen with 19 and Davies with 15, eliminated the Zollners, 97–78.[13]

Next, the Royals faced their nemesis—the Lakers—in the western division playoff finals. The two powerhouse teams had split their season series, each winning four games, including a Lakers double overtime victory. But this time the Royals got a break. Mikan suffered a hairline ankle fracture in the next-to-last regular season game. He could score, but not run, rebound, or defend up to par.[14]

Playing the opening game in the Minneapolis State Armory, because a sportsman's show had been booked into the auditorium, the Lakers shaded the Royals, 76–73. Making a brilliant coaching move in the second game, Maestro Les Harrison started Red Holzman, instructed the "Little Strategist" to control the ball, and told his team-mates that they could either let Red have the ball or sit on the bench. Indefatigable Red responded magnificently, played the entire game, and directed a patient weaving offense resulting in high percent-age shot opportunities. Red hit 10 of 13 set shot attempts, out-scored Mikan, and limited Slater Martin to one bucket. As effectively as Red performed, Mikan believed that Arnie Johnson's control of the back-boards and keying fast breaks determined the outcome. The Royals prevailed, 70–66, and negated the Lakers' home court advantage. [15]

Traveling to Rochester on the same plane, Jack Coleman told Mikan that ethyl chloride might numb his ankle pain. George tried the remedy and "it worked like a charm," but the Royals won their two home games anyway. Despite Mikan's 32-point effort, the Royals took the clincher, 80–75, thanks to 6' 6", 210-pound University of San Francisco rookie forward Joe McNamee's tip-in with 35 seconds remaining.[16]

NBA FINALS

The Royals opponent in the Finals, the New York Knicks, had finished third in the eastern division and eliminated the Boston Celtics and Syracuse Nationals in the divisional playoffs. New York *Daily Compass* sports writer Stan Isaacs viewed Royals–Knicks games as showdowns between two of the NBA's premier ball handlers, Bob Davies and 6', 180-pound Richard "Tricky Dick" McGuire. Isaacs described Bob as the only NBA little man "an effective drawing card in himself" and stated that many fans idolized him as "the greatest thing to come out of Jersey since [President] Woodrow Wilson." Isaacs quoted another scribe: "You begin to think McGuire knows every trick in the book, until Davies comes to town and, all over again, shows you he's the guy who wrote it."[17]

Although basketball historian Roland Lazenby has described the Royals–Knicks match-up as "the most entertaining Finals" in the

NBA's brief history, Gotham newspapers afforded it scant coverage. *The New York Times*, in effect, ignored the "Basketball World Series." None of the "Sports of the Times" columns by Arthur Daley, who had covered Bob's scintillating NIT Halley's Comet performance, mentioned the NBA, the playoffs, the Knicks, the Royals, or their stars. Stories about preseason Grapefruit League baseball games, such as the Brooklyn Dodgers losing to the Atlanta Crackers and Greensboro (NC) Patriots on their trip home from spring training, took precedence over NBA Finals coverage. *The New York Times* relegated three Knicks–Royals game stories to the sports section's third page and one account to the fifth page, printed no game pictures, and published no stories on travel days. New York City and Rochester radio stations broadcast the games, but there was no TV coverage. [18]

In the Edgerton Park Sports Arena opening game, the Knicks suffered their worst defeat of the season, a kingly 92–65 trouncing. *The New York Times* reporter opined that "only the Royals looked like they belonged in the final." The Royals poured it on again in the second encounter, drubbing the Knicks, 99–84, as Jack Coleman grabbed an Arena record 28 rebounds and dished out eight assists, five more than either McGuire or Davies, who led the Royals in scoring with 24 points. [19]

Returning to New York City, their backs literally "against the drill shed wall," the Knicks hosted the Royals in the 69th Regiment Armory because a circus had been booked into Madison Square Garden. Led by Arnie Risen with 27 points and 18 rebounds, the Royals won the third contest, 78–71, extending their playoff winning streak to six games. Bob Davies converted four key free throws down the stretch as the Knicks fouled trying to get the ball back. After the game, Bob made a rare appearance for a visiting NBA player on the Jimmy Powers TV show. [20]

New York City reporters predicted that the Royals would wrap up the championship the next night. Desperate Knicks coach Joe Lapchick replaced star playmaker Dick McGuire with 6' 3", 190-pound Columbia University Medical School student Ernest Maurice "Doc" Vandeweghe Jr. (father of future NBA star and executive vice president of basketball operations Ernest Maurice "Kiki" Vandeweghe

III), who was playing professional basketball part time. Vandeweghe scored ten points and the Knicks won, 79–73.[21]

Undaunted, the overconfident Royals believed that they would clinch the crown in the fifth game, because the Knicks had not won in Rochester for three years, and had lost 11 consecutive games there. Champagne bottles chilled in ice buckets near the Royals locker room. But the Knicks prevailed, 92–89, despite Bob Davies' ten assists. Back in the 69th Regiment Armory, the Knicks, overcoming Arnie Johnson's 27 and Bob Davies' 17 points, won again and tied the series, the only time in NBA Finals history that a team has recovered from a 3–0 deficit and forced a seventh game.[22]

On April 21, 1951, in Edgerton Park Sports Arena, the Royals and Knicks met in the decisive contest. Six decades later, *USA Today* on *YouTube* featured this showdown as one of the five best all-time NBA Final seventh games. The Royals bolted to a 13–3 lead, increased the margin to 32–18, and at half-time maintained a 40–34 advantage. But with six minutes and 15 seconds left in the fourth quarter, the visitors tied the score, 69–69, and, at the four-minute mark, led 71–70.[23]

There is a time-worn cliché that the NBA Finals bring out the best in the greatest players. With two and a half minutes remaining and the Knicks leading 74–72, Bob Davies stole the ball from All-Star Max Zaslofsky. With 44 seconds remaining and the score tied at 75–all, Davies drove to the basket, and Dick McGuire knocked him hard to the floor. The referees allowed a timeout for medical attention.

And then came the ultimate moment. Bob Davies stepped to the foul line. "These were," wrote Leonard Koppett in his official NBA playoffs history, "by definition, the two most pressure-packed free throws anyone had yet been asked to make in the history of the NBA." *Democrat & Chronicle* columnist George Beahon believed that Bob did not know the meaning of pressure. "I had two tries and made them both for a two-point lead," recalled Bob, not mentioning that neither under-hand shot touched the rim. "It was a great personal thrill for me to be so effective at such a trying time."[24]

Bob's clutch foul shots sealed the NBA championship. Under the rules, a jump ball was held after a successful foul shot in the last two minutes. Against the Lakers, this rule too often worked to the

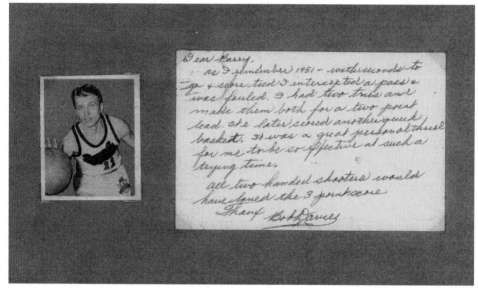

It was a great personal thrill for Bob Davies to sink two clutch free throws in the last minute of the first NBA Final Playoff seventh game and clinch the championship. (April 21, 1951, Author's Collection)

Royals' disadvantage. Mikan or Pollard would foul a Royals little man and win the jump, at worst trading one point for an opportunity for two points. Against the Knicks, justice prevailed. The Royals controlled the tip, Red Holzman dribbled out most of the clock, and Jack Coleman netted a field goal to close out a pulse-pounding 79–75 Finals victory.[25]

Asked about the Knicks' startling comeback from three games down and near win on the Royals' home court in the championship game, Bob Davies said, "I always believe the game takes care of itself. You know the fourth phrase of The Lord's Prayer ["Thy will be done"]! Well, that's good enough for me." [26]

During these Finals, the Royals played their typical balanced team basketball. In the deciding game, Risen scored 24, Davies 20, Wanzer 13, and Coleman 9 points. For the seven-game series, Risen averaged 21.7 PPG and Davies, still shooting with an injured left little finger, 17 PPG; Coleman contributed 44 assists and Davies 37; and Risen grabbed 100 rebounds followed by Coleman with 92. [27]

The Rochester Royals were one of two great early NBA teams. Front Row, left to right, Bob Davies, Bobby Wanzer, William Holzman, Paul Noel, Frank (Pep) Saul, Back Row- from left to right, Bill Calhoun, Joe McNamee, Arnie Risen, Jack Coleman, Arnitz Johnson. (1951, NBAE/Getty Images)

"They'll wear the mantle well," said gentlemanly Knicks coach Joe Lapchick about the Royals. "I'm talking from the heart now. This is a fine Rochester club. A good, clean bunch of kids. Good sports... wonderful opponents.... When you play them...you play basketball. All the way."[28]

Attendance for the seven NBA Finals games totaled 30,300 (compared to 39,554 on June 18, 1999 at a San Antonio Spurs–New York Knicks Finals game in the Alamo Dome). Thirteen thousand five hundred fans (90% of capacity) attended the three 69th Regiment Armory games, 2,500 fewer than the Madison Square Garden "Bobby Davies Night," and almost 5,000 fewer than his NIT Halley's Comet performance. Sellout crowds, however, totaling 16,800, filled Edgerton Park Arena for the four contests in Rochester.[29]

After battling all season and then through 14 playoff games for extra spending money, the Royals split a $14,750 ($134,000 today) playoff bonus. Unlike today, the NBA did not present them with a trophy, a banner, or rings. However, in 1984, the NBA belatedly honored the champion Royals by presenting Les Harrison and his former players a silver bowl in connection with their being recognized as the Rochester professional sports team of the century.[30]

COLLEGE ALL-STAR GAME

As reigning NBA champions, the Royals met the College All-Stars on October 19, 1951, before 16,805 fans (3,305 more than the Knicks' combined three home playoff game attendance) in Chicago Stadium. "It was General MacArthur who said old soldiers never die," wrote *Chicago Herald-American* reporter James E. Enright. "Had he so desired the general could have added old pros in basketball too—and hit the nail on the head where Bob Davies of the Rochester Royals is concerned." Calling Bob "a truly great pro by any means of measuring," Enright described him as "a boy who became a man, and never lost his magic touch with a basketball." [31]

Accounting for a third of the Royals' scoring with 25 points, Bob's 10-point third quarter outburst spurred the NBA champions to a lead that they never relinquished. Reporter Wendell Smith called Bob's performance "one of the greatest shooting exhibitions" ever seen in the stadium. "But there is more to this Davies' story than just his potent shot-making," pointed out Enright. "What about his sensational playmaking? Also his deft dribbling, the likes of which the full-of-fight but awed collegians had never seen before?" The "more mature but still fiery Davies," wrote *Rochester Times-Union* sports writer Al C. Weber, made the difference between winning and losing a 76–70 game. "We did everything we could," said College All-Stars coach Adolph Rupp, "but didn't have the answer to the hot hand of Davies." In the 16 College All-Star Games, only Bob Davies was collegiate MVP and professional champion high scorer in different contests.[32]

All-Star Game Night turned into a nightmare for Coach Rupp and University of Kentucky Wildcat basketball devotees. Law enforcement officials took into custody former Kentucky stars Alex Groza and Ralph Beard, who were watching the game, for questioning about illegal betting on Wildcat basketball games. Groza, Beard, and other college players had taken bribes to shave game-winning margins around bookmakers' point spreads. Clair Bee's LIU All-American Sherman White and two teammates, as well as seven players from Nat Holman's CCNY 1950 NCAA Tournament and NIT champion team, were indicted for accepting bribes. Bee and Holman, two of the greatest all-time college basketball coaches, were not involved, but accepted responsibility for what happened on their watch, resigned, and never coached again at that level. [33]

It was the darkest moment in American sports history since the 1919 Black Sox scandal when eight Chicago White Sox players allegedly accepted bribes and allowed the Cincinnati Reds to win the Baseball World Series. That was the occasion, as legend tells it, that a small boy implored his hero, White Sox hitting star "Shoeless Joe" Jackson, "Say it ain't so, Joe." As part of his rationale for banishing guilty White Sox players from MLB, Commissioner Kennesaw Mountain Landis emphasized the importance of sports in providing role models for youth. "Baseball is something more than a game to an American boy;" said the Commissioner, "it is his training field for life work. Destroy his faith in its squareness and honesty and you have destroyed something more; you have planted suspicion of all things in his heart." Groza and Beard's arrests devastated Kentucky school children who idolized them and had donated pennies, nickels, and dimes for a University of Kentucky Memorial Coliseum mural glorifying their Olympian basketball heroes. The NBA banned the two All-NBA First Team and former U.S. Olympic Team members for life.[34]

"There are too many deals made," commented Bob Davies, who never associated with gamblers and advised his younger brother Dick not to play for a major university basketball program that was breaking NCAA rules. "Some kids make a deal to get into college, then make a deal to shave points, then make a deal with the D.A. afterwards…. The most ridiculous thing is the excuse these kids give," concluded Bob, who had experienced the Great Depression and post-World War II austerity. "'I needed the money.' Who doesn't?"[35]

NOTES

1   Shouler et al., *Total Basketball,* 80–81; "the post-war": Jimmy Powers, "The Powerhouse," *NY Daily News,* Feb. 23, 1954; John Devaney, *Bob Cousy,* 173.

2   "a real": Bob Ajemian, "Cousy Will Have to Drop Fancy Stuff If He Plays Pro, Says Rochester Ace," *Boston Evening American,* Feb. 18, 1950. "One of Bob's": "Cousy Is Fancier Than Ever As Pro," *Minneapolis Laker News 1952–1953* (#5896), 4, LeBov Collection, Sacramento, CA.

3   Al C. Weber, "First Half Kayo Wins for Royals: Risen Paces Royals To Opening Victory," *T-U,* Nov. 1, 1950; Kenneth Shouler, "Chapter 9: The NBA's First African-Americans," in Shouler et al., *Total Basketball,* 140; Measuring Worth.

4   "What a game": Glen Gaff, "Lakers Succumb to Royals 82–72," *Minneapolis Tribune,* Dec. 14, 1950; "He was driving" and "It did get": "Davies Hits 28, Mikan 43 As Royals Upset Lakers," *T-U,* Dec. 14, 1950.

5   "Royals Trip Zollners, 74 to 68, But Lose Bob Davies by Injury; Lakers Spurt to Defeat Bullets," *D&C,* Dec. 28, 1950; "The Thing": Matt Jackson, "Cage Reform: Rule Changes Needed to Prevent Recurrence Of the 'Big Stall'," *T-U,* Jan. 8, 1951; George Beahon, "Olympians Trip Royals, 75–73, Win Record 6-Overtime Contest: Basket by Beard In Last Second Ends Drama," *D&C,* Jan.7, 1951; "Olympians Win In 6 Overtimes: Beard Ends Marathon At Rochester, 75 To 73," *Indianapolis Star,* Jan. 7, 1951.

6   Jack Clary, *Basketball's Great Moments,* 40–43; "one feat": Goldaper, *Great Moments,* 28; Isaacs, *Vintage NBA,* 83, cf. "NBA Encyclopedia Playoff Edition: Regular Season Records: Personal Fouls: Fewest personal fouls, both teams, game," http://www.nba.com/history/records/regular_personalfouls.html (21 fouls — Phoenix [9] at Portland [12], Dec. 1, 2001).

7   "Johnson's Late Basket in Overtime Nips Bullets, 80 to 78, *D&C,* Jan. 11, 1951; "Knicks Lose by 102–92: Beaten by Royals' Quintet in Fourth Overtime Period," *NYT,* Jan. 24, 1951; Al C. Weber, "Davies, Risen Pace Royals To 5-Point Win over Bullets: Victors Hit .493 Field Goal Mark," *T-U,* Jan. 31, 1951; "that darned Davies": "Head Westward: Harrisonmen Battle Olymps In Indianapolis," *D&C,* Jan. 31, 1951; Elliot Cushing," Macauley, Cousy Pace Celtics: Royals Quint Collapses in 2d Half as Boston Captures 93–77 Triumph," *D&C,* Feb. 12, 1951; George Beahon, "Royals Turn Back Lakers, 87 to 82, Keep Division Title Hopes Alive," *D&C,* Feb. 18, 1951.

8   "I'm sure": George Beahon, "'Good, Winning Job': Davies Sees All-Stars Playing Best in Boston," *D&C,* Feb. 27, 1951.

9   George Beahon, "East Subdues West in NBA Star Tilt By 111–94 as Macauley Halts Mikan: Underdogs Take Early Margin Before 10,094 Crowd—Davies Registers 13," *D&C,* March 3, 1951; Joe McKenney, "Eastern All-Star Five Beats West: 10,094 at Garden See Macauley Spark 111–94 Victory With 20 Points—Mikan Held to 12," *Boston Post,* March 3, 1951; "special favorites": Maurice Podoloff to Mr. Robert E. Davies, March 30, 1951, BDSHOF; Measuring Worth.

10   "lithe, blond" and "ranked far": "best all-around professional: mikan or davies?" *Sports Album* (Winter, Dec. 1950–Feb. 1951): 16, 17; Michael MacCambridge, *The Franchise: A History of Sports Illustrated Magazine,* 18; "If not": John H. Travers, "Meet the Royal Member of the Royals' Family—Bob Davies: Bob Davies Does It with Houdini Art," *Harrisburg Sunday Patriot-News,* Dec. 23, 1951.

11   Arata, ed., *2006–07 Sacramento Kings Media Guide,* 139; Shouler et al., *Total Basketball,* 81–82.

12   "People Today Picks All-Star Pro Basket [sic] Team," BDSHOF; Glen Gaff, "Lakers Choose All-Opponents," *Minneapolis Tribune,* March 2, 1951; Hubbard, *NBA Encyclopedia,* 3rd ed., 428 (Calhoun).

13   Shouler et al., *Total Basketball,* 81; George Beahon, "Davies' Scoring, Playmaking Spark Royals to 110–81 Win Over Fort Wayne Zollners in Inaugural Play-Off: Locals Jump To Big Lead At Start," *D&C,* March 21, 1951; "In six": Elliot Cushing, "Sports Eye View," *D&C,* March 23, 1951; George Beahon, "Zollners Stop Royals, 83–78, Even Division Playoff Series; Locals 'Black Out' from Field," *D&C,* March 23, 1951; George Beahon, "Royals Subdue Zollners, 97 to 78, Gain Finals in NBA Western Division: Wanzer Sparks Victory—3rd Period Attack Stops Ft. Wayne," *D&C,* March 25, 1951.

14   Arata, ed., *2006–07 Sacramento Kings Media Guide,* 139; Schumacher, *Mr. Basketball,* 187–90.

15   Al C. Weber, "Lakers Trip Royals: Royals Hopeful Despite Loss to Sub-Par Lakers," *T-U,* March 30, 1951; George Beahon, "Royals Upend Lakers, 70–66, Even Western Division Series As Holzman Dominates Tilt," *D&C,* April 1, 1951; George Beahon, "Rochester's championship season," *T-U,* May 22, 1982.

16   George Beahon, "Royals Take Western Playoffs at Arena, Eliminate Lakers, 80–75, in Close Battle," *D&C*, April 4, 1951; George Beahon, "Tense Tilt Sees Lakers Lose Their 1st Playoff Series in 4 Years of Pro League Play: Injured Mikan Scores 32 in Valiant Try," *D&C*, April 4, 1951.

17   Hubbard, *NBA Encyclopedia*, 3rd ed., 640 (McGuire); "an effective" and "You begin": Stan Isaacs, "Davies, Best Thing From New Jersey Since Woodrow Wilson," BDSHOF.

18   "the most entertaining": Lazenby, *NBA Finals*, 46; Matt Jackson, "Gotham Gossip: Knicks Get Minor Play In Press... Big Town School Sports Dead," *T-U*, April 12, 1951; Fisher, "Rochester Royals," 38.

19   George Beahon, "Royals Trounce Knicks, 92 to 65, To Take Lead in NBA Playoff Finals: RR-Men Outgun Foes, With Risen, Wanzer Tops in Scoring," *D&C*, April 8, 1951; "only the Royals": Louis Effrat, "Royals Turn Back Knicks Five, 92–65: Rochester Takes First Game in Final Play-Off Series for Pro League Title," *NYT*, April 8, 1951; George Beahon, "Royals Drub Knickerbockers Again, To Take 2–0 Lead in NBA Championship: Coleman Cracks Rebound Mark—Bob Davies Leads RR-Men in Scoring with 24," *D&C*, April 9, 1951.

20   George Beahon, "Royals Spill Knicks, 78–71, For 3–0 Lead in Title Race; Risen Stars, Hits 27 Points," *D&C*, April 12, 1951.

21   George Beahon, "Knicks' Closing Rally Shades Royals, 79-73, Forces 5th NBA Playoff Game Here Tomorrow: Risen Leads Great Comeback In 2d Half by Rochester after Trailing, 40–28," *D&C*, April 14, 1951.

22   Elliot Cushing, "Knicks Upset Royals at Sport Arena, 92–89, Playoffs for NBA Crown Back to New York: Connie Simmons, Team Play Won, Lapchick States," *D&C*, April 16, 1951; George Beahon, "Knicks Square Title Series By Humbling Royals, 80–73, Final Game Here Saturday," *D&C*, April 19, 1951; http://www.nba.com/encyclopedia/rochester_royals_1951.html.

23   http://ftw.usatoday.com/2013/06/the-5-best-finals-game-7s-in-nba-history/; George Beahon, "Royals Grab NBA Title With 79–75 Win over Knicks: 4,200 Witness Thrilling Climax," *D&C*, April 22, 1951; Louis Effrat, "Royals Top Knicks For Crown, 79–75, Win Seventh Game of NBA Finals in the Last Minute After New York Rally," *NYT*, April 22, 1951.

24   "These were": Koppett, *Championship NBA*, 22; George Beahon, "In this Corner," BDSHOF; "I had two": Davies postcard to author.

25   George Beahon, "Rochester's championship season," *T-U*, May 22, 1982.

26   "I always believe": Elliot Cushing, "'It's Fine Rochester Club,' Lapchick, Losing Coach Says," *D&C*, April 22, 1951; Dick Davies, telephone conversation with author, Dec. 30, 2011 (quote clarification).

27   "Composite Box Score Of Finals in Playoffs," BDSHOF.

28   "They'll wear": Elliot Cushing, "'It's Fine Rochester Club,' Lapchick, Losing Coach Says," *D&C*, April 22, 1951.

29   Arata, ed., *2006–07 Sacramento Kings Media Guide*, 139; https://en.wikipedia.org/wiki/San_Antonio_Spurs#1999.

30   Arata, ed., *2006–07 Sacramento Kings Media Guide*, 139; "Composite Box Score Of Finals in Playoffs," BDSHOF; Measuring Worth; Fisher, "Lester Harrison," 240.

31   "It was General" and "a boy": James E. Enright, "Royals Win All-Star Game," *Converse Basketball Yearbook 1952*, 37.

32   "one of the": Wendell Smith, "Pros Win, 76 to 70, on Davies' 25 Points," *Chicago Herald-American*, Oct. 20, 1951; "But there": James E. Enright, "Royals Win All-Star Game," *Converse Basketball Yearbook 1952*, 37; "more mature" and "We did": Al C. Weber, "Davies Draws Rupp's Praise In Wake of Royals' Win," *T-U*, Oct. 20, 1951; Schleppi, *Chicago's Showcase*, 149–50, 167–70 (Mikan not 1946 College All-Star Game MVP).

33   "Groza, Beard Seized in Basketball Fix: Ex-Kentucky Stars Nabbed In Stadium, 33 Players Now Involved," *Chicago Tribune*, Oct. 20, 1951; "Beard And Groza Are Quizzed In Net Fix Scandal," *Indianapolis Star*, Oct. 20, 1951; "They Were Toast of Town: Stunned Bluegrass Cage Fans Stutter over 'Fix' Disclosure," *D&C*, Oct. 21, 1951; "Pros Suspend Groza, Beard for Fix Roles, *Chicago Tribune*, Oct. 21, 1951; McCallum, *College Basketball*, 93–97.

34   "Say": http://www.thisdayinquotes.com/2009/09/it-ain-so-joe-actually-wasnt-so.html; "Baseball is": John Helyar, *Lords Of The Realm: The Real History of Baseball*, 6.

35   "There are": Bill Carroll, "Basketball Great Bob Davies Says: Too Many Deals Made," *Lancaster New Era*, July 6, 1961; Dick Davies, telephone conversation with author, Jan. 29, 2009.

NBA'S GRAND OLD MAN

AS AL CERVI, JOE FULKS, RED HOLZMAN, IRON MAN ARNIE JOHNSON (with the consecutive game record of 326), and other veterans retired, Bob Davies, the NBA's "oldest teen-ager," assumed the role of a legendary grand old man. *Philadelphia Inquirer* sports writer Gene Courtney remarked that Bob, despite his age, could still "easily model for Jack Armstrong, the All-American Boy." "Whether it is a comic strip character or a loyal old hard-driving pro," wrote New York City sports columnist Jimmy Powers about Davies, "your eyes light up when you see an old friend day in and day out. He 'wears well,' as the phrase goes, like old bed-room slippers." In his first product endorsement, "All Star" and "All Action" Bob Davies promoted American Amoco Gas that kept "Going Strong... Going Farther and Smoother for Less." An Associated Press cartoon portrayed Bob as "Rochester's Amazing Veteran," still "improving all the time."[1]

Bob attributed his basketball longevity to sleeping ten hours a night, not imbibing alcoholic beverages or smoking cigarettes, and keeping his legs in shape during the summer playing golf and semi-professional baseball and softball. Les Harrison believed that Bob continued to play at a high level because he constantly studied the game and each season added new offensive and defensive wrinkles to his formidable arsenal of skills.[2]

1951–52 SEASON
Although Rochester's mayor, Samuel Dicker, proclaimed November

All Star and All Action Bob Davies, here seated in his Buick Roadmaster presented by Seton Hall and Royals fans, promoted AMOCO gas in his first product endorsement. (1951, Courtesy of Mary Davies)

1, 1951 "Rochester Royals Day" in honor of their NBA championship, only 2,136 spectators welcomed Davies, Wanzer & company back to Edgerton Park Sports Arena for the 1951–52 season opener. Taking advantage of the opportunity to watch the first locally televised Royals game, many fans stayed home and followed the action on their snowy, 17-inch black-and-white TV screens. Davies, scoring 20 points, led the Royals to a 101–97 victory over the Baltimore Bullets.[3]

A quarter of the way into the season, Bob Davies joined Syracuse Nat Alex Hannum as co-holder of a dubious all-time NBA record: most personal fouls committed in a regulation-length game—seven. With 40 seconds remaining in a game against the Philadelphia Warriors, the Royals had only five available players. Three had been disqualified for personal fouls, one had been ejected for abusive language, and one was injured. When Bob committed his sixth foul, he remained in the game because the NBA rules required five men on the floor and the Warriors were awarded a technical foul shot. Bob fouled once more trying to get the ball back.[4]

Midway through the season, "Rochester's Rapid Roberts," Davies and Wanzer, were unanimous choices for the West Team in the second NBA All-Star Game. Davies turned in another fine performance, scoring eight points and dishing out five assists. Wanzer held Cousy scoreless in the first half. Playing 19 minutes as Mikan's substitute, Arnie Risen scored six points. Led by Philadelphia Warriors forward Paul Arizin, the East prevailed, 108–91.[5]

Near the end of the season, Bob Davies matched his career high game scoring record—33 points. The "classiest operator" on the Baltimore Coliseum court, he hit 12 of 20 attempts, mostly long, fadeaway two-hand set shots. "Snap your fingers!" wrote *Baltimore News-Post* reporter John Steadman. "That's about how long it took him [Davies] to focus on the target and flash the ball on its way. Whether he's personally popular or not, Davies deserves any professional tribute you want to pay him."[6]

The Royals finished the 1951–52 campaign with the best win-loss record (41–25). And the Royals with Davies, Wanzer, and Risen, and the Lakers with Mikan, Mikkelsen, and Pollard, became the first NBA teams with three players scoring over 1,000 points in a season. In another milestone achievement, Arnie Johnson, by averaging ten points per game, enabled the Royals to become the first NBA team to have all five starters average in double figures. Although the NBA widened the three-second lane from 6 feet to 12 feet, primarily to hold down Mikan, Big George still led the league in scoring with a 23.9 PPG average and set a new single game record of 61 points against the Royals. Among all NBA players, Davies, Wanzer, and Risen ranked fifth, eighth, and ninth in scoring average; Wanzer and Coleman fourth and sixth in field goal percentage; Davies and Wanzer third and seventh in assists per game (APG); and Risen and Coleman fourth and seventh in rebounds per game (RPG). Davies joined Mikan, Cousy, Macauley, and Arizin on the All-NBA First Team. Wanzer, an All-NBA Second Team member, converted 90 percent of his foul shots, an NBA first.[7]

The Royals quickly eliminated the Zollners in the western division playoff opening round. "Long ball hitters" Wanzer and Davies scored

26 and 23 points respectively in the first game 95–78 win. In the second and deciding encounter, a 92–86 victory, Davies scored 29 points, many on difficult floating jumpers, and Wanzer contributed 23.[8]

Outside finesse overcame inside strength in the opening game of the western division playoff finals against the Lakers in Edgerton Park Sports Arena. Davies (26) and Wanzer (24), combined for 50 points, outscoring Mikan, who set a playoff single-game scoring record of 47 points, and the Royals won, 88–78. But in the second game, the Lakers prevailed in overtime, 83–78, as Davies' protégé and Wanzer's college teammate, Pep Saul, who had been traded to the Baltimore Bullets and then to the Lakers, drove around his former college coach four times, scored 17 points, and sank the clinching basket. Davies tallied 20 points. [9]

Back in Minneapolis for the third game, Bob Davies turned in one of the worst performances of his career in a 77–67 Royals loss. On the court just 18 minutes, he missed three awry shots against Slater Martin's tenacious defense. "When you shut out Bob Davies," noted Minneapolis sports writer Bill Carlson, "it's like blanking Ted Williams and Stan Musial in the same day." [10]

"If you're a pro," commented Davies, "you take your lumps one night and give 'em the next. You make a sucker of an opponent one game, and he makes you look bad the next. If you can't take the game on those terms, you don't belong in it."[11]

Quickly regaining his form, Davies led the Royals with 21 points in a last-ditch fight that Lakers coach John Kundla called the greatest professional game ever played in the Minneapolis Auditorium. The lead changed 15 times and the score was tied 18 times. Pep Saul and Vern Mikkelsen led the Lakers with 18 points each. Jim Pollard's tip-in with two seconds left on the clock clinched the western division final championship 82–80, and the Lakers went on to defeat the New York Knicks in the NBA Finals.[12]

NBA IMAGE

Bob Davies' movie-star good looks, strong moral character, and colorful style of play made him a natural for endorsements aimed at selling products to boys and girls who admired sports heroes. Confirming

The "famous blond bomber" portrayed a "Father Knows Best" image in an early Wheaties TV commercial (Oct. 1, 1954, Courtesy of General Mills Archives/Courtesy of Mary Davies)

Bob's popularity in NBA cities, Minneapolis-based General Mills signed him as the third professional basketball player, following local Laker heroes Jim Pollard and George Mikan, to endorse their breakfast cereal, "Wheaties—The Breakfast of Champions." Portraying Mr. "Main Street USA," Bob, in one of three 60-second TV commercials, sat at a breakfast table, wearing a polo shirt, and ate a bowl of Wheaties while reading a newspaper. He perfectly reflected the wholesome 1950s American middle-class family values and lifestyle popularized in the beloved radio and TV network situation comedy series, the "Adventures of Ozzie and Harriet" and "Father Knows Best," in which everything worked out fine in the end. Bob projected the best player image that the NBA never realized it had.[13]

Even if their families did not yet own TV sets, juvenile readers of

26 million *Tarzan, Red Ryder, Little Lulu, Looney Tunes, Tom & Jerry*, and other March 1954 Dell comic issues were introduced to Bob Davies by a full-page back-cover Wheaties advertisement. Wearing a sweat-shirt and jeans, Bob showed a boy named Tommy how to receive a pass with his back to the defender, turn quickly, and dribble for a lay-up. After their workout, Bob and Tommy enjoyed a bowl of Wheaties. "You can't spark unless you're in shape!" said Bob. "Get proper rest and food. Notice—I choose energy food like Wheaties." In the last cartoon frame, Bob, seated in the stands and dressed in a business suit, watched Tommy sink a basket in a high school game. "That's the old spark," yelled nice guy Bob.[14]

General Mills paid Bob Davies $500 ($4,400 today) and provided his family 50 cartons of small individual Wheaties packages for the rights to use his bubble-gum-card-sized picture on a Wheaties box. His compensation exceeded the $75 that Baseball Hall of Famer Honus Wagner received around the turn of the 20th century for endorsing a Louisville Slugger baseball bat, but pales by comparison with the $2.5 million Nike paid modern NBA icon Michael Jordan for lending his name to the Air Jordan sneaker. No wag dare say, however, that this Davies biography (even though Bob sold Chuck Taylor basketball shoes for twenty-seven years), is less an account of a man than a his-tory of a sneaker, as has been intimated about Jordan's autobiographi-cal *Driven from Within*.[15]

Another food manufacturer took advantage of Bob's All-American image to promote its product sold in 15 midwestern, great plains, southwestern, and southern states. His image appeared on Junge Bread end labels in a Movie and Athletic Stars series that included actor Lex Barker (Tarzan), cowboy actors John Wayne and Tim Holt, crooner Bing Crosby, ventriloquist Edgar Bergen, football quarter-back Johnny Lujack, African-American running back Buddy Young, boxers Rocky Marciano and Kid Gavilan, and the other two of the early NBA Big Three, George Mikan and Joe Fulks.[16]

1952–53 SEASON

Before the 1952–53 season opened, nice guy Bob Davies tried to help an African-American player get an NBA job. Four blacks had played

This Wheaties advertisement featuring Bob Davies appeared on the back of twenty-six million Dell comic books including Tarzan, Red Ryder, Little Lulu, and Tom & Jerry. (March 1954, Courtesy of General Mills Archives/ Courtesy of Mary Davies)

in the NBA during the 1950–51 season and three more the following season. Davies arranged a Royals tryout for 6' 2", 185-pound Harlem Globetrotters reserve Robert "Bobby" Knight. Davies regarded Knight as good a dribbler as flamboyant Globetrotter Marques Haynes, who, pivoting on a knee, dribbled as low as six inches from the floor and kept the ball away from opponents. But a white player, Jack McMahon, a 6' 1", 185-pound former St. John's University captain and College All-Star team member, beat out Knight for the Royals' only open guard slot, and during the 1952–53 season the NBA added only one more African American player. Knight eventually signed with the New York Knicks and appeared in two games during the 1954–55 NBA season. [17]

Shortly before 1952 pre-season training ended, Bob Davies left his teammates in order to attend his father's funeral. Edris Davies had been disabled several years due to a broken hip and a heart condition. Devoted son Bob and daughter-in-law Mary assisted his parents financially, buying them a car, television set, and heating coal, paying their rent several times, and purchasing sneakers for Dick so he could play high school basketball. "He was a wonderful big brother," said Dick. "I don't know where we would have been if it hadn't been for Bob."[18]

Although Davies was again a unanimous choice for the mid-January NBA All-Star Game staged in Fort Wayne's new Allen County Memorial Coliseum, West Coach John Kundla slated him for spot duty because he had suffered a groin injury in another melee with the Zollner Pistons, had missed three games, and had been seeing limited action. In the first half, Davies played only eight minutes, as Wanzer scored all his nine points and clamped down on Cousy defensively. Davies re-entered the game with eight minutes remaining in the fourth quarter and the West trailing by a point. As usually hostile Fort Wayne fans cheered wildly, their "friendly enemy" swished a set shot to put the West ahead for keeps, drove into the lane and hit a floating one-hander, and made a driving hook and a free throw, capping an eight consecutive point outburst. He also intercepted two passes and fed Slater Martin and Vern Mikkelsen for buckets. "Bob was the kind of guy that crowds liked to cheer," said Bobby Wanzer, "and he would react to the cheering and try to give them more to cheer for." Kundla thought that Davies had turned in the best individual short spurt performance in the three All Star Games. As the buzzer sounded on a West 79–75 victory, Davies tucked the ball under his arm, raced to the locker room, and packed it in his traveling bag. Kundla told reporters that Bob deserved the game ball. Rochester *Times-Union* Sports Editor Matt Jackson thought that Bob would have been selected MVP, rather than Mikan, if the vote had not been taken before Bob broke open the game.[19]

This All-Star Game was not televised over a national network or by a Fort Wayne station. Veteran announcer Marty Glickman, the "Voice of the New York Knicks," did the play by play over the Mutual Broadcasting System, which had 500 affiliated radio stations. A few TV viewers may have seen snippets of Davies' legendary short spurt performance, because two national TV services, Telra of Philadelphia and Telenews of New York, provided taped game segments to their subscribing stations. The week following the game, Movietone News, Paramount News, and Pathé News showed brief NBA All-Star Game clips in movie theater newsreel sports segments.[20]

As team captain, the only player allowed under NBA rules to talk to a referee, Bob Davies complained too often and too vociferously, and, under a new "mouth-shut" rule, was assessed "technical-personal" misconduct fouls that counted toward disqualification from the game and carried fines ranging from $25 to $100. Les Harrison hit on a clever solution to protect his superstar; he named Arnie Johnson team captain. In seven seasons, Arnie had been assessed one technical foul and that had been for inadvertently kicking the ball into the stands as he turned to run down court. Appropriately, the referee apologized for whistling the undeserved technical. Harrison reasoned that taciturn Arnie never complained to officials, perhaps had won their respect, and might get a hearing if he argued a point. Asked about his new responsibility, Arnie, in an unprecedented outburst of oratory, said, "It must be awful miserable being a referee. How do I feel about being captain? Well, it's okay with me if the boys want me. We'll have to wait and see what happens." Under the "Johnson Regime," the Royals, avoiding misconduct calls, won six of eight games.[21]

The Royals finished the 1952–53 season in second place in the western division, four games behind the Lakers. The Rochester men were second in team scoring average, canning 86.3 PPG to the Boston Celtics 88.1 PPG, but sixth in team defense. Leading team scorer Bob Davies ranked eighth in the NBA with a 15.6 point average and sixth in assists with 4.2 per game. Coleman ranked seventh in field goal percentage, and Coleman sixth and Risen ninth in total rebounds. Wanzer ranked tenth in two categories with 14.6 PPG and 3.6 APG. The Royals' Davies and Wanzer were chosen for the 1952–1953 NBA All-Star Second Team.[22]

Not surprisingly, the western division opening playoff round with the Fort Wayne Zollner Pistons deteriorated into a donnybrook. In the first game in Rochester, the Zollners concentrated on smothering Davies and Wanzer, who scored 12 and 15 points respectively, and defeated the Royals 84–77. Two nights later, in Fort Wayne, Davies suffered a slight ankle sprain late in the second quarter. Playing sparingly thereafter, he scored only eight points, but limited Andy Phillip to two field goals and controlled the ball the last six minutes against a desperate, physical full-court press. Three Royals and two Zollners fouled out, and the referees called six injury time-outs. The Royals won, 83–71, boarded a late-night train, and arrived in Rochester early the next morning. The Zollners enjoyed a restful night's sleep in their own beds and flew into Rochester on game day in Mr. Zollner's private DC-2. That night, Bob Davies, who scored only six points, tied the game on a driving lay-up with ten seconds left, but the Zollners scored with four seconds remaining and ousted the Royals from the playoffs, 67–65. Good sportsmen Bob Davies, Arnie Risen, and Jack Coleman visited the Zollners' locker room, shook hands, and wished them luck. But the Lakers eliminated the Zollners, three games to two, and then defeated the Knicks in the Finals.[23]

1953–54 SEASON

Even though Bob Davies did not miss a game for the first time in his pro career, the 1953–54 season marked the nadir of his NBA stardom and a shift into a new role as a sixth man (another term not yet coined). According to Red Auerbach, who claimed credit for inventing the concept five seasons later with Frank Ramsey, the sixth man is one of the team's best players, who is held in reserve to provide scoring punch off the bench, and is on the court in the final minutes when the game is on the line. "Davies," said Les Harrison, "can get off the bench and fire up a club better than any man I know." Second-year guard Jack McMahon took over Bob's starting position. As sixth man, Bob averaged 29.7 minutes, 12.3 points, and 4.5 assists per game, compared to starter McMahon's 26.6 minutes, 10.0 points, and 3.4 APG. [24]

Attendance at Royals home games declined along with Bob Davies' floor time. In the nine of the first ten 1953–54 season Edgerton Park Sports Arena games for which figures are available, the Royals averaged 1,380 spectators. Top-price ticket fans, men who wore business suits and women who dressed in furs as if going to a dinner and concert, became tired of the inadequate building and watching an aging team, and stopped showing up. Home games on Tuesday and

Saturday nights competed with the new entertainment fad, television, particularly the tremendously popular Milton Berle and Sid Caesar–Imogene Coca comedy shows. Average game and total season attendance at Edgerton Park Sports Arena dropped about 50 percent from the 1950–51 championship season level of 2,408 and 81,872 to 1,254 and 45,150 in the 1953–54 season. Four and a half decades later (1998), 62,046 fans, almost 17,000 more than for the entire Royals 1953–54 home season, jammed into the Georgia Dome to witness Michael Jordan's farewell appearance against the Atlanta Hawks.[25]

Striving to boost attendance, team captain and ticket sales campaign committee chairman Bob Davies, "whose fiery spirit and daring play" had made him the darling of Rochester fans, led teammates and businessmen on a four-day door-to-door ticket-selling campaign in downtown Rochester. Wearing overcoats, suits, and ties, the players canvassed potential ticket buyers. Anyone calling the Royals' office could request a favorite player to visit her or him and make ticket arrangements. However, not even the future great St. Louis Cardinals baseball broadcaster Jack Buck, recreating Royals road games over a local radio station from minimal Western Union wire details, could arouse enough interest to lure wayward fans back into the aging Edgerton Park barn with its poor sight lines. Worried owner Les Harrison might well have heeded Bob Davies' advice in the Royals' program advertisement: "'Ease the tension with Beech-Nut gum!'.... No matter what you do—driving in for a lay-up, bowling for that strike, or working in an office, chewing Beech-Nut Gum really eases the tension."[26]

Based largely on reputation and popularity, Bob Davies was the first sixth man selected to play in an NBA All-Star Game. A Cousy biographer stated that some basketball experts at that time still considered Davies "the best of the NBA's backcourt men." The wily veteran Davies and rising superstar Cousy dazzled a Madison Square Garden crowd in the Fourth NBA All-Star Game, which took place on January 21, 1954 and was not televised. Davies did not enter the game until the second quarter. In a ten-minute stint, he made two successive three-point plays and finished the period with ten points. In the last two minutes of the fourth quarter, he hit a floating jump shot

"**Ease the tension** with **BEECH-NUT GUM!**"

says BOB DAVIES
(star player — Rochester Royals)

"I've read that scientists at a leading university have proved chewing Beech-Nut Gum eases the tension. Anyone who plays basketball knows how true that is. Practically all the fellows I know chew gum from the opening whistle. No matter what you do—driving in for a lay-up, bowling for that strike, or working in an office, chewing Beech-Nut Gum really eases the tension."

BEECH-NUT PACKING CO.

Bob advised everyone based on scientific study and basketball players' experience to ease the tension with Beech-Nut gum. (1953–1954, Courtesy of Mary Davies)

that tied the score. At this point, Cousy, smothered by Bobby Wanzer, had scored only eight points and turned over the ball twice. And then Davies upstaged Cousy and almost made him the goat of the first NBA All-Star Game in Cousy's hometown. With 33 seconds remaining, the East leading by two points, and Cousy trying to dribble out the clock, Davies stole the ball from him and drove for a bucket to tie the game. Cousy responded with a field goal and George Mikan converted two pressure-filled foul shots to end regulation time in an 84–84 tie. In overtime, Cousy redeemed himself. He opened the period with a field goal, controlled the ball the rest of the way, and scored eight more points for a total of 20 as the East won, 98–93. Fouling Cousy to get the ball, Bobby Wanzer earned the dubious distinction of being the first player to foul out of an NBA All-Star Game. The sports writers took another vote and awarded Cousy the MVP instead of Jim Pollard, whom they had selected prior to the end of the fourth quarter. Converting 8 of 16 field goal attempts, Davies finished with 18 points. In four All-Star Game appearances, Davies connected on 19 of 40 field goal attempts, an incredible .475 percentage in that era for a long-range shooting guard.[27]

Two days after the All-Star Game, the Royals debuted on national television over the DuMont "Forgotten Network," which, in the early 1950s, briefly competed with NBC, CBS, and ABC for the U.S. television market. DuMont broadcast 13 unsponsored NBA Game of the Week programs over 65 stations, mostly in eastern and a few midwestern and southern states. Marty Glickman, promoted to the "Voice of Basketball," did the play by play. The Philadelphia DuMont affiliate blacked out the Royals game with the Warriors due to a conflict with the March of Dimes telethon. When the Warriors cut the Royals' lead to four points, Davies and Wanzer, collaborating on set shots and nifty cut-in plays, put the game out of reach. Falling out of bounds, Davies passed for a basket that extended the lead to 11 points. Davies and Coleman paced the Royals with 14 points each in their 71–61 victory.[28]

Unfortunately, NBA basketball turned off many TV sports fans who did not appreciate views of the game taken from poor (one or two) camera angles and flickering reception on small screens, nor griping to referees, muggings, parades to the foul line, and stalling tactics that cut down scoring in what should have been exciting closing minutes. According to Hall of Famer Bill Sharman, the games often resembled National Hockey League frays. NBA team owners did not encourage fighting, but did not discourage it either. Referees did not eject players for fisticuffs. If a player did not protect himself, opponents took advantage of him. Bullies strong-armed several good players who did not fight back out of the league. Team enforcers devoted special physical attention to the opponent's superstar or high scorer. In his nine-season pro career, George Mikan, basically a stationary target, suffered through 166 stitches; a BB imbedded in a leg; broken bones in both elbows and feet, as well as an arm, nose, and several fingers; lost teeth; and a damaged kneecap. Incredibly, Big George, who probably administered more punishment than he absorbed, missed only two games and those because of viral infections. In his ten-season pro career, moving target Bob Davies played through torn knee ligaments, ankle sprains, fractured and bruised ribs, a groin strain, and a broken finger, as well uncounted black eyes and cut lips.[29]

"Fair Game" Bob Davies did not alter his slashing style of play because he happened to be the target for the night. He continued driving into the area under the basket—a no man's land for less determined guards. He never became gun shy, never backed off. He looked like an average-sized guy, but could get just as rough as the bullies. At the end of the 1951–52 season, Davies ranked fourth in personal fouls (269) behind perennial NBA leading foulers Mikan (286) and Mikkelsen (282).[30]

"Bobby Davies was a tough son of a bitch," said Hall of Fame coach Bob Knight. "He didn't go out there like Caspar Milquetoast. Bobby Davies was as tough as they came."[31]

If an opposing team's enforcer roughed him up, Davies asked the guy whether he did it on purpose or whether it was an accident. If the response was on purpose, Bob did not turn the other cheek. In a Lakers game, Bob twice fought through a big man's screens. Both times he took an elbow and yelled, "You can't hurt other players." After a third elbowing, Bob slugged the big guy. And Red Auerbach told a story about the Celtic enforcer mugging Bob several times and Bob calling time-out, walking over to Red, pointing at the enforcer, and warning Red that, if he did not call off the guy, Bob would take care of Red. After all, Lieutenant (JG) Robert E. Davies had once outranked Acting Petty Officer Arnold Auerbach.[32]

During the 1953–54 season, the Royals won six of nine games from the Lakers, but, with 44 wins and 28 losses, finished four games behind them in the four-team western division. The Rochester men ranked fourth in team offense and second in team defense. Leading team scorer Bobby Wanzer ranked tenth in the league with a 13.3 PPG average followed by Risen with 13.2 PPG and sixth man Davies with 12.3 PPG. Davies ranked fifth in the league in assists and Risen seventh in rebounds.[33]

In a wacky, six-game round-robin playoff format, each division's top three teams played each other home and away until the one with the worst record was eliminated. The Royals played six games in 13 days. Bob Davies could no longer hop off a train at 5:30 a.m. the morning after a tough game in Rochester, walk to the Green Parrot Restaurant, and compete effectively that night in Fort Wayne. Nor could he play in Rochester, board a 10:30 p.m. sleeper to Chicago, get up at 7 a.m. and catch a connecting 9 a.m. train to Minneapolis, and perform at a high level at 7:30 p.m. after a 1,200 mile, 18-hour train trip. Now he needed two days' rest to recover. Nonetheless, he totaled 14 points in two games as the Royals eliminated the Zollners.[34]

Although no longer a starter, Bob Davies still worried the Lakers. Coach Kundla described him as a coach on the floor and always thinking, aware of his opponents' idiosyncrasies, and taking advantage of every opportunity. With Davies playing a "spot" role and converting only two free throws, the Royals lost the first game in Minneapolis. In the do-or-die second clash in Edgerton Park Sports Arena, which DuMont televised over 60 stations, Davies scored 11 points, and Jack Coleman sank a hook shot with eight seconds remaining to clinch a thrilling 74–73 Royals victory. But the Lakers won the deciding contest in Minneapolis despite Risen (24) outscoring Mikan (11); Davies and Wanzer contributed eight points each. The Lakers then defeated the Syracuse Nationals to achieve the first NBA playoff championship three-peat.[35]

A summer Harlem Globetrotters northeastern states "Basketball under the Stars" tour provided Bob Davies a last hurrah as a basketball showman. He performed for the Boston Whirlwinds against an aggregation of former college stars dubbed the House of David on a doubleheader card staged on a six-ton portable court set up in baseball stadiums. His primary job was to feed the ball to former Rio Grande College (OH) star Clarence "Bevo" Francis, who had scored 113 points in a college game. As a crowd gasped, Bob, dribbling full speed on a fast break, leapt, brought the ball in his right hand across the front of his body, and dropped it behind his back to a teammate cutting in from the right side for a lay-up. After the tour ended, Globetrotters owner Abe Saperstein wrote Bob a letter complimenting him on his exemplary character: "The hell of this business is that there are so few people who are in our books 'real people,' and it is always a refreshing surprise to find those who can be classified in that category... of which I am happy to say I must include you."[36]

During the 1952, 1953, and 1954 pre-seasons, the Boston Celtics, suffering at the gate like most NBA teams and struggling to expand their New England region fan base, played a series of exhibition games against the Royals in small communities such as Houlton, Ellsworth, Millinocket, and Rumford, Maine, as well as cities such as Hanover and Manchester, New Hampshire and Hartford and Bristol, Connecticut. According to the *Bangor (Maine) Daily News,* these exhibitions featured Bob Davies, "one of basketball's all-time greats," and Bob Cousy, "the greatest player in the history of basketball." Motivated by their personal rivalry, Cousy some nights played uncharacteristically tenacious defense against Davies. In the 1954 pre-season series, Cousy complained that Davies, shamefully for a Bible reader, employed obnoxious and irritating defensive tactics such as pulling on his shorts (a Red Auerbach-endorsed dirty trick). Familiarity bred contempt and the two superstars tired of each other.[37]

NOTES

1   Jack Barry, "Cousy to Face Philly, See Limited Service," *Boston Sunday Globe,* Jan. 23, 1955; "oldest teen–ager": "Davies Disdains To Act His Age," *Philadelphia Inquirer,* Dec. 24, 1952; "easily model": Gene Courtney, "Prospects of NBA Teams: Davies' Legs Hold the Key To Royals' Title Chances," RRSHOF 1954–1955 Season; "Whether it": Jimmy Powers, "The Powerhouse," *N.Y. Daily News,* Feb. 23, 1954; "All Star": Rochester Royals Season 1951–52 Official Program, 6; "Rochester's amazing veteran": "Court Comet" by Pap, *Fort Wayne News-Sentinel,* Jan. 29, 1953.

2   Bob Davies as told to Al C. Weber, "How to Play Basketball: Top Physical Condition," *T-U,* Dec. 6, 1951; George Beahon, "In This Corner," *D&C,* Jan. 21, 1954; John H. Travers, "Meet the Royal Member of the Royals' Family — Bob Davies: Bob Davies Does It With Houdini Art," *Harrisburg Sunday Patriot-News,* Dec. 23, 1951.

3   Samuel B. Dicker, Mayor, City of Rochester, Proclamation, Nov. 1, 1951, PMHOF; "Royals' .493 Shooting KOs Bullets," *T-U,* Nov. 2, 1951; Fisher, "Lester Harrison," 220.

4   Hal Freeman, "Warriors Jar Royals To End Streak, 96–80: Fulks Scores
    26 Points, Arizin 22 As Rochester Loses 1st in 6 Games," *Philadelphia
    Inquirer*, Dec. 5, 1951; http:www.apbr.org/forum/viewtopic.php?t=1356;
    National Basketball Association 1952–53 Record Book: Press, Radio and
    Television Brochure, 5.
        On Dec. 26, 1950, Syracuse Nat Alex Hannum committed seven
    fouls in a game against Boston. On Nov. 13, 1999, Atlanta Hawk Cal
    Bowdler was whistled for seven fouls due to referees' error in a game
    against the Portland Trail Blazers.
5   Jack Barry, "East All-Stars Score Second Win Over West: Arizin, Star of
    Night, Paces Victors; Shares Scoring Honors with Mikan," *Boston Daily
    Globe*, Feb. 12, 1952; George Beahon, "Underdog East All-Stars Polish
    Off West, 108–91 For 2d in Row Before 10,211 Fans at Boston Garden,"
    D&C, Feb.12, 1952.
6   "Snap": John Steadman, "Kudelka's Shot Stirs Bullet Court Fans,"
    Baltimore News-Post, March 4, 1952.
7   Arata, ed., *2006–07 Sacramento Kings Media Guide,* 140; Dolph Grundman,
    Jim Pollard: The Kangaroo Kid, 108; Bob Matthews, "Former Royals
    forward 'Arnie' Johnson dies at 80," *D&C*, April 8, 2000; Shouler et al.,
    Total Basketball, 83–85.
8   George Beahon, "Wanzer, Davies Lead Royals To 95–78 Win over
    Zollners In Division Playoff Opener," *D&C*, March 19, 1952; George
    Beahon, "Royals Eliminate Zollners in Playoffs, 92–86, Davies Hits for
    29, Wanzer 23, Risen 21 Points," *D&C*, March 21, 1952.
9   Al C. Weber, "Lakers Bank on 'Inside' Attack Against Royals' 'Outside'
    Power'," *T-U*, March 29, 1952; George Beahon, "It's Bob, Bob, Bob as
    Royals Top Lakers, 88–78, In Opener of Western Title Series; Mikan Hits
    47," *D&C*, March 30, 1952; George Beahon, "Lakers Topple Royals, 83 to
    78, In Overtime Thriller, Even Series," *D&C*, March 31, 1952; Pep Saul,
    telephone conversation with author, Nov. 27, 2009.
10 George Beahon, "They Must Win Tonight!: Minneapolis Defeats
    Royals, 77–67 To Take Lead in Division Playoff," *D&C*, April 6, 1952;
    "When you shut out": Bill Carlson, "Royals' Davies Held Scoreless,"
    Minneapolis Sunday Tribune, April 6, 1952.
11 "If you're": "Bobby Bows Out: Fans Bid Farewell To Davies Saturday,"
    RRSHOF 1954–55 Season.

12   Charlie Wagner, "Ex-Mate Saul Helps Oust Royals from NBA Playoffs; Pollard's Bucket Decides," *T-U*, April 7, 1952.

13   Anderson, "His Career," *Miami Herald*, April 6, 1980; Imee B. Roberts, General Mills Consumer Services, e-mail message to author, Jan. 6, 2009; "Champions are made, not born," General Mills Wheaties TV commercial W-118 (Oct. 1, 1954), courtesy of General Mills Archives, Minneapolis, MN; John Dunning, *On the Air: The Encyclopedia of Old-Time Radio*, 243–44; http://fatherknowsbest.com; Bernard Weinraub, "Dousing the Glow Of TV's First Family; Time for the Truth About Ozzie and Harriet," *NYT*, June 18, 1998.

14   Susan Wakefield, General Mills Corporate Archivist, e-mail message to author, Jan. 8, 2014; "'Spark Up to get a clear shot!' says Bob Davies, Shooting Star Of The Rochester Royals," *Tarzan*, March 1954.

15   "Good friends for him…and mother, too…in Dell Comics!" *Saturday Evening Post*, Jan. 10, 1953, 90; Bob Bishop, telephone conversation with author, Jan. 13, 2010 (reviewed all March 1954 Dell comics back covers); Dick Davies, telephone conversation with author, Dec. 22, 2009; Mary Davies, telephone conversation with author, March 13, 2007; Measuring Worth; Bernard J. Mullin, Stephen Hardy and William A. Sutton, *Sport Marketing*, 3rd ed., 255; Sarah Skidmore, "23 years later, Air Jordans maintain mystique," *Seattle (WA) Times*, Jan. 10, 2008; Jack McCallum, "Air and Space: And the Brand Played On," *Sports Illustrated*, Nov. 7, 2005, 19.

   Bob Davies and 59 other players' individual cards are in the first Bowman Bubble Gum basketball card set issued in 1948. www.sportscards.info/Basketball/1948Bowman/1948Bowman.htm; "The Card Corner: Bob Davies," *Buffalo (NY) News*, Jan. 22, 1992.

16   http://cgi.ebay.com/1952-Bread-Energy-labels-PROOF-Strip-w-Bob-Davies; http://www.joplinglobe.com/local/.

17   "Knight Shows Promise As Royal Cage Rookie," *T-U*, Oct.13, 1952; Menville, *Harlem Globetrotters*, 185; Marques Haynes: George, *Elevating the Game*, 52–55; Shouler et al., *Total Basketball*, 143; Hubbard, *NBA Encyclopedia, 3rd ed.*, 594 (Knight).

18   "Edris Davies, Bob's Dad, Dies," *T-U*, Oct. 25, 1952; Dick Davies, telephone conversations with author, Jan. 29 and April 4, 2009; "He was": David Jones, "Meet The Davies: Davies inspired many with play," *Harrisburg Patriot-News*, Aug. 6, 2009.

19   George Beahon, "Lakers Tip Royals In Overtime, 83–80, For 3-Game
     Lead," *D&C*, Jan. 5, 1953; Glen Gaff, "Mikan Paces West to Win,"
     Minneapolis Tribune, Jan. 14, 1953; "friendly enemy": Bob Reed, "West
     All-Stars Nose Out East By 79–75," *Fort Wayne Journal-Gazette*, Jan. 14,
     1953; "Bob was": Wanzer, telephone conversation with author, Sept.
     15, 2014; Al C. Weber, "Davies' Spurt Wins for West All-Stars," and
     Matt Jackson, "Royal Touch: Davies, Wanzer, Risen Play Leading Roles
     In West Win," *T-U*, Jan., 14, 1953; "Kundla Banks on 'Enemy' Davies
     to Spring Upset," *Minneapolis Star*, Jan. 21, 1954; Matt Jackson, "Cage
     Classic: Bob Davies Was '53 Star But Premature Ballot Picked Mikan,"
     T-U, Jan. 20, 1954; Carl Weigman, "A Mere Six-Foot-One-Inch 'Giant'
     Cracks a Tight Game: Bob Davies Paces West Pro All-Stars," *Fort Wayne
     Journal-Gazette Special to the Evening News,* Jan. 14, 1953.
         Hampered by a bad back, Risen played 19 minutes as Mikan's
     backup, snared nine rebounds and scored five points.
20   Gould, *Pioneers of the Hardwood*, 206–7.
21   "It must": George Beahon, "In This Corner," *D&C*, Feb. 9, 1953.
22   Shouler et al., *Total Basketball,* 86–88; Neft and Cohen, *Sports
     Encyclopedia: Pro Basketball*, 5th ed., 105.
23   Dave Warner, "Ft. Wayne Defeats Royals For Division Playoff Lead In
     84-to-77 Arena Battle," *D&C*, March 21, 1953; Dave Warner, "Royals
     Jolt Zollners at Home, 83–71, To Knot Western Division Playoffs," *D&C*,
     March 23, 1953; Al C. Weber, "Royals Win Fight for Survival, Beat
     Zollners in Rough Contest," *T-U*, March 23, 1953; Ben Tenney, "Pistons
     Remain Hopeful Despite Setback," *Fort Wayne News-Sentinel*, March
     23, 1953; Dave Warner, "Zollners Oust Royals from Playoffs: Royals
     Drop Playoff 'Rubber Tilt' With Brian's Last Seconds Arena Shot, 67–65,"
     D&C, March 25, 1953; Ben Tenny, "Rhubarb in Rochester Quite a
     Hassle," *Fort Wayne News-Sentinel*, March 25, 1953.
24   Hubbard, *NBA Encyclopedia*, 3rd ed., 460; Red Auerbach, *On And Off
     the Court*, 18–19; "Davies can": incomplete clipping, RRSHOF 1954–55
     Season; Arata, ed., 2006–07 *Sacramento Kings Media Guide*, 142.
25   Cook, "Rochester Royals," *Rochester History* (Winter, 1996): 11, 13–14;
     http://basketball-reference.com; http//wiki.answers.com; Shouler et al.,
     Total Basketball, 323 (March 27, 1998 game).
26   "Royals to Mail Ticket Sale Letters," BDSHOF; "Davies Gives Royals

Spark And Spirit," *Minneapolis Laker News 1952–1953* (#5896), 19, LeBov Collection, Sacramento, CA; George Beahon, "Royals Defeat Hawks in 76–64 Contest As Risen Leads in Scoring, Rebounding," *D&C*, Dec. 16, 1953; Jack Buck, Bob Rains, and Bob Broeg, *Jack Buck: "That's a Winner,"* 75; "Ease the tension," Beech-Nut gum ad, BDSHOF.

27   "the best": Steve Gelman, *Bob Cousy: Magician Of Pro Basketball*, 76; Al C. Weber, "Rochester Trio Stars in Defeat Before 16, 478: East Edges West in Overtime Thriller," *T-U*, Jan. 22, 1954; George Beahon, "East Beats West in Overtime Tingler, 98–93, Before 16, 478 Fans as Cousy Breaks Loose," *D&C*, Jan. 22, 1954; Joseph M. Sheehan, "East Defeats West in Overtime Pro All-Star Game at Garden: 16,478 See Cousy Pace 98–93 Victory," *NYT*, Jan. 22, 1954; Devaney, *Bob Cousy*, 27–28, 111–15; Isaacs, *Vintage NBA*, 139–40; "NBA East-West All-Star All-Time Players Record," BDSHOF.

28   Paul Pinckney, "In the Pink," *D&C*, Dec. 13, 1953; http:/www. dumonthistory.tv/3.html; https://en.wikipedia.org/wiki/NBA_on_ DuMont; "Slow Start Hurts Warriors as Royals Triumph," *Philadelphia Inquirer*, Jan. 24, 1954; Glickman, *Fastest Kid*, 85; https://www.nba.com/ knicks/history/glickman 010107.html; "Royals Play Philly Here And on TV," RRSHOF 1953–54 Season; "Royals Hand Nats Third Straight Loss: Baltimore Here This Afternoon," *Syracuse Herald-American*, Feb. 14, 1954 (Royals' second DuMont Network appearance).

29   Roland Lazenby, *Jerry West: The Life And Legend Of A Basketball Icon*, 307; Koppett, *24 Seconds*,18, 67–70; Schumacher, *Mr. Basketball*, 154.

30   George Beahon, "Lakers Tip Royals In Overtime, 83–80, For 3-Game Lead," *D&C*, Jan. 5, 1953; Matt Jackson, "Still On Top: New Yorkers Talk Causes For Continued Success Of Injury-Hit Royals," *T-U*, Jan. 9, 1952; Salzberg, *Set Shot*, 56; Neft and Cohen, *Sports Encyclopedia: Pro Basketball*, 5th ed., 100.

31   "Bobby Davies was": David Jones, "Davies inspired many with play," *Harrisburg Patriot-News*, Aug. 6, 2009.

32   "You can't": Ed Frierson, telephone conversation with author, April 8, 2009; Dick Davies, telephone conversation with author, April 15, 2008; Red Auerbach with Joe Fitzgerald, *Red Auerbach On And Off The Court*, 7.

33   Shouler et al., *Total Basketball*, 91; Arata, ed., *2006–07 Sacramento Kings Media Guide*, 142.

34 Salzberg, *Set Shot*, 58; Bob Davies, interview by Charles Salzberg, Coral
    Springs, FL, 1986, tape recording and Bob Davies-edited transcript,
    Joseph M. O'Brien Historical Resource Center, Naismith Memorial
    Basketball Hall of Fame, Springfield, MA; Dave Warner, "Off to Good
    Start: Royals Topple Fort Wayne In Playoff Opener, 82–75," *D&C*,
    March 17, 1954; Dave Warner, "Royals Oust Zollners, 89 to 71; Open
    with Lakers Wednesday," *D&C*, March 22, 1954.

35 Bill Carlson, "Royals' Davies Big Worry for Lakers Here Tonight,"
    Minneapolis Sunday Tribune, Feb. 14, 1954; Dave Warner, "Royals Open
    Playoffs: Lakers Rip Royals, 89–76, As Mikan, Pollard Shine," *D&C*,
    March 25, 1954; Dave Warner, "Royals Defeat Lakers, 74–73, Invade
    Minneapolis," *D&C*, March 28, 1954; Dave Warner, "Lakers Erase
    Royals From Playoffs, 82–72," *D&C*, March 29, 1954.

36 "Bobby Davies Joins Boston Whirlwinds," *T-U,* July 20, 1954; Ike
    Shynook, "Trotters, Whirlwinds Win In Outdoor Cage Twin Bill,"
    D&C, Aug. 13, 1954; Paul Pinckney, "In the Pink," *D&C*, Aug. 15, 1954;
    Kyle Keiderling, *Shooting Star: The Bevo Francis Story,* 218–19; Clary,
    Basketball's Great Moments, 58–62; Wolff, *One Hundred Years,* 88; "The
    hell": Abe Saperstein to Bob Davies, Nov. 27, 1954, BDSHOF.

37 "one of": Bud Leavitt, "Boston Celtics And Rochester Begin Five Game
    Maine Series Tonight On Houlton Court At 8:30 PM," *Bangor (ME) Daily
    News*, Oct. 12, 1953; Reynolds, *Cousy*, 135–36; Arnold "Red" Auerbach,
    Basketball For The Player, The Fan And The Coach, 187 ("Strategic Move
    #11: Grabbing or pulling the pants or shirt of the opponent can be very
    aggravating.").

FAREWELL TOUR

1954–55 SEASON

BEFORE THE 1954–55 NBA SEASON COMMENCED, TWO OF THE early NBA Big Three superstars, 30-year-old George Mikan and 32-year-old Jumping Joe Fulks, retired. Bob Davies, 34 and still going strong, had to cope with a schedule of 72 games in 135 days, some in out-of-the-way localities. Striving to interest fans in NBA basketball and increase gate receipts, the Royals played 12 games in non-league communities such as Saratoga Springs and Endicott, New York; Hershey, Pennsylvania; Toledo, Ohio; and Spencer, Iowa.[1]

"Little Bobby Wanzer" was replacing Bob Davies as the face of the Royals franchise. Wanzer's picture appeared on the front cover of *This Week Magazine*, the Sunday supplement tucked into 36 newspapers coast to coast with a total circulation of almost 11 million. In the article entitled "Wanzer's a Wizard," writer Bob Shoemaker called him "the most valuable man on the Royals squad" and praised his set shooting, surprising rebounding for his size, and defensive tenacity, especially against Bob Cousy. "The guy's a pest," said the Cooz, perhaps recalling the game in which Wanzer scored 30 points and held him to two field goals.[2]

Ten-year-old Jimmy Davies debuted as the Royals water boy—a season-long highlight for his father. Bob presented Jimmy with a Royals warm-up jacket numbered 7. "Seven," Bob would say, "come eleven." On his part, Jimmy acted very professionally and refrained from commenting about his father's performance, whether good, bad, or indifferent. Jimmy said, "Nice game, Daddy," when the Royals won, or "Too bad you had to lose, Daddy," when they lost.[3]

The Royals' opening game on October 30, 1954, is a very significant one in basketball history. Appropriately, the NBA's two greatest ball handlers, Bob Davies and Bob Cousy, opposed each other in the first regular season game in which the 24-second shot rule applied. With fans turned off by boring stalling exhibitions, such as a Zollners 19–17 victory over the Lakers, the Royals' six-overtime and four-overtime marathons against the Olympians and Knicks, and the Celtics holding the ball to prevent the Royals from surpassing the Celtics' NBA single-game scoring record (Commissioner Podoloff fined Red Auerbach $100 for making "a mockery of the game"), the NBA adopted the rule that forced a team to shoot the ball within 24 seconds or lose possession of it. NBC-TV, with Lindsey Nelson doing the play-by-play, broadcast the game over 110 stations. Neither team lost the ball due to a shot clock violation. Wanzer scored 25 points and limited Cousy to four field goals as Davies netted 13 points. The Royals won, 98–95.[4]

The moment that signaled the end of the professional basketball trail for Bob Davies occurred in an unforgiving venue: Syracuse, New York. Known for shaking backboard guy wires as visiting players attempted foul shots, mixing into player fights, and terrorizing referees, Nats supporters reveled in their rowdy reputation. A character nicknamed "The Gorilla" tried to intimidate visiting players. A fan had once confronted Bob Davies and told him not to expect to leave the arena alive if the Royals won.[5]

In the 13th game of the 1954–55 season, Bob Davies, taunted by raucous Nats fans, scored a pitiful two points. Commenting on this lackluster performance, *Syracuse-Herald Journal* sports columnist Jack Slattery commented that it was sad to see how far "the once great Bobby Davies has faded. The fans of short memory jeered him for his ineffective play.... Davies has been one of the most colorful players in the game's history.... But without guys like him we couldn't get anyone into the auditoriums. He's always been a great competitor.... It just doesn't seem right to hear the fans hoot at a fellow who has done the things Davies has accomplished."[6]

Three days later Bob announced his retirement from the NBA

effective the end of the season. He had deep needs to compete, excel, and win. He had played on undefeated Edison Junior High School, Franklin & Marshall, Seton Hall, and Sub Chaser Training Center teams. Now, he had relinquished his starting role, and the Royals were losing more games than they were winning. Adjusting to defeat was too painful. He felt terrible after each loss and, unrealistically, vowed never to lose again. He could no longer take charge and control a game. Basketball was no longer fun for him.[7]

Wife Mary, expecting their third child, rejoiced at his retirement decision. "Bob will be home every night," she said. "It'll be wonderful. This basketball is no kind of life for a family man."[8]

"It's nice to see Bobby get out of the game as a competitor while he's still an outstanding performer," commented *Rochester Times-Union* sports columnist Matt Jackson. "There's nothing quite so pathetic as watching a great sports performer stay in the game until the customers start telling him it's time to quit."[9]

"We will be sorry to see Bobby leave us;" said Les Harrison, "but I think he is making the right move…. I would like to emphasize that the decision to retire was strictly Bobby's. We would have liked to have him with us as long as he would stay."[10]

The next home game Davies proved that he still had enough gas in his tank to compete at the NBA level. "Bob Davies," exclaimed a Rochester sports writer, "was the whirling dervish of old. He set up plays, played solid defense, stole the ball and made himself generally a nuisance." Upon leaving the game, a 105–78 whipping of the Syracuse Nationals, Bob, who scored 12 points, received a tremendous ovation.[11]

On Christmas night 1954, Bob Davies, in his opinion, played the best game of his decade-long professional career. The Zollners had defeated the Royals five of their last six games, including three straight in Edgerton Park Sports Arena. Bob's pride would not allow him to lose four consecutive times at home to an archrival like the Zollners or Lakers. But, at half-time, the listless Royals trailed, 39–27. Starting the second half, Bob Davies scored eight and Jack Coleman seven points as the Royals made a 17–2 run. When the Zollners pulled within three points in the fourth period, Bob contributed his best assist—a backhand feed for a lay-up. Caught guarding high-scoring 6' 5", 195-pound Hall of Fame forward George Yardley, Bob spun him around with a stiff arm. In an 80–73 victory, Bob tallied 25 points. "I thought it might have been one of my best games," said Bob. "But it's hard to judge when you're playing. Some of my teammates told me it was my greatest game"[12]

As the season progressed, venerable Bob Davies adjusted masterfully to the 24-second shot clock. In a New Year's Day game, the Warriors, in the fourth quarter, rallied within two points of the Royals. As the shot clock ticked down to two seconds, Bob, "a great favorite in Philadelphia," held the ball and, with nobody open for a pass, swished a long set shot. Less than a minute later, again with two seconds to shoot, he looked boxed in, but made an offbalance lay-up. His long set shot clinched the Royals' victory with seconds left in the game. The next night, with two and a half minutes remaining and the Royals trailing the Lakers by three points, Bob sank a free throw, then passed for two buckets, and finally stole the ball to seal a two-point victory.[13]

Midway through his final professional basketball season, legendary Bob Davies still had the right stuff to set a landmark NBA record. On January 22, 1955, in Edgerton Park Sports Arena, he became the first NBA playmaker to distribute 20 assists in a game. Ironically, he accomplished this feat against Bob Cousy and the Boston Celtics. No TV cameras or ESPN pundits, however, memorialized his historic performance. Hampered by a knee injury, Cousy played only in the first half, but did help prevent Davies from crashing into a wall following a drive to the basket. Playing all but three minutes in the first three quarters, Davies, sporting an ugly-looking black eye and using "eyes in the back of his head," garnered 18 assists. After an eight-minute rest in the fourth quarter, he notched his 20th assist with 25 seconds remaining in the game. He scored 25 points and converted 17 free throws, eclipsing Mikan's Edgerton Park Sports Arena single-game free throw record, in a 121–110 Royals victory.[14]

The national media overlooked Davies' milestone achievement. *Sports Illustrated*, *Sport*, *Newsweek*, and *Time* magazines did not mention it. *The New York Times* published the game box score without assist totals, and the *Chicago Tribune* listed only the game score. A

Boston Globe article mentioned Davies' feat in the fourth paragraph. But the *Los Angeles Times,* under the headline "Rochester Cage Star Breaks Assists Record," reported that "Veteran Bob Davies ... hung up a new (NBA) record for assists when he was credited with 20." Tinseltown would have loved the Harrisburg Houdini.[15]

DAVIES VS. COUSY

The two greatest ball handlers of their time, Bob Davies and Bob Cousy, definitely appreciated each other's skills. "He had no weakness," commented Cousy about Davies. "He had such imagination and control—the perfect playmaker." In Davies' opinion, Cousy was the quickest thinker and best dribbler in the NBA, and it was very difficult to steal the ball from him.[16]

It is difficult to compare Davies and Cousy because their styles of play were so different, and they rarely played each other head to head. Except for Cousy's rookie season, Davies usually guarded Sharman, and Wanzer hounded Cousy. Slashing driver Davies took more of a physical beating and missed more games due to injury; Cousy played 316 consecutive games until a knee injury sidelined him for one game halfway through his fifth NBA season. Cousy utilized a foul-line jump shot in addition to an outside one-hand push shot and a variety of drives. Davies shot long-range two-hand set shots or drove to the basket. Cousy controlled the ball while Sharman ran around screens and tried to get open for a pass from Cousy. On the other hand, the Royals' guards shared playmaking duties. Holzman, Wanzer, and McMahon, as well as forward Jack Coleman, could efficiently initiate the offense. As Hall of Fame point guard New York Knick Walt "Clyde" Frazier has pointed out, the top assist makers have to handle the ball "a lot." After the opposing team took a shot, Davies blocked out his man, but Cousy usually ran to an open space for an outlet pass to start a fast break. Unquestionably, Davies, who often tried to steal the ball, defended better than Cousy. A Rochester sportswriter labeled Cousy "Mr. Nolo Contendere" defensively. Later in his career, Cousy, when he lost or left his man, relied on the great Celtics center Bill Russell to block his man's shot or intimidate him from shooting.[17]

Cousy, who played in a higher scoring era and controlled and shot the ball more than Davies did, posted the better career offensive statistics. During Davies' first NBL season, teams averaged 50.9 points per 40-minute game. During Cousy's first NBA season, teams averaged 84.1 points per 48 minute game, and, during his last season, 115 PPG. The widening of the foul lane from 6 to 12 feet beginning with the 1951–52 season opened up more space for guards to penetrate. During the five seasons they both played in the NBA, Cousy and Davies respectively took 18.32 and 12.75 shots per game, a difference of five and a half more attempts by Cousy. Over their NBA careers, Cousy averaged 18.4 points and 7.5 assists per game and Davies 14.3 PPG and 4.9 APG. Davies converted .378 of his field goal attempts, improving two percentage points after the NBA switched from a leather ball with a valve tucked under latex-covered rawhide laces to a molded and pebbled ball, and Cousy converted .375. Cousy made .803 of his foul shots to .759 for Davies.[18]

Another way to compare Davies and Cousy is to evaluate their teams' performances when Davies played with Hall of Fame center Arnie Risen (1947–55) and Cousy with Hall of Fame center "Easy Ed" Macauley (1950–56). Macauley was the better scorer and Risen the better rebounder; neither was a shot blocker. Risen was selected for the All-NBA Second Team once, ranked fourth, ninth, and tenth in league scoring once each, and fourth and ninth in rebounding twice and seventh once. Macauley was named to the All-NBA First Team three times and ranked third and fourth in league scoring twice each and eighth and tenth once and ninth in rebounding once. Competing against the George Mikan-Minneapolis Lakers dynasty, the Royals won an NBA championship, as well as posted the best NBA regular season record twice and tied for best once. The Cousy-Macauley Celtics were perennial bridesmaids in the weaker eastern division except for one third-place finish and were eliminated from the playoffs three times in the opening round and three times in the division final. The Royals won 18 and the Celtics 17 of the 35 regular-season games in which both Davies and Cousy participated.[19]

Some observers rated Bob Davies a better player than Bob Cousy.

Lee Williams, former director of the Naismith Memorial Basketball Hall of Fame, observed both Davies and Cousy in their prime. "Place

Cousy as high as you want," said Williams, "because he was a great player. Don't take anything away from Cousy, but just think of it this way: as good as Cousy was, Davies was better. He could do everything Cousy could do, and he was better in a couple of departments."[20]

Hall of Fame college coach Bob Knight rates Bob Davies as great as any player in his era, and better than Cousy. In Knight's opinion, Davies was the best guard to play basketball before Sam Jones, Oscar Robertson, and Jerry West.[21]

"I'd take Davies over Cousy any time," said 1952 NBA Co-Rookie of the Year William "Tosh" Tosheff, who guarded both men three seasons. "Cousy had big guys blocking for him. Davies only had one guy—Arnie Johnson. And Davies could back door you. Cousy couldn't play defense."[22]

Naismith Memorial Basketball Hall of Fame inductee Ben Kerner, who observed NBL, BAA, and NBA basketball as owner of the Tri-Cities Black Hawks, Milwaukee Hawks, St. Louis Hawks and Atlanta Hawks, called Davies the "first superstar of basketball," the "pioneer of playmaking," and the "best backcourt man" he had ever seen.[23]

Cementing his reputation, Bob Davies, in his third NBC and sixth and last nationally televised game, netted three field goals in a five-minute overtime period and finished the game with 21 points and 10 assists, but the Royals lost to the Lakers, 107–104.[24]

FAREWELL TOUR

"When Bob announced his retirement," recalled Les Harrison in 1990, "everyplace we played that last season paid their respects to him. There are a lot of those retirement deals now, but Bobby's was the first."[25]

In Fort Wayne, owner Fred Zollner on Piston Appreciation Day presented "Veteran Bob Davies," sporting another black eye, a plaque in appreciation for ten years of brilliant basketball and fine entertainment.[26]

In Syracuse, the Nats Ladies' Fan Club, more genteel than their male counterparts, presented Bob a traveling bag. "[T]he league has known few players with more color and greater ability to pack the fans in the seats," wrote a Syracuse columnist. "True, many came to hurl abuse on Davies because he represented the enemy. But no honest minded fan of basketball will deny that Bob has provided some of the greatest thrills one can find in pro basketball. It's the spectacular performers like Davies and Bob Cousy who have thrilled thousands of fans and helped bring professional basketball from a barnstorming, one-night stand kind of thing to the major league status it enjoys today.... He'll be missed."[27]

New York City columnist Leonard Lewin paid tribute to legendary Bob Davies in a Knicks game program article entitled "This May Be Davies' Garden Farewell":

Another great basketball player is preparing to fire his last shot before Father Time's buzzer sounds. George Mikan became the first of the modern super-stars to hang 'em up. Now it's Bobby Davies' turn....

Nobody ever created more excitement in his Garden debut than Davies did that night. Cousy still startles people with what he does, even though they've seen him do it so many times. So you can imagine the reaction to Davies' antics in an era when such a thing was unheard of....

But no one who saw it will ever forget Davies' Garden debut. Just like no one who saw Joe DiMaggio's first major league game, or Ty Cobb's, or even Willie Mays', will ever forget it. The start and finish of careers like Davies' are monuments erected only for the sports greats....

You'd never know that Davies is the grand old man of the game. Yes, older than Fred Scolari and Jim Pollard [both 32]. Yet, he looks and plays like a kid. That's because he has never lost the one thing that distinguishes the class from the rest of the field—desire. The best you can wish any basketball player is to hope that some day he might become another Bob Davies.[28]

Midway through the fourth quarter of a Royals–Knicks doubleheader game in Boston Garden, Celtics owner Walter Brown realized that Bob Davies probably would never again play in the Bay City because it was unlikely that the Royals and Celtics would meet in the playoff final round. Brown considered announcing Bob's retirement at the end of the game, but then, because Bob, who scored 23 points, was playing so well, instructed the public address announcer to mention his retirement during a timeout. Bob received a three-minute standing ovation. Gentleman Celtic owner Walter Brown described the applause as "a great tribute to a great player."[29]

Laker Nation also appreciated the legendary Bob Davies. A writer for the *Minneapolis Laker News*, in an article entitled "Davies Will Be Missed," stated that he was "as personable a fellow as ever walked the pro court," never "failed to excite the crowd when he got in the game," and few were his equal in igniting a rally, but "probably nobody in the paid ranks [apparently unaware of Mikan's greetings from hostile fans on the road] had been alternately booed and cheered as much as Bob. Fans either love him or hate him."[30]

In Rochester, Bob Davies Appreciation Night attracted the largest Edgerton Park Sports Arena crowd of the season, a mere 2,932 (70 percent of capacity) admirers. During the half-time ceremony, Les Harrison retired Bob's Royal jersey number 11 (it now hangs from the Sacramento Kings Arena rafters); the NBA presented him a gold basketball; and Bobby Wanzer gave him a plaque and clock from his teammates. "To me," said Wanzer, "he was always, in essence, a complete team player. With him the team came first. That's why I think we had such a fine record."[31]

"Thanks for ten years of loyalty," said Bob, the only active player remaining from the Royals' 1945–46 NBL championship team. "And a very special thanks to Les Harrison for bringing me to Rochester. My wife and sons always will remember you." Bob always expressed gratitude for the opportunities that basketball provided him. "How could I have ever come so far," he reflected, "been able to have met so many wonderful people and have helped my family without basketball?"

Playing about half the game, Davies turned in a credible performance. He scored 12 points, making four of seven attempts from the floor and four of five from the free throw line. Just before he fouled out with a minute and a half to play, Bob dished out an assist to give his team a three-point lead. The Royals defeated the Celtics, 105–103.[32]

Not missing a game and averaging 25 minutes per contest, sixth man Bob Davies ranked third on the Royals in scoring average with

Rochester Royals owner Les Harrison retired Bob's number 11 with wife Mary and son Jimmy, the Royals ball boy, by his side. (March 13, 1955, Courtesy of Mary Davies)

12.1 points (only a bucket and change below his NBA career 14.3 average) and first in assists with 4.9 per game (his NBA career average). His .415 FGM percentage was the best of his NBA career. Despite numerous injuries, he retired holding the combined NBL-NBA most regular-season games played record of 569 games.[33]

PLAYOFFS

The third-place Royals, who won 29 games and lost 43 (their first losing season and the struggling eight-team NBA's second worst record), faced the second place "Mikan-less" Lakers in the western division opening playoff series. Sports reporter Don Riley wrote that "yellow-haired Bob Davies will be the oldest man on the court tonight" and continued, this "veteran of the tough professional basketball wars is the man around whom Rochester will rally as he makes his last stand in the National Basketball Association…. But he's far from over the hill. The gent who has been described as 'the coach on the floor' and the 'best blue-chip player in the business' is still averaging 12 points per game.... His feared set shots, far beyond the realm of percentage guarding, and his brilliant passing and floor generalship, have left behind an enviable record."[34]

"You never know what to expect of Davies," said Lakers coach John Kundla, recalling Bob's neat give-and-go bucket earlier in the season with 15 seconds left in overtime that cinched a Royals victory. "On a good night he can probably still do more things better than any man in the league. He's brainy and he's a mean competitor. I have a hunch since this is his swan song he'll shoot the works. He has to be rated with the all time pro greats and we've got to be ready to handle him." But Davies, Risen, and Coleman played poorly, and the Royals lost, 82–78.[35]

Back in Rochester before only 2,280 Royals fans for his last home game, Bob Davies swished five set shots in five minutes and sparked a third quarter rally in contributing to a 94–92 victory. But the Royals lost the deciding game in Minneapolis with Bob scoring eight points, and his professional basketball career ended away from home on a negative note.[36]

THE DAVIES LEGEND

As the curtain fell on the greatest ten years in Rochester sports history, journalist Ralph Hyman, who had written a three-part series about Bob's life in the *Times-Union*, summarized the legendary "Davies Story":

> There are the John Barrymores of the theater, the Cole Porters in music, the Ernest Hemingways in writing, the Joe DiMaggios in baseball. They were all a little better in their trade than most. Davies belongs in this category.
>
> He made the great play without thinking about it. His movement on the court was a thing of beauty. He would throw the bounce pass and his man would be there. He would flick a set shot in from near half-court, breaking his competitor's spirit. He thrilled the spectator and left him limp.
>
> This man—Davies—was one of the game's all-time greats.[37]

NOTES

1   Hubbard, *NBA Encyclopedia*, 3rd ed., 503 (Fulks), 649 (Mikan); Arata, ed., *2006–2007 Sacramento Kings Media Guide*, 143.

2   "Little Bobby" and "The guy's": Bob Shoemaker, "Wanzer's A Wizard," *This Week Magazine*, March 13, 1955, 23; *N. W. Ayer & Sons Directory of Newspapers and Periodicals* (1955), 722 (10,899,759); "Wanzer Scores 30 As Royals Whip Celts," *T-U*, Feb. 2, 1953; "Royals Thump Celtics, 109–86, on Foul Strategy," *D&C*, Feb. 2, 1953.

3   "Seven": Jim Davies, telephone conversation with author, Sept. 18, 2011; "Nice game": Ralph Hyman, "Davies Story: Ike Will Be Coach Davies' Neighbor," *T-U*, March 13, 1955.

4   George Beahon, "Off on Right Foot: Royals Tip Celtics, 98–95, In Opening NBA Contest," *D&C*, Oct. 31, 1954; "Knicks Lose By 102–92: Beaten by Royals' Quintet in Fourth Overtime Period," *NYT*, Jan. 24, 1951; "Punishment by Podoloff: Auerbach Draws Fine of $100 For Stall in Celtic-Royal Tiff," *D&C*, Jan. 9, 1952; "Royals Edge Celts With Late Fouls," *Boston Sunday Post*, Oct. 31, 1954; Lindsey Nelson, *Hello Everybody, I'm Lindsey Nelson*, 260–61.

5   Jack Andrews, "Nats Down Royals in Torrid Contest, 82–78: Schayes Sinks 24 to Spark Syracuse Club," *Syracuse Post-Standard*, Dec. 3, 1954; Jack Newcombe, "Old Pro From Syracuse," *Sport*, April 1952, 49; Salzberg, *Set Shot*, 56.

6   "the once": Jack Slattery, "Highlighting Sports," *Syracuse Herald-Journal*, Dec. 5, 1954.

7   Al C. Weber, "Finish: Davies Will retire From Royals For Coaching Job next Season," *T-U*, Dec. 6, 1954; Salzberg, *Set Shot*, 58.

8   "Bob will be": Bill Pulsifer, "Davies' New Home Adjacent to Golf Course: Husband's Plans Please Mary Davies," BDSHOF.

9   "It's nice": Matt Jackson, "End of Trail… A Great Pro, Our Own Bobby, to Retire At Season's End," *T-U*, Dec. 6, 1954.

10 "We will be": Al C. Weber, "Davies Will Retire from Royals For Coaching Job Next Season," *T-U*, Dec. 6, 1954.

11 "Bob Davies": Al C. Weber, "Trail by 13 Points, Win by 27: Royals Do Job, Smothering Nats," *T-U*, Dec. 9, 1954.

12 "I thought": Dave Warner, "Davies' Brilliant Play Paces Royals To 80–73 Arena Win over Zollners," *D&C*, Dec. 26, 1954.

13 "Royals 3d Period Drive Brings Victory Over Warriors, 96–92,"
    Philadelphia Inquirer, Jan. 2, 1955; "Break Minneapolis Jinx: Royals' Win
    over Lakers Fifth in Last Six Games," *T-U,* Jan. 3, 1955; "Royals Win,
    102–100, on Spears' Basket, Ending 9-Game Lakers' Victory Streak,"
    D&C, Jan. 3, 1955.

14 George Beahon, "Davies Sets Assist Record as Royals Win, 121–110: Old
    Pro Records 20, Plus 25 Points," *D&C,* Jan. 23, 1955.

15 "Pat on the Back," "Pro Basketball at Midseason" and "Scoreboard,"
    Sports Illustrated, Jan. 24, 1955, 1, 46–49 and 59; "Hotbox" and
    "Scoreboard," *Sports Illustrated,* Jan. 31, 1955, 2 and 61; *Newsweek,* Jan. 31,
    1955, 64–65; "Sports," *Time,* Jan. 31, 1955, 56–57; "National Basketball
    Association At Rochester," *NYT,* Jan. 23, 1955; "Pro Basketball standings:
    yesterday's scores," *Chicago Tribune,* Jan. 23, 1955; "Cousy Used
    Sparingly as Celts Lose, 121–110," *Boston Globe,* Jan. 23, 1955; "Rochester
    Cage Star Breaks Assist Record (AP)," *Los Angeles Times,* Jan. 23, 1955.
    The modern single game assists record is 30 set by the Orlando
    Magic's Scott Skiles on Dec. 30, 1990. http://www.basketball-reference.
    com/leagues/stats.html.

16 "He had": Zander Hollander, ed., *Pro Basketball Encyclopedia,* 200;
    Salzberg, *Set Shot,* 53; George Beahon, "Ashcan Hoop Started Davies,"
    RRSHOF 1953–54 season.

17 Bob Davies, interview by Charles Salzberg, Coral Springs, FL, 1986,
    tape recording and Bob Davies-edited transcript, Joseph M. O'Brien
    Historical Resource Center, Naismith Memorial Basketball Hall of Fame,
    Springfield, MA; Jack Barry, "Cousy to Face Philly, See Limited Service,"
    Boston Sunday Globe, Jan. 23, 1955; Frazier, *Rockin' Steady,* 64; "Mr. Nolo
    Contendere": George Beahon, "In This Corner," *D&C,* March 2, 1955.

18 http://www.basketball-reference.com/leagues/NBA_stats.html.

19 Hubbard, NBA *Encyclopedia,* 3rd ed., 451 (Cousy), 461 (Davies), 621
    (Macauley); 714 (Risen); Shouler et al., *Total Basketball,* 74–97, 376.

20 "Place Cousy": Garry Brown, "The Morning Line: Who's Bob Davies?"
    Springfield (MA) Union, Feb. 4, 1970.

21 David Jones, "Meet The Davies: Davies inspired many with play,"
    Harrisburg Patriot-News, Aug. 6, 2009.

22 "I'd take": Bill Tosheff, telephone conversation with author, Nov. 30,
    2009; Isaacs, *Vintage NBA,* 175.

23   Hubbard, *NBA Encyclopedia, 3rd ed.*, 783; Garry Brown, "Morning Line," *Springfield Union*, Feb. 4, 1970; Goldaper, *Great Moments*, 29.

24   Dave Warner, "Lakers Take Overtime Win by 107 to 104," *D&C*, March 6, 1955; "Rochester Gets 2 Cage Games of 18 on NBA TV Program," RRSHOF 1954–55 Season.
    Davies scored 15 points in his second NBC and fifth national TV appearance. "Kerr, Kenville Provide Spark in Nats' Victory," *Syracuse Post-Standard*, Nov. 21, 1954..

25   "When Bob": Bob Matthews, "Royals star Bob Davies was innovator," *T-U*, April 24, 1990.

26   "Weary Royals Again Bow To Fort Wayne, 105–84," *D&C*, Jan. 24, 1955; "Pistons Win Easily, 105–84, In Appreciation Day Game," *Fort Wayne Journal-Gazette*, Jan. 24, 1955.

27   "Royals at Syracuse: Net Fans Will Honor Bobby Davies," *T-U*, Feb. 24, 1955; "[T]he league": Jack Slattery, "Highlighting Sports," *Syracuse Herald-Journal*, Feb. 24, 1955; Jack Andrews, "Nationals Explode in Final Period to Beat Royals, 97 to 83: Victory Lifts Division Lead To Four Games," *Syracuse Post-Standard*, Feb. 25, 1955 (Davies scored four points); "Nats Outspeed Royals for 97–83 Win, 7th Victory in 8 Contests on Season," *D&C*, Feb. 25, 1955.

28   "Another great": Leonard Lewin, "This May Be Davies' Garden Farewell," BDSHOF; William J. Briordy, "Knicks Triumph Over Rochester: They Score 32 Points in 4th Period to Win, 101–96, on Garden Court," *NYT*, March 7, 1955 (Davies scored two points).

29   "Royals Lose to Knicks, 95–92; Face Lakers at Arena Today," *D&C*, March 5, 1955; Joe Looney, "Celtics Routed, 121–106: Ramsey Nets 24; Knicks Win, Land in Second Place," *Boston Herald*, March 5, 1955; Nick Del Ninno, "Brown Unleashes Blast At Celtics," *Boston Traveler*, March 5, 1955; "a great": Walter A. Brown to Les Harrison, March 8, 1955, BDSHOF.

30   "as personable," "failed to," and "probably nobody": "Davies Will Be Missed," *Minneapolis Laker News: Philadelphia vs. Minneapolis* (1955), 35, LeBov Collection, Sacramento, CA.

31   Dave Warner, "Royals Defeat Celts, 105–103, Before 2, 932," *D&C*, March 14, 1955; "To me": Pete Reinwald, "Rochester Royals' Davies dies; NBA Hall-of-Famer was 70," *D&C*, April 24, 1990.

32 "Thanks for": Dave Warner, "Royals Defeat Celts, 105–103, Before 2, 932,"
    D&C, March 14, 1955; "How could": Dave Warner, "Bobby Bows Out:
    Fans Bid Farewell To Davies Saturday," BDSHOF.

33 Arata, ed., *2006–07 Sacramento Kings Media Guide*, 143; Hubbard, *NBA
    Encyclopedia, 3rd ed.*, 460; Shouler et al., *Total Basketball*, 543.

34 "yellow-haired": Don Riley, "Royals' Star In Last Stand Tonight—Lakers
    Fear Davies," *St. Paul (MN) Pioneer Press*, March 16, 1955.

35 "You never": Don Riley, "Royals' Star In Last Stand Tonight—Lakers
    Fear Davies," *St. Paul (MN) Pioneer Press*, March 16, 1955; "Royals Tip
    Lakers, 99–97, In Buffalo Overtime Fray," *D&C*, Dec. 16, 1954; "Lakers
    Beat Royals, 82–78, Take Lead in Playoffs," *D&C*, March 17, 1955.

36 Dave Warner, "Royals Rally to Trip Lakers, 94–92, Play Rubber Tilt
    Tonight at St. Paul," *D&C*, March 19, 1955; Al C. Weber, "Still Alive as
    Lakers Found Out: Royals Seek 2d Clutch Win to Survive," *T-U*, March
    19, 1955; "Lakers Oust Royals from Playoffs With 119–110 Victory in 3rd
    Game," *D&C*, March 20, 1955.

37 "There are": Ralph Hyman, "The Davies Story: Bob Forsook Baseball for
    Cage Career," *T-U*, March 11, 1955.

LIFE OFF THE COURT

BEFORE BOB DAVIES RETIRED AS A PLAYER IN MARCH 1954, LES Harrison offered him the Royals coaching job, but Bob turned it down because he and Mary believed that his absences on road trips would be too detrimental to their family life. The young couple wanted to reside close to Bob's widowed mother in Harrisburg, Pennsylvania, and Mary's parents in nearby York, and Bob hoped to work with young people at a small college and instill in them religious values. Lutheran-affiliated Gettysburg College in Central Pennsylvania satisfied their criteria. Bob accepted an assistant professorship of physical education and coaching position. After 13 years residing in apartments, Mary and Bob looked forward to living the American middle-class dream life in a custom-built, split-level house overlooking a golf course.[1]

But Bob's super-competitiveness and religious idealism clashed in his new position. He had retired from professional basketball partly because the Royals were losing more games than they were winning. He did not adjust well to coaching a small college basketball team with limited talent that lost 30 games and won 18 in two seasons. He practiced with the second team against the starters and, on one occasion, in frustration, punted the ball into the rafters and left the gym. The Gettysburg College athletic director admonished him for arguing with referees during games.[2]

And Bob's other coaching assignments were not satisfying. He had never played soccer or even seen a game, and his Gettysburg Booters in two seasons won five, lost 14, and tied one game. "He stayed about three pages ahead of his players in a book," recalled Mary. An unorthodox, one-handicap golfer and two-time New York State Amateur Golf Tournament qualifier, Bob fared better coaching the links team to 15 wins and 20 losses in three seasons.[3]

Oldest son Jimmy caddied for President Dwight D. "Ike" Eisenhower, who owned a farm near Gettysburg. When Ike was president, Jimmy and three other caddies for the foursome ran alongside the president's blue Cushman golf cart, about 75-yards behind two secret service agents on each side of the fairway carrying golf club bags with three or four clubs and a rifle butt sticking out. Golfers ahead on the course stepped aside, and Ike always thanked them for their courtesy in allowing him to play through. After Ike retired from the Oval Office, he liked to play in mid or late afternoon after most caddies had gone home. A club official would call Jimmy, who lived nearby, and he would hustle to the first tee. Jimmy rode alone in the cart with Ike driving, and without any secret service protection.[4]

The Davies loved their bucolic life style, but it was difficult for a family of five to subsist on Bob's $4,000 ($33,600 today) annual salary. Chuck Taylor conducted a basketball clinic at Gettysburg College and offered Bob a job he could not refuse as a Converse sneaker sales and promotion representative, at almost double his academic annual salary, $7,500 ($63,100 in today's money), a new leased Oldsmobile every year, and an expense account. [5]

It is ironic that in his 27-year career with Converse, Bob Davies probably spent more time away from his family than he would have as an NBA coach. His first sales area covered Pennsylvania, New Jersey, Delaware, Washington, DC, Maryland, and part of New York state. He left home Monday morning, returned Thursday evening, and processed paperwork on Friday. When he was home, the family always ate dinner in the dining room because it was a "very special" occasion, comparable to Sunday dinner for many families at that time. On the road, he checked store inventories and took orders, called on college and high school coaches, and conducted basketball clinics. A child of the Depression, he skipped breakfast, ate fast food for lunch, and enjoyed a good dinner on his expense account, often entertaining

Bob Davies worked twenty-seven years for Converse as a sales and promotion representative among other duties conducting basketball clinics. (Courtesy of Mary Davies)

a customer. Whenever possible, he turned in a "business" round of golf. When Converse needed a southeastern states area representative, he took over that territory, taking two six-week trips a year. [6]

"Davies was one of the most genteel individuals I've ever had the pleasure of knowing," said Bill Bolton, a fellow Converse sales rep. [7]

"Bob Davies was quite the gentleman," recalled customer Jerry Phipps. "I thought a lot of him. He was a good soul. I always enjoyed talking with him. He didn't talk about himself. You would never know meeting him he was the kind of player he was."[8]

Traveling his sales territory, Bob stayed in touch with old friends. In Harrisburg, he called on former John Harris High School African-American star Dick Felton, whose style of play had influenced him. In New Jersey, he visited former Seton Hall Athletic Director James Carey in his parish and former Pirates player Whitey Macknowski, the basketball coach at Drew University. In Maryland, often with sons in tow, Bob enjoyed pizza with Baltimore sportswriter Seymour Smith. In New York state, he called on West Point basketball coach Bob Knight and former LIU coach Clair Bee. Visiting Rochester, he took Les Harrison on business trips and assisted Al Cervi in his basketball camps. [9]

Bob enjoyed combining his job and love of sports. An AP photo showed him dressed in a business suit in the Yankee Stadium left field stands during the 1957 World Series, catching a home-run ball bare-handed. He promoted Converse products at major sports events, including the Montreal Olympics and several NCAA Eastern Regional, NIT, and Atlantic Coast Conference (ACC) basketball tournaments.[10]

Briefly back on the basketball court, Bob competed in Old-Timers Games held in conjunction with NBA All-Star Games. Two years after his retirement from the Royals, he was co-high scorer with ten points in the first NBA Old-Timers Game in 1957. Seven years later, *Boston Globe* sportswriter Cliff Keane noted that 44-year-old Bob, the oldest participant in the second NBA Old-Timers Game, was one of the best conditioned "gaffers" on the court. Bob unleashed his legendary 30-foot set shot and, like in the old days, back-pedaled toward the other end of the court as the ball swished through the net. By far the oldest player in the 1985 Schick Legends Classic at age 65, Bob competed against NBA legends as young as 36-year-old Pistol Pete Maravich and took perhaps the last two-hand set shot in an NBA All-Star weekend. Legends West Team Coach Bobby Leonard reminded the media that pioneers like Bob Davies, Bob Cousy, and George Yardley had laid the foundation for the modern NBA.[11]

During the 1980 ABC-TV Wide World of Sports Super Star Contest that pitted elite athletes from different sports in a decathlon-like series of events to determine a hypothetical world's best athlete, 60-year-old Bob Davies and 52-year-old Bob Cousy defeated all comers, including future four-time Super Star Champion Renaldo Nehemiah and his partner, in tennis doubles. Davies and daughter Camy, a ranked junior tennis player, paired against Baseball Hall of Famers George Brett and Mike Schmidt, as well as Bob Cousy and a friend, and beat them. With the passage of time, Cousy and Davies had mellowed in

Bob and Mary Davies raised their own All American family. From left, Bob, Mary, Jimmy and Bo with Camy and Dick in front. (Courtesy of Mary Davies)

their attitudes toward each other and had become good friends.[12]

During the summer, Bob's job was less demanding, and he spent more time with his family. He played any sport that his kids wanted. "We were the most competitive family in the world," recalled youngest son, Dick. Bob taught each child the "Davies" behind-the-back dribble, and each child requested number 11 for their high school and university team uniforms. [13]

Bob was a role model for his children. "I would say that my Mom was just as much a role model as my Dad," said Camy, "but she followed his lead. He was definitely the spiritual leader and overall leader of the family. They worked well together. We all knew that Dad made the final decision on most everything and Mom would support him. We all knew that Dad expected us to respect Mom as well."[14]

"Dad was a very humble man," recalled son Dick. "He was pretty much focused solely on attitude, effort and performance. Being a positive role model was all part of attitude." [15]

All four Davies children participated in high school sports and graduated from college. During his sophomore and junior years at Syracuse University, Jim commuted two hours each way and worked 42 hours a week at a radio station. Bo set a University of South Carolina Gamecock season pass-interception record, and was drafted by the NFL New Orleans Saints. Dick competed on a nationally ranked James Madison University Archery Team and qualified for the U.S. Olympic Team tryouts. And Camy played on a Florida state champion high school basketball team, garnered all-state volleyball honors, and received a Florida State University full-ride volleyball scholarship.[16]

But Bob's super-competitiveness and perfectionism sometimes strained the parent-child relationship. "He'd go out in the backyard," recalled Mary, "and work with the kids. He was a tough master. He'd tell the kids what they did wrong after they'd played a game." An "A" tennis player, Bob hit tennis balls nightly with Camy. "He was too hard on her," said Mary. "I told him to give her a pat on the back." Ultimately, Camy lost her passion for the sport, but continued playing to please her father.[17]

Like his own father, Bob attended as many of his children's sporting events as possible. Several times after Dick showered following a Gettysburg High School Friday night football game, the family drove 550 miles to Columbia, South Carolina, watched Bo play football for the University of South Carolina Gamecocks, dined with him, and returned to Gettysburg on Sunday.[18]

In addition to devoting time to his children, Bob Davies contributed generously to the community. "The pro athlete spends his career taking," said Bob, "being looked up to as a hero, idolized. When he's through he should have time to give, especially to young people." Deeply involved in the interdenominational Fellowship of Christian Athletes (FCA) that challenges athletes and coaches to commit their lives to Jesus Christ and stresses service to God, integrity, excellence, and teamwork, Bob founded Gettysburg High School and Gettysburg

Bob Davies was active in the Fellowship of Christian Athletes and volunteered at several summer camps. (Courtesy of Mary Davies)

College Huddle Bible Study Groups and led their meetings. The Davies family attended several FCA summer camps, and Bob acted as dean at one of them. "Bob loved what those camps did for kids," recalled Mary. "Ghetto kids would come with an attitude and want to fight over anything and at the end of camp didn't want to leave and had their arms around each other." [19]

While teaching a Sunday school class, Bob Davies befriended U.S. Navy officer Bill Lewis, provided him a copy of the FCA *Christian Athlete* magazine, and suggested that he "might like this outfit." Assigned to the Pentagon, Lewis, with the assistance of Bob's former Royals teammate Otto Graham, founded the Greater Washington (DC) FCA chapter. After retiring from the navy, Lewis led the effort to establish an FCA Golf Ministry that challenges male and female golfers and coaches to follow Jesus Christ as their Savior. This Ministry still conducts youth camps and sponsors events in conjunction with the Professional Golf Association tournament schedule. [20]

The legendary Bob Davies returned to the limelight on April 11, 1970, when he was inducted into the Naismith Memorial Basketball

Bob Davies' Naismith Memorial Basketball Hall of Fame plaque identifies him as the "First Super Star of Modern Pro Basketball." (1970, Monsignor William Noel Field Archives and Special Collections Center, Seton Hall University)

Hall of Fame. The dinner program and his plaque identified him as the "first Super Star of Modern Pro Basketball." Appropriately, the principal speaker, United Nations (UN) Under Secretary Dr. Ralph Bunche, the first African-American to win the Nobel Peace Prize and a former UCLA basketball player, spoke about playing basketball and development of character. Dr. Bunche pointed out that participating in that sport, a young person learns perseverance, patience, poise, and teamwork. Honey Russell introduced Bob, and Clair Bee unveiled his plaque. "I really feel great for Bob," said Honey. "He was a fantastic player, but more than that, he's a terrific individual. You'd want him for a son.... I would have loved to see Bobby play with a guy like Russell or Chamberlain or Alcindor [Kareem Abdul Jabbar]. Bob Cousy had Bill Russell, but all Davies had was Honey Russell, and I was on the bench." In his remarks, Bob said, "Basketball is a team sport. Any honors a player gets, he owes to the team and the coach."[21]

During the January 1971 NBA All-Star game festivities in San Diego, California, Bob received his Silver Anniversary NBA All-Star

Lifelong friend Chuck "The Rifleman" Connors presented Bob his NBA Silver Anniversary Top Ten Player Award. (April 11, 1970, Courtesy of Mary Davies)

Team award. Former teammate and then-movie-and-TV-star Chuck Connors presented him with the plaque. The local press ignored the basketball legend and quoted the screen star in their stories.[22]

Two years later, Bob and Mary moved to Coral Springs, Florida in order to escape wintry Pennsylvania weather and enjoy golf and tennis year-round. With a smaller sales area (Florida, Georgia, and North and South Carolina), Bob spent more time at home. Mary looked after Bob's mother, who moved into a nearby condominium. Bob helped found the Coral Springs Baptist Church, served as senior elder, taught Sunday school, and in the Evangelism Explosion program, spoke about Christianity.[23]

Through daughter Camy and her grammar-school teacher, Arilee Pollard, Bob reconnected with Arilee's husband, long-time Laker rival Jim Pollard who had migrated to Florida as coach of the American Basketball Association (ABA) Miami Dolphins. Bob nominated Jim for the Naismith Memorial Basketball Hall of Fame and attended his enshrinement ceremony. Jim asked Bob to coach the opposing team in

Bob presented his lifelong friend Les Harrison at his Hall of Fame induction ceremony. (April 1980, Courtesy of Mary Davies)

an annual high school basketball charity fundraiser basketball game, and they enjoyed doing this together seven times.[24]

Les Harrison remained a close friend of Bob and Mary, and Bob introduced him at Les's Hall of Fame induction ceremony in 1980. Every winter, Les visited the Davieses in Florida, and they played fiercely competitive gin games. Les, a real card shark, enjoyed trouncing Bob and watching him throw his cards on the floor. Mary liked to take Les shopping. "He sure knew his vegetables," she said about the former Rochester Public Market wheeler and dealer.[25]

After retiring from Converse in 1985, Bob played seven-handicap golf. "I beat him at one thing," said feisty Mary. "I won the women's championship at all three golf clubs we joined." No husband and wife competed more fiercely on the links than Bob and Mary. "It was like war," remembered Bob's brother Bill. Sermonizing about activities for married couples, Bill, a Presbyterian minister, started to suggest golf, remembered Bob and Mary, thought "Oh, no, don't do that," and stopped in mid-sentence.[26]

In May 1987, Bob Davies introduced Bobby Wanzer at his Hall of Fame induction ceremony. "We worked well together," remembered the senior partner of the first great NBA guard combination, in a speech limited to two minutes. "Most teams won with their big men," pointed out Les Harrison on that occasion, "we won with our backcourt."[27]

In August 1989, Todd Caso interviewed Bob for an NBA history documentary in which he commented about the trials and tribulations of travel in the league's early days. Bob was able to watch the opening segment of a pre-broadcast VHS of the show before he left home to enter a hospital at Hilton Head, South Carolina. He had never been hospitalized in his life and had procrastinated about seeking medical attention for prostate cancer. Chuck Connors called and inquired about his condition. As the end neared, Bob gathered his family in his hospital room and prayed for them. On April 22, 1990, Robert Edris Davies, age 70, died.[28]

In an obituary on national TV, Keith Olberman said: "The basketball world has lost one of its immortals. Davies was conceded to be the best ball handler in basketball's first half century."[29]

Les Harrison and Bobby Wanzer traveled from upstate New York and Bob and Missy Cousy from Massachusetts to Florida for the funeral. Retired NBA referee Steve Honzo escorted Mary Davies into the service. No members of the media were present.[30]

"The One Great Scorer," as sports columnist Grantland Rice characterized God, must have awarded Bob Davies high marks for his life of good deeds. Pennsylvania Governor Robert B. Casey issued a statement memorializing Bob "for not only his athletic achievements, but the joy he brought to others and his devotion to making God's work here on earth truly his own." Harrisburg Mayor Stephen R. Reed proclaimed October 22, 1990 as Bob Davies Memorial Golf Classic Day and urged citizens "to further strive to live their lives in as an exemplary manner as he did." The Fellowship of Christian Athletes renamed their Harrisburg chapter the Bob Davies Memorial Chapter.[31]

"My Bob was the most humble person I've ever known," said Mary Davies. "He was a good Christian guy. He never promoted himself. He would do anything for anybody. He would drive a hundred miles if somebody asked him to speak at a banquet. He visited sick children in hospitals." [32]

"He was like the All-American boy," said Bobby Wanzer. "Blond, clean cut, lived a good clean life. He was what you could call today a hero for the kids."[33]

"I had a lot of great players," said Les Harrison, "but Bob Davies was one in a lifetime—as a competitor and as a person…. He was my pride and joy. He was pure class on the court. He was the first at practice and the last to leave…. He was a gentleman and a credit to the game. He didn't smoke, he didn't drink, he taught Sunday school and he signed autographs for youngsters all day long. He was the true all-American boy."[34]

"He [Davies] was probably years ahead of his time," Red Holzman told a *New York Times* reporter. "He was one of the few guys that could have been playing today. He was a great player."[35]

"Actually," said Bob a decade after his NBA retirement, ""today's brand of play would have suited me better. I liked the break, or what you might call the current 'confusion' state of ball."[36]

Les Harrison believed that 6' 1½", 175-pound Bob Davies compared favorably in natural ability and skill with 6' 1", 175-pound John Stockton, the all-time NBA assists and steals leader. "Stockton was slo-mo compared to Bob," said not unbiased brother Dick Davies. Both of these speedy, instinctive but disciplined, tenacious and tough-as-nails guards were clever passers who put their teams first. Their NBA career scoring averages were similar: 14.3 PPG for Davies and 13.3 PPG for Stockton. Stockton's assist totals (11.0 APG) were much higher than Davies' (4.9 APG), but he was the Jazz's principal ball handler in a higher scoring era and Davies shared ball handling duties with triumvirates, consisting first of himself with Holzman and Cervi, then with Wanzer and Holzman, and finally with Wanzer and McMahon. Unfortunately for this comparison and for Davies, who had a penchant for stealing the ball in critical game situations, steals were not recorded until after he retired. If this statistic had been kept, the chief criticism of his defense, gambling to steal the ball, might have been regarded as a positive. [37]

Even though he had not spoken to Bob in over 40 years, former sub chaser crewman James Thomas cried when he read about his former officer's death. Shortly after World War II ended, Thomas brought five Southside Chicago tough guys to the Royals' locker room in the Chicago International Amphitheater. "You'd better stay away from those boys," warned Bob, "if you want to make anything of your life." Thomas accepted Bob's advice. He married, operated a milk delivery route, and put three children through college. "I owed 40 percent of my life to Bob," said Thomas. "Without him I would have ended up in the penitentiary."[38]

"My friendship with your husband," wrote Hall of Fame basketball coach Bob Knight to Mary, "was one of the most enjoyable things that has happened to me in sports. There is no one I have met that I respected or admired more than him."[39]

Sports writer George Beahon, who covered most of Bob's career in Rochester, wrote "Remembrances of Bob Davies": "Simply a total class act. Classic build. Classic athlete. Classic work habits. Classic personal life and habits. A man who made kids love him, and actually shuddered when he first heard about athletes charging money for autographs."[40]

"Bob Davies was one of a kind," said African-American NBA pioneer Earl Lloyd. "They don't make them like him anymore. He was a class act, a great, great basketball player. He was doing things then nobody else did. There was no controversy about him. He was not good copy like Dr. J [Philadelphia 76ers Julius Erving] or Magic [L.A. Lakers Ervin Johnson]. He just showed up and played." [41]

Bob Davies certainly deserves the accolades, basketball legend and sports-hero role model.

NOTES

1   Bruce Whitman, "Bob Davies Says 'No, Thanks' To Chicago's New NBA Entry," "Davies Will Retire from Royals For Coaching Job Next Season," "Starring Days Past, Royals' Bob Davies Maps Plan of Future," Walter

Consuelo Langsam, President, to Mr. Robert Davies, April 22, 1954, and "Davies' Wish Now Is Reality With Post as Bullet Mentor," BDSHOF; Gettysburg College Faculty Form: Robert E. Davies, Special Collections, Musselman Library, Gettysburg College, Gettysburg, PA.

2   Gettysburg College, *Spectrum* (1956): 92–95, and *Spectrum* (1957): 88–91; Frank Capitani, telephone conversation with author, April 11, 2009.

3   Gettysburg College, *Spectrum* (1956): 32–33, 173; *Spectrum* (1957): 92–93, 100, and *Spectrum* (1958): 103 "He stayed": Mary Davies, telephone conversation with author, Jan. 19, 2007.

4   Jim Davies, telephone conversation with author, April 6, 2009 and e-mail to author, July 24, 2015; Ralph Hyman, "The Davies Story: Ike Will Be Coach Davies' Neighbor," *T-U*, March 13, 1955.

5   Dick Davies, telephone conversation with author, May 6, 2009; Measuring Worth.

6   Mary Davies, interview with author, Lake Mary, FL, Dec. 3, 2007; Mary Davies, telephone conversations with author, March 13, 2007, Oct. 6, 2008, May 20, 2009, and May 30, 2011.

7   "Davies was one": http://www.bcallstarsbasketball.net/history/converse/bob_davies.html.

8   "Bob Davies was quite": Jerry Phipps, telephone conversation with author, Nov. 5, 2014.

9   Fredrico, e-mail message to Calobe Jackson Jr., July 12, 2008; Mary Davies, telephone conversations with author, Oct. 6, 2008, Jan. 22, 2009, and Aug. 18, 2009; John Macknowski, telephone conversation with author, May 14, 2011; Seymour Smith to author, June 4, 2011; Bo Davies, telephone conversation with author, May 24, 2009; George Beahon, "Bob Davies," *T-U*, Aug. 21, 1982.

10   "Hank Doesn't, Davies Does" (AP Wire photo caption), *D&C*, Oct. 10, 1957; Mary Davies, telephone conversations with author, Oct. 6, 2008, Jan. 22, 2009, and Aug. 18, 2009.

11   Louis Effrat, "Host Five Winner At Boston, 109–97: East Overcomes Slow Start and Routs West as Cousy and Johnson Excel," *NYT*, Jan.16, 1957; Jack Barry, "East All-Stars Hand West 109–107 Loss: Cousy Selected 'Most Valuable'," *Boston Daily Globe*, Jan.16, 1957; Cliff Keane, "Old Timers Game Makes Buddies of Ex-Enemies," *Boston Globe,* Jan. 15, 1964; Dave Overpeck, "Legends Classic a bit of the past for 'Oldtimers',"

Indianapolis Star, Feb. 9, 1985; Dave Overpeck, "Familiar, legendary moves highlight East's victory," *Indianapolis Star,* Feb.10, 1985.

12 https://en.wikipedia.org/wiki/Superstars; Mary Davies, telephone conversation with author, Aug. 18, 2009; Camy Keck, telephone conversation with author, Jan. 18, 2012.

13 "We were": Dick Davies, telephone conversation with author, April 20, 2009; Bo Davies, telephone conversation with author, May 24, 2009.

14 "I would say": Camy Keck e-mail message to author, April 8, 2014.

15 "Dad was": Dick Davies, e-mail to author, April 19, 2013.

16 Jim Davies, telephone conversation with author, April 6, 2009; Bo Davies, telephone conversation with author, May 24, 2009; Dick Davies, telephone conversation with author, April 20, 2009; Camy Keck, telephone conversations with author, April 17, 2009 and Jan. 18, 2012; Camy Keck e-mail message to author, May 27, 2009.

17 "He'd go" and "He was": Mary Davies, telephone conversation with author, Sept. 28, 2009; Camy Keck, telephone conversation with author, Jan. 18, 2012.

18 Dick Davies, telephone conversation with author, April 20, 2009.

19 "The pro": McKenzie, "Bob Davies: A Pioneer in the Backcourt," *Basketball Digest,* Jan. 1975, 61; http://www.fca.org/AboutFCA/; Bob Baldridge, "200 Hear Davies At FCA Luncheon," *Nashville Tennessean,* Dec. 20, 1964; Camy Keck, telephone conversation with author, April 17, 2009; "Bob loved": Mary Davies, telephone conversation with author, Oct. 6, 2008.

20 "might like": Joseph Dunn, *Sharing the Victory: The Twenty-five Years Of the Fellowship Of Christian Athletes,* 132–34, 143; Jim Esary, Director, FCA Golf Ministry, telephone conversation with author, Jan. 11, 2011.

21 Jerry Radding, "Davies and Carnevale Inducted into Cage Hall of Fame," *Springfield (MA) Sunday Republican,* April 12, 1970; "first Super Star": "Naismith Memorial Basketball Hall of Fame 3rd Annual Enshrinement Dinner Program, April 11, 1970," Ralph Bunche Papers, Bx. 24, Schomburg Center for Research in Black Culture, New York, NY; John A. Garraty and Mark C. Carnes, gen. eds., *American National Biography,* s.v. "Bunche, Ralph Johnson"; Garry Brown, "The Morning Line: Starry Night," *Springfield Republican,* April 13, 1970; "I really feel" and "Basketball is": Garry Brown, "The Morning Line: Honey and Bob,"

Springfield Sunday Republican, April 12, 1970.

22 "1, 400 Honor All-Time Stars At NBA Fete," *San Diego Union,* Jan. 12, 1971; Jack Murphy, "The Others Ran And Ran But Fulks Put Ball Through Net" and Wayne Lockwood, "25 Years And Many One-Nighters: All-Stars Take Stroll Down Memory Lane," *San Diego Union,* Jan. 13, 1971.

23 Mary Davies, telephone conversation with author, Oct. 6, 2008.

24 Arilee Pollard, interview by author, Lodi, CA, Feb. 9, 2010; Jerry Radding, "It all started here… Hall of fame (sic) grows," *Springfield Morning Union,* May 2, 1978; Grundman, *Jim Pollard,* 165–66.

25 Jerry Radding, "Superstars head cage enshrinees," *Springfield Union-News,* April 29, 1980; "He sure": Mary Davies, telephone conversation with author, March 13, 2007.

26 "I beat": Mary Davies, telephone conversation with author, Jan. 19, 2007; "It was": Bill Davies, telephone conversation with author, Sept. 14, 2011.

27 "We worked" and "Most teams": Jerry Radding, "Five more stars enter Hall of Fame: Barry, Frazier, Maravich, Houbregs, Wanzer inducted," *Springfield Morning Union,* May 6, 1987.

28 Todd Caso to Mary Davies, April 24, 1990 (in possession of Mary Davies, Longwood, FL); Bob Matthews, "Royals' star Bob Davies was innovator," *T-U,* April 24, 1990; Mary Davies, telephone conversation with author, Sept. 8, 2011; Bill Davies, telephone conversation with author, May 21, 2008; Dick Davies, telephone conversation with author, June 21, 2011.

29 "The basketball world": "Basketball Hall of Famer – Rochester Royals (Inventor of the behind the back dribble and pass)" addendum to "Bob Davies (NBA Hall of Fame) Talks About Travel in the Early Days," https:www.youtube.com/watch?v=uL.AqMZNBghE.

30 Camy Keck, telephone conversation with author, April 17, 2009, and e-mail message to author, Feb. 11, 2011.

31 "The One": Mark Inabinett, *Grantland Rice and His Heroes: The Sportswriter As Mythmaker In the 1920s,* 2; "for not": Commonwealth of Pennsylvania: Governor's Office, "Greetings," Oct. 22, 1990, and "to further": Office of the Mayor, Harrisburg, Pennsylvania, "Proclamation," Oct. 22, 1990 (in possession of Mary Davies, Longwood, FL).

32 "My Bob": Mary Davies, telephone conversation with author, Aug. 18, 2009.

33 "He was": Pete Reinwald, "Rochester Royals' Davies dies; NBA Hall-of-Famer was 70," *D&C*, April 24, 1990.

34 "I had": Bob Matthews, "Royals' star Bob Davies was innovator," *T-U*, April 24, 1990.

35 "He was": Thomas Rogers, "Bob Davies, 70, Star On Basketball Court In the 40's and 50's," *NYT*, April 24, 1990.

36 "Actually": Gene Levy, "The Pro Way: Davies Finds Current NBA Aces 'Too Good'," *Star-Gazette (Elmira, NY)*, Dec. 18, 1964.

37 Matthews, "Royals' star Bob Davies was innovator," *T-U*, April 24, 1990; "Stockman was": Dick Davies, telephone conversation with author, Jan. 27, 2012; Hubbard, *NBA Encyclopedia*, 3rd ed., 460 (Davies), 765 (Stockton).

38 "You'd better" and "I owed": James Thomas, telephone conversation with author, Jan. 19, 2009.

39 "My friendship": Bob Knight to Mary Davies, Sept. 30, 2004 (in possession of Mary Davies, Longwood, FL).

40 "Remembrances": George Beahon, "Mr. Frisky looks like Derby favorite," *T-U*, May 1, 1990.

41 "Bob Davies was": Earl Lloyd, telephone conversation with author, July 19, 2008.

CHAPTER 14

POSTSCRIPT: THE LITERARY LEGACY OF BOB DAVIES

AMERICAN YOUTH FOR A CENTURY AND A HALF HAVE READ STORIES about heroes, real and fictional, and identified with their exploits, and, in too few cases, moral character. The legendary Bob Davies is a rarity among genuine American sports hero-role models. As Father James Carey recognized in the inspirational Seton Hall Prep School bulletin testament to his character, Bob developed into a role model before he became a national sports hero. Among great American athletes only Bob Davies has been the prototype for a fictional sports-hero role model character, not in one book, but in many, 23 in the juvenile fiction series *Chip Hilton*.

The first American sports-hero role model was a fictional character. Between 1896 and 1912 *Frank Merriwell*, known as the "unreal ideal," captured the imagination of adult and teenage readers of weekly and biweekly dime novels. Future U.S. president Woodrow Wilson and presidential candidates Al Smith and Wendell Wilkie, as well as journalist Westbrook Pegler and *Hopalong Cassidy* creator Clarence E. Mulford, heavyweight boxing champions Jack Dempsey and Jess Willard, baseball slugger Babe Ruth and pitcher Christy Mathewson, and crooner Rudy Vallee and actor Frederic March, avidly read Frank Merriwell stories. Girls like future syndicated gossip columnist Louella Parsons absolutely adored him. Eminent literary critic George Nathan noted, "For one who read Mark Twain's 'Huckleberry Finn,' or 'Tom Sawyer,' there were 10,000 who read Standish's 'Frank Merriwell's Dilemma' or 'The Rescue of Inza' and 'Frank Merriwell at Yale,' or 'The Winning Last Quarter-Mile'." "We're now teaching readin', writin', 'rithmetic and *Merriwell*," commented an educator. At the height of Frank's popularity, 300,000 dime novels, many shared by several teenagers, were published weekly.

Author Gilbert Patten, writing under the pseudonym Burt L. Standish, emphasized that Frank succeeded as an athlete because of his strong moral character. In Frank, a clean mind functioned in a healthy body with a heart of gold. He was a paragon of manly virtues—modest, clean-living, patriotic, smart, tolerant, sportsmanlike, friendly, chivalrous, fair, well-mannered, kind, generous, and loyal to family and alma mater. Frank performed "deeds of derring-do" for the mythical Fairdale Academy and later Yale University teams. He specialized in striking out batters with the bases loaded, scoring the winning touchdown on the last play of the game, and nipping his rivals at the finish lines of track races. Caught in the Merriwell mystique, sports writers described similar real-life performances with the metaphor, "a Frank Merriwell finish."[1]

By candlelight late into the night, young Clair Bee (born 1896) read Frank Merriwell novels. Clair yearned for a role model. His mother had died at a young age. His father remarried and Clair did not fit into the new family structure, so he spent periods of his boyhood on an uncle's farm and in a military academy. Reading Frank Merriwell stories inspired Clair to overcome personal hardship and graduate from high school in his 20s, work his way through college, earn two advanced degrees, and succeed as a man, athlete, coach, and university administrator.[2]

During the 1920s, newspaper sports writers idealized nationally known star athletes as heroes. "When a sportswriter stops making heroes out of athletes," noted Grantland Rice, the nation's leading sports columnist, "it's time to get out of the business." Rice added the qualifier that God, "The One Great Scorer," valued the way an athlete conducted his personal life more highly than his sports achievements.[3]

It did not take American business long to capitalize on the national infatuation with sports heroes and pay star athletes for endorsing their products. In 1934, General Mills contracted with New York Yankee slugger Lou Gehrig, incidentally a man of strong character, to vouch for its cereal, "Wheaties—The Breakfast of Champions." As time passed, sports writers mostly ignored mentioning professional athletes' moral shortcomings and peccadilloes, so that sports-hero endorser misbehavior did not impact negatively on product images and corporate bottom lines. [4]

Shortly after World War II, Clair Bee, who had written three technical basketball books, decided to write a boy's sports-hero role model novel in the Frank Merriwell-Jack Armstrong genre. He wanted to demonstrate that boys participating in athletics could develop religious and social values that would be useful all their lives. He thought it best to base the principal character on a real person. Impressed over the years with Bob Davies' modesty, integrity, and particularly sportsmanship during and after Seton Hall's two demoralizing losses to Long Island University, Bee decided to model his fictional Chip Hilton character on Bob, who exemplified the type of boy that he liked to coach. [5]

Before Bee encountered Bob, he had been a role model for his brothers and sister.

"Bob was the oldest and quietest," remembered the late Ed Davies, a Wheaton College (IL) Little All-American football star. "He was like he was a nobody, just the guy next door. He set an example for his four brothers and sister."[6]

"Bob was the epitome of a competitor," said Bill Davies, a Wheaton College track team captain and Presbyterian minister. "He would play tiddlywinks for blood. But he was always a sportsman to the nth degree. He played sports so his brothers and sister played sports. He went to college so we went to college. As the oldest brother, he set a precedent which we never reached, but we always aspired to it."[7]

"Bob was like a father to me," said the late Dick Davies, who retired as a Goodyear Rubber Company vice president. "Without him I would have ended up driving a laundry truck. No good person was better than Bob at being good. He was just good." A worldwide newspaper wire photo showed Dick, the 1964 U.S. Olympic basketball team's only armed services veteran, kneeling in prayer after the team won the gold medal. Bob and Dick Davies are the only brothers, one to have played on an NBA championship team and the other on an Olympic championship team.[8]

Not to be outdone by her brothers, Bettye Davies excelled as an acrobatic high school drum majorette and cheerleader who performed back and front flips from a standing start. She cleaned houses to earn money and graduated from Akron University.[9]

"Bob would have fit the Frank Merriwell character to a T," said former sub chaser crewman James Thomas, who met Bob during World War II.[10]

"I think, in Coach Bee's mind, Bobby Davies was the consummate athlete," said Hall of Fame Coach Bob Knight. "Plus, he was such a high integrity person. Chip Hilton is Superman and Jack Armstrong and Ted Williams combined. And I don't think I heard [Bee] speak about a player more respectfully than he did about Bobby Davies." [11]

"The fictional Chip Hilton was the stereotype one expected from the brush of Norman Rockwell," wrote sports historian Sandy Padwe. "Blond, blue-eyed, virtuous, intelligent, hardworking, a fine athlete with a strong sense of responsibility to his family, his church, his school, his friends and even his enemies, Chip Hilton belonged on Main Street, USA."[12]

And before Clair Bee wrote his first Chip Hilton book, Bob Davies had experienced many Frank Merriwell moments—swishing all 13 foul shots in his most important high school game, stealing the ball and scoring after the buzzer sounded to preserve the Seton Hall Pirates' 42-game win streak, electrifying a sell-out Madison Square Garden crowd when he unveiled the behind-the-back dribble, starring in the College All-Star Game, and drop-kicking a basket.

Bee described his visual image of Chip Hilton to the publisher's artist. The pictures of Chip on the book dust jackets and bindings are spitting images of Bob Davies. Blond, blue-eyed, handsome and slope-shouldered, 6' 1 ½" Bob and 6' 2" Chip, both nicknamed the Blond Bomber, weighed 175 and 170 pounds, respectively. Both dribbled behind their backs, drained two-hand set shots, drew comparisons to Hank Luisetti, and earned All-American basketball honors. [13]

Eight of the 23 Chip Hilton books focus on basketball. *Championship Ball* (1948) is dedicated to Sy Lobello, the LIU basketball team co-captain killed during World War II. *Hoop Crazy* (1950) is dedicated to

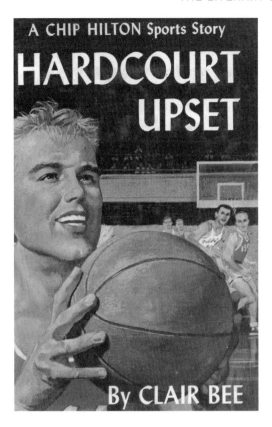

A CHIP HILTON Sports Story

HARDCOURT UPSET

By CLAIR BEE

Fictional sports hero-role model Chip Hilton is based on the life, and is the spitting image, of Bob Davies. (1961, Courtesy of Chip Hilton Sports: Cynthia Bee Farley)

William "Dolly" King, "student, athlete, gentleman, and friend" and examines difficulties confronting a black joining an all-white basketball team in a town reluctant to accept him. In *Comeback Cagers* (1963), Chip sank a free throw with time expired to win the conference championship and earn an NCAA Tournament invitation.[14]

Between 1948 and 1966, Grosset and Dunlap published 2.2 million copies of the Chip Hilton books. Department store juvenile book sections displayed them next to the best-selling Hardy Boys and Nancy Drew series. As boys, author John Grisham, sportscaster Bob Costas, and basketball coach Bob Knight read the Hilton books. Like other young readers, they wanted to emulate Chip's character and achievements. In Chip's world, boys did things the right way, played fair, worked hard, and succeeded. Chip balanced sports, studies, and helping to support his widowed mother. He declined a college scholarship

so a needier boy could accept it, and turned down a professional baseball contract so he could complete his education. Chip and his Valley
Falls High School and State University teammates coped with losing
games, season-ending injuries, physically superior opponents, crimi-
nal conduct, biased sportswriters, and tournament selection politics.[15]

"Chip was as much a part of my boyhood as radio characters such
as the Lone Ranger and Straight Arrow," reminisced novelist James K.
Fitzpatrick. "One came from reading the stories fully believing that in
the United States, a boy who played fair, worked hard and listened to
his parents could grow up to be as strong and good and decent—and
as admired—as Chip Hilton."[16]

As the Chip Hilton books rolled off the printing presses, NBA
marquee attraction Bob Davies continued to conduct his personal life
in an exemplary manner. "We are all really servants of God," Bob
emphasized. "We must act like it." He wrote a YMCA official, "Boys
grow up fast! It's up to men like you and me to help these boys grow
into real men, who can be useful citizens in a democracy."[17]

During one NBA off-season, Bob Davies helped the "Christian
Team." He introduced evangelist Jack Shuler at a "Tide of Salvation"
Revival in Rochester and spoke on Shuler's "Crusade for Christ"
program in Kansas City, Missouri. At the Hartwick College Athletic
Dinner in Oneonta, New York, Bob outlined his Christian formula for
success—faith, work, conditioning, and promotion of God. "You can't
get anywhere without knowing the Bible," he emphasized. "Know
the rules of life. Read the Bible to know where you're going and how
you're going." Speaking at a high school banquet, soft-spoken Bob
said, "All brotherhoods, especially if they are based on brotherhood—
the word of God—are wonderful." His advice to young athletes:
"Live the way you should with emphasis on faith in God and your
fellow-man."[18]

After Bob retired from the NBA, teenagers in the cynical 1960s,
dealing with the Vietnam War, racism, civil rights, women's lib-
eration, environmental pollution, and other important social issues,
tuned out Chip Hilton as unreal and irrelevant and began admiring
anti-heroes such as football quarterback "Broadway Joe" Namath and
heavyweight boxing champion Muhammad Ali and bad-boy role

movie actors James Dean and Marlon Brando. All-American Boy hero types, à la Bob Davies, became passé. Historian Arthur Schlesinger characterized the decade as "an age without heroes." Magazines published articles with titles like "Where Have Our Heroes Gone?", "What's Happened to Our Heroes?", and "Youth Heroes Have No Haloes." Alice Childress wrote an award-winning young adult novel tellingly titled *A Hero Ain't Nothing but a Sandwich,* which became even more popular when it was adapted into a movie starring Cicely Tyson and Paul Winfield. The sports media dug deeper and uncovered sports-hero misconduct unbecoming an image as a role model. "Where have you gone, Joe DiMaggio, a nation turns its lonely eyes to you...," lamented a Simon and Garfunkel hit song. The price of a Chip Hilton novel rose from one dollar to two dollars and the books stopped selling.[19]

During a Converse business trip, Bob Davies called on Clair Bee in Roscoe, New York. Bee told Bob that he had modeled the character Chip Hilton on him and gave him a copy of *Backcourt Ace* inscribed: "To Dickie Davies son of one of America's greatest athletes—May you be as great an athlete and gentleman and sportsman." Bob had known about the books, but had never heard himself connected with Chip. He had read a chapter or two of a Chip Hilton book, but did not finish it because he was too old for reading juvenile fiction. It was not publicly revealed that Bob Davies was the prototype for Chip Hilton until January 1980 when *Sports Illustrated* published Jack McCallum's wonderful article, "A Hero for All Times."[20]

On a subsequent visit, Bob interrupted Clair Bee, blinded by glaucoma, listening to his grandson reading aloud a Chip Hilton book. "Hi, Coach," said Bob, "it's Chip Hilton." The grandson's "eyes got as big as teacups." He believed that Chip Hilton really existed![21]

During the Naismith Memorial Basketball Hall of Fame induction festivities in 1983, Bob walked up to Clair. "It's Bob Davies, coach," he said. Bee corrected him, "It's Chip Hilton." Asked on another occasion whether athletes like Chip Hilton still existed, Bee reflected a moment and responded, "Yes, I believe there are. I believe there are."[22]

The Bob Davies sports-hero role model legend lives on. Teenagers still read about Chip Hilton. The Chip Hilton Sport Series originally

The legendary Bob Davies' retired jersey number 11 hangs from the
Sacramento Kings Arena rafters. (2007, R. Widner)

published by Grossett and Dunlap has been reissued by Broadman and Holman in both paperback and electronic updates reflecting 21st-century realities. Chip and his best buddy, Speed Morris, an African American, now watch ESPN-TV, read *Sports Illustrated*, e-mail friends, complete homework on a computer, and take three-point shots. They even tackle drug issues at home, school, and in sports. The books have not lost their emphasis on basic values—moral and physical courage, self-reliance, persistence, selflessness, sportsmanship, and teamwork.[23]

Since 1997, the Chip Hilton Player of the Year Award has been pre-sented to a graduating NCAA Division I men's basketball player who has demonstrated outstanding character, leadership, integrity, humil-ity, and sportsmanship. Tim Duncan of Wake Forest University won the inaugural award. Keeping a promise to his mother made before her death, Tim graduated from Wake Forest. Humbly and modestly, he has since led the San Antonio Spurs to five NBA championships.

The Tim Duncan Foundation Character Program annually rewards 3,000 San Antonio area K–12 students with achievement certificates, Spurs game tickets, Sea World passes, and Character Program t-shirts for demonstrating good character traits (integrity, respect, dependability, fairness, caring, and civic responsibility) and making good life choices.[24]

But Charles Barkley, the Hall of Fame basketball player and now TV pundit, does not believe that sports heroes have an obligation as role models. "I'm not paid to be a role model," he observed in a widely seen TV commercial while still an NBA star. "I'm paid to wreak havoc on the basketball court."[25]

And after four decades searching for, and writing about, sports-hero role models, only to lose faith in them, long-time *New York Times* sports columnist George Vecsey has retired from "the role-model business." He asks why "should the public retain high moral expectations for athletes, who are famous mostly because of hand-eye coordination? Who elected them role models?"[26]

American youth do not need to rely on professional athletes or fictional characters for role models. Although a boy or girl may not have an exceptional sibling like Bob Davies or a remarkable parent like Mary or Bob Davies, there are outstanding adults and young persons involved in youth athletic, school, church, temple, and synagogue activities, as well as the Fellowship of Christian Athletes, YMCA, YWCA, Girl Scouts, Boy Scouts, Campfire Girls, Boys and Girls Clubs, and similar organizations. A young person seeking a role model should follow sports hero Bob Cousy's advice to his daughters—emulate someone you know and admire who consistently sets a good example and can respond to your questions and concerns.[27]

NOTES

1   Robert H. Boyle, "Frank Merriwell's Triumph, OR, How Yale's Great Athlete Captured America's Fancy, Purified The Penny Dreadfuls And Became Immortal," *Sports Illustrated*, Dec. 24, 1962, 86–92, 95–96; "For one": George Jean Nathan, "Suggestions for a Biography," The *American Mercury*, Sept. 1925, 109–10; "We're now": Irving Wallace, "The Return

Of Frank Merriwell," *Esquire*, Aug. 1952, 105; ibid., 32; "finish": Stewart H. Holbrook, "Frank Merriwell At Yale Again – And Again And Again," *American Heritage*, June 1961, 25; ibid, 24–71, 78–81.

2   John A. Garraty and Mark C. Carnes, gen. eds., *American National Biography*, s.v. "Bee, Clair Francis"; Padwe, *Basketball's Hall Of Fame*, 145–47; McCallum, "A Hero For All Times," *Sports Illustrated*, Jan. 7, 1980, 55–56; Dr. Rogers McAvoy introduction to *Chip Hilton Sports Series: Backcourt Ace* by Clair Bee, ix.

3   "When a": Inabinett, *Grantland Rice*, ix; ibid., 2.

4   Robert Lipsyte and Peter Levine, *Idols Of The Game: A Sporting History Of The American Century*, 93.

5   https://en.wikipedia.org/wiki/Wheaties; McCallum, "A Hero," *Sports Illustrated*, Jan. 7, 1980, 58, 60.

6   "Bob was": Ed Davies, telephone conversation with author, July 24, 2008.

7   "Bob was": Bill Davies, telephone conversations with author, May 21, 2008, and July 17, 2013.

8   "Bob was like": Dick Davies, telephone conversation with author, April 15, 2008; "U.S. Olympic Basketball Victory Brings Player's Prayer" (caption), AP sports wire story, Tokyo Olympics Oct. 23, 1964 (pr61233rce).

9   Bettye Davies Frierson, telephone conversation with author, April 8, 2009.
   The outbreak of World War II altered many young Americans' lives, among them Bob's brother Tom, who served in the Army Air Corps and after the war, deciding he had lost too much time to attend college, embarked on a successful career as a licensed civil engineer.

10 "Bob would": James Thomas, telephone conversation with author, Jan. 19, 2009.

11 "I think": David Jones, "Davies inspired many with play," *Harrisburg Patriot-News*, Aug. 6, 2009.

12 "The fictional": Padwe, *Basketball's Hall Of Fame*, 147.

13 See the eight Chip Hilton basketball books listed in the bibliography under "Bee, Clair."

14 McCallum, "A Hero," *Sports Illustrated*, Jan. 7, 1980, 60.

15 James Fitzpatrick, "What Would Chip Hilton Do?" http://catholicexchange.com/2007/03/22/96679/print/; "Farley works to keep legacy of father, coach, author Clair Bee alive," *Lubbock (TX)*

Avalanche-Journal, April 3, 2010.

16 "Chip was": James K. Fitzpatrick, "What Would Chip Hilton Do?" http://catholic exchange.com/2007/03/22/96679/print/.

17 "We are": Ralph Hyman, "The Davies Story: Ike Will Be Coach Davies' Neighbor," *T-U,* March 13, 1955; "Boys grow up": "Here it is, Fellows," clipping, BDSHOF.

18 Harry Schmeck, "'Tide of Salvation' Meetings Begin," Bill Richardson, "Star Cager Turns His Talents To Helping 'Christian Team'," and "You can't": "Hard Work, Faith Key Success Points, Rochester Cage Star Tells Hartwick Sports Dinner," BDSHOF; "All brotherhoods": "Royal Bob Davies Addresses Brotherhood," Webster (NY) Central School *Courier* (June 12, 1952): 5.

19 Benjamin G. Rader, *In Its Own Image: How Television Has Transformed Sports,* 185–87; Benjamin G. Rader, *American Sports: From the Age of Folk Games to the Age of Televised Sports,* 315–17; "Where have": Craig Muder, "Linked in Song: Paul Simon's Homage To Joe DiMaggio To Be Part Of Aug. 2 Anniversary Concert," Baseball Hall of Fame *Memories and Dreams* (Opening Day 2014): 43; McCallum, "A Hero," *Sports Illustrated,* Jan. 7, 1980, 60.

20 "To Dickie": *Backcourt Ace* copy in possession of Dick Davies, Winchester, VA; McCallum, "A Hero," *Sports Illustrated,* Jan. 7, 1980, 58.

21 "Hi Coach": Eric Hillstrom, "New Book a Chip Off the Old Block," *USA Today,* July 3, 2002.

22 "It's Bob": Gergen, "Showtime," *Newsday,* April 26, 1990; "Yes, I": McCallum. "A Hero," *Sports Illustrated,* Jan. 7, 1980, 60.

23 Jack McCallum, "Scorecard: Back to School for Chip Hilton," *Sports Illustrated,* Oct. 18, 1999.

24 https://en.wikipedia.org/wiki/Chip_Hilton_Player_of_the_Year_Award; J. Chris Roselius, Sports Stars With Heart: *Tim Duncan: Champion On And Off The Court,* 13–14, 26, 28, 54, 77–78.

25 "I'm not paid": http://www.thedailybeast.com/newsweek/1993/06/27/i-m-not-a-role-model.html.

26 "should the public": George Vecsey (*New York Times*), "Commentary: There's no need for outrage: Athletes are lousy role models anyway – so what's the fuss over their misdeeds?" *Sacramento Bee,* Dec. 23, 2007.

27 John Devaney, *Bob Cousy,* 71.

ACKNOWLEDGMENTS

A VERY SPECIAL THANKS TO THE DAVIES FAMILY—BOB'S WIDOW Mary, brothers Dick (deceased), Ed (deceased), and Bill, sister Bettye and husband Ed Frierson, daughter Camy Keck, and sons Jim, Bo, and Dick for sharing their wonderful stories. The other half of the NBA's first great backcourt combination, the late Bobby Wanzer, cannot be thanked enough for steering the author "in bounds." Also, thanks to Bob's friend and coach Les Harrison (deceased), teammates Frank "Pep" Saul, Red Holzman (deceased), Fuzzy Levane (deceased), and Al Cervi (deceased), as well as Seton Hall player Johnny Macknowski, African-American NBA pioneer Earl Lloyd (deceased), and archrival Minneapolis Laker Jim Pollard's widow Arilee, for their special insights. Jack L. Coleman II graciously lent the author his father's scrapbook, and Arvin Odegaard provided information about his uncle Arnie Johnson

Without the help of my fellow Sacramento NBA history aficionados, Ray LeBov, executive director, Association for Professional Basketball Research (APBR) and founder of the "Basketball Intelligence" blog (basketballintelligence.net), and the late Joe Cronin, Sacramento Kings historian and sports archivist hobbyist extraordinaire, this book might still be a work in process. John Grasso reviewed the manuscript, made valuable suggestions, and assisted with statistical analysis. Charles Salzberg graciously lent the author his Bob Davies interview tape and transcript.

Two professional archivists have gone beyond the call of duty in assisting with this project. Alan Delozier, Special Collections, Seton Hall University, encouraged me from the start, suggested improvements in the Seton Hall chapters, provided statistical information, and located pictures. Curator and historian Matt Zeysing directed me to important files in the Naismith Memorial Basketball Hall of Fame Archives and responded to research requests.

From the RIT Press, Director Bruce Austin suggested the title, and Managing Editor Molly Cort, Design and Marketing Specialist Marnie Soom, and copyeditor Ann Stevens, improved the quality of the book in all aspects.

Several individuals helped immensely on specific topics. Michael C. Cohill of Akron Toy & Marble Co, Akron, Ohio, educated me about the game of marbles. Outstanding local historian Calobe Jackson provided significant information about Harrisburg, PA, schools and race relations. Jim Lacey, Jack McDermott, and Pete Sheridan described Bob's importance as a role model to Seton Hall Prep School boys. Roger Gogan and Seymour Smith contributed significantly to the Great Lakes Naval Station Bluejackets' story. James Thomas (deceased) alerted me to Bob Davies' human side as a U.S. Navy officer. University of Rochester History Professor Jessie Moore and Librarians Phyllis Andrews, Margaret Becket, Melissa Mead, and Alan Unser, as well as Monroe Community College Librarian Debbie Moore, led me to sources on Rochester race relations. Cindy and Randy Farley read and suggested changes to the chapter about the Chip Hilton books.

Assisting in a multitude of special ways were Bob Bishop, Paradise, CA; Albert Bryson, Catalog Librarian, Lincoln University, PA; Lindita Cani, South Orange Public Library, South Orange, NJ; Frank Capitani (deceased), Hershey, PA; Rick Coles, Director of Alumni Relations, Seton Hall Preparatory School, West Orange, NJ; David Cox, Kansas City Public Library, Kansas City, MO; Kim Dalhaimer, Mead Public Library, Sheboygan, WI; Anita Danigelis, Fletcher Free Library, Burlington, VT; Karen Drickamer, Director of Special Collections and Archivist, Gettysburg College Library; Tamara Edevold, Gonvick Historical Society, Gonvick, MN; Deborah Edge, Jodi Foor, Nathaniel Patch, and Barry L. Zerby, National Archives at College Park, MD; Harris Freedman, Harrisburg, PA; Ken Frew, Historical Society of Dauphin County, Harrisburg, PA; Debbie Gambrall, Anderson Public Library, Anderson, IN; Anne Therese Gonzalez, Great Lakes Naval Station, Chicago, IL; Allan Holtzman, Enoch Pratt Free Library, Baltimore, MD; Scott Johnson, Director of Public Relations, Harlem Globetrotters, Phoenix, AZ; Noel Kalenian, Denver Public Library, Denver, CO; Frank Keetz, Schenectady, NY; Lea Kemp, Librarian/ Archivist, and Carol Baumeister, volunteer, Rochester Museum and Science Center, Rochester, NY; Kimberly Kleinhans, Onondaga County Public Library, Syracuse, NY; Shirley Ann Knight, Manager, Annie E. Sterline Library, Lewisberry, PA; Richard E. Kolb, Publisher and Editor-in-Chief, *VFW Magazine*, Kansas City, MO; Anne Marie Lane, Curator, Rare Books, American Heritage Center, University of Wyoming, Laramie, WY; Michael R. Lear, Archives and Special Collections Assistant, Martin Library of the Sciences, Franklin & Marshall College, Lancaster, PA; Alice L. Lubrecht, Director, and Iren Snavely, Rare Books Librarian, Bureau of State Library, Harrisburg, PA; Kelly Martinka, Bemidji State University Alumni Association, Bemidji, MN; Jeff Mead, Athletic Dept., Long Island University, Brooklyn, NY; Allison Moonitz, Ocean City Free Public Library, Ocean City, NJ; Newt Oliver, Springfield, OH; Jesse Pears, Rochester Public Library, Rochester, NY; Jerry Phipps, Bridgeville, DE; Sue Porter, VP, Scripps Howard Foundation, Cincinnati, OH; Jim Roan, National Museum of American History Library, Smithsonian Institution, Washington, DC; Imee B. Roberts, General Mills Consumer Services, Minneapolis, MN; Michele Rowe, City Archives, Rochester, NY; George Rugg, Curator, Dept. of Special Collections, Hesburgh Library, University of Notre Dame, Gary, IN; Michael Salmon, LA84 Foundation Library, Los Angeles, CA; Carol Sandler, Strong National Museum of Play, Rochester, NY; Jim Sargent, Virginia Western Community College, Roanoke, VA; Barbara Scheibel, Onondaga County Public Library, Syracuse, NY; Jon Scott, Schwenksville, PA; Diane Shaffer, Harrisburg, PA; Bill Shaman, Archivist, Bemidji State University, Bemidji, MN; Eileen L. Summers, NCAA Library, Indianapolis, IN; Jason E. Tomberlin, Special Projects Librarian, Wilson Library, Chapel Hill, NC; Dan Treadwell, Takoma Park, MD; and André D. Vann, Coordinator of University Archives and Records, North Carolina Central University, Durham, NC.

A debt of gratitude is owed to librarians at the Arden-Dimick, Sacramento Main and California State University Libraries, Sacramento, CA, and the Shields Library, University of California, Davis, CA.

My niece Katy Warren and friend Jim Morris read early versions of the manuscript and made valuable suggestions.

Most of all, my wife Carolyn, who is a jack-of-all-trades equal to Les Harrison, but in editing, formatting, picture selection, and marketing.

Any errors and omissions are due to the foibles and failings of an old set-shot artist who misses "the game."

ROBERT EDRIS (BOB) DAVIES

BACKGROUND

Born on January 15, 1920, in Harrisburg, Pennsylvania
Died on April 22, 1990, in Hilton Head, South Carolina
Height: 6′ 1½″ Weight: 175 pounds
Family: Married Mary Helfrich on August 8, 1942—four children
Education:
    B.S. in Physical Education from Seton Hall College, 1942
    M.S. in Physical Education from Columbia Teachers College, 1948
Military Service:
    U.S. Navy 1942–1945, Honorable Discharge,
    Lieutenant Junior Grade
Employment:
    Assist. Professor of P.E. and Coach, Seton Hall College 1946–47
    Assist. Professor of P.E. and Coach, Gettysburg College 1955–57
    Sales and Promotion Representative, Converse Rubber Co. 1957–85

HONORS

NCAA Consensus All-American First Team 1941, 1942
Collyer's Eye Magazine All-American First Team 1942
Converse All-American Third Team 1942
PIC Magazine All-American Second Team 1942
Madison Square Garden All-American Second Team 1942
College All-Star Game Most Valuable Player 1942
National Basketball League (NBL) Most Valuable Player 1947
NBL All-Star First Team 1947

NBL All-Star Second Team 1948

Basketball Association of American (BAA) All-Star First Team 1949

National Basketball Association (NBA) All-Star First Team 1950, 1951, 1952

NBA All-Star Second Team 1953

NBA All-Star Games 1951, 1952, 1953, 1954

Sport Magazine—sixth greatest college player in first half of 20th century

Pennsylvania Sports Hall of Fame 1967

NBA 25th Anniversary All-Time Team 1970

Naismith Memorial Basketball Hall of Fame 1970

Seton Hall University Athletic Hall of Fame 1973

Madison Square Garden College Basketball 50th Anniversary All-Time Team 1984

Sports Hall of Fame of New Jersey 1997

SEASON	TEAM	GAMES	POINTS	SCORING AVERAGE	ASSISTS AVERAGE
1934–35	John Harris High School	N/A		N/A	N/A
1935–36	John Harris High School	N/A		N/A	N/A
1936–37	John Harris High School	16	162	10.0	N/A
1937–38	Franklin & Marshall College	11	242	22	N/A
1938–39	Seton Hall College	15	N/A	N/A	N/A
1939–40	Seton Hall College	18	212	11.8	N/A
1940–41	Seton Hall College	18	185	10.2	N/A
1941–42	Seton Hall College	19	225	11.8	N/A
1940–41	National Invitational Tournament	3	34	11.3	N/A
1942–43	Great Lakes Naval Station	37	269	7.3	N/A
1945–46	Rochester Royals (NBL)	27	242	7.5	N/A
1946–47	Rochester Royals (NBL)	32	462	14.4	N/A
1947–48	Rochester Royals (NBL)	48	472	9.9	N/A
1948–49	Rochester Royals (BAA)	60	904	15.1	5.4
1949–50	Rochester Royals (NBA)	64	895	14.2	4.6
1950–51	Rochester Royals (NBA)	63	955	15.2	4.6
1951–52	Rochester Royals (NBA)	65	1,052	16.2	6
1952–53	Rochester Royals (NBA)	66	1,029	15.6	4.2
1953–54	Rochester Royals (NBA)	72	887	12.3	4.5
1954–55	Rochester Royals (NBA)	72	872	12.1	4.9

COACHING RECORD

Seton Hall—Basketball 1946–47	Won 24/Lost 3
Seton Hall—Baseball 1946 & 1947	Won 28/Lost 10
Gettysburg College Basketball 1955–56 & 1956–57	Won 18/Lost 30

ABBREVIATIONS

AAU	Amateur Athletic Union
APG	Assists per game
BAA	Basketball Association of America (1946-49)
BDSHOF	Bob Davies Scrapbook, Joseph M. O'Brien Historical Resource Center, Naismith Memorial Basketball Hall of Fame, Springfield, MA
CCNY	City College of New York, New York, NY
D&C	Rochester (NY) *Democrat & Chronicle*
FCA	Fellowship of Christian Athletes
FGM	Field goals made
GLNTS	Great Lakes Naval Training Station, Chicago, IL
LIU	Long Island University, Brooklyn, NY
LSU	Louisiana State University, Baton Rouge, LA
MLB	Major League Baseball
Measuring Worth	Samuel H. Williamson. "Seven Ways to Compute the Relative Value of a U.S. Dollar amount, 1774 to the present," Measuring Worth, 2015, URL: www.measuringworth.com/uscompare/
MVP	Most valuable player
NACP	National Archives & Records Administration, College Park, MD
NAIB	National Association of Intercollegiate Basketball (est. 1939)

NBA	National Basketball Association (est. 1949)
NBL	National Basketball League (est. 1938)
NCAA	National Collegiate Athletic Association
NIT	National Invitational Tournament (est. 1938)
NYCRR	New York Central Railroad
NYT	*The New York Times*
NYU	New York University, New York, NY
PMHOF	Professional Men File, Joseph M. O'Brien Historical Resource Center, Naismith Memorial Basketball Hall of Fame, Springfield, MA
PPG	Points per game
RG	Record Group
RPG	Rebounds per game
RRSHOF	Rochester Royals Scrapbook copy, Joseph M. O'Brien Historical Resource Center, Naismith Memorial Basketball Hall of Fame, Springfield, MA
SCTC	U.S. Navy Submarine Chaser Training Center, Miami, FL
SHUAC	Athletic Collection, Monsignor William Noe Field Archives & Special Collections Center, Seton Hall University, South Orange, NJ
T-U	Rochester (NY) *Times-Union*

SELECTED BIBLIOGRAPHY

Aamidor, Abraham. *Chuck Taylor, All Star: The True Story of the Man Behind the Most Famous Athletic Shoe in History.* Bloomington: Indiana Univ. Press, 2006.

Abdul-Jabbar, Kareem. *On the Shoulders of Giants: My Journey through the Harlem Renaissance.* With the assistance of Raymond Obstfeld. New York: Simon and Schuster, 2007.

Ambrose, Stephen E. *Band of Brothers: E Company, 506th Regiment, 101st Airborne from Normandy to Hitler's Eagle's Nest* (3d Touchstone ed.). New York: Simon & Schuster, 2001.

Anderson, Bruce. "His Career Still Reads Like a Novel." *Miami (FL) Herald,* April 6, 1980.

Angevine, Elbert. *Basketball in Rochester.* Rochester, NY: H.P. Bittner, 1951.

Arata, Darryl. *2006–07 Sacramento Kings Media Guide.* Sacramento, CA: Maloof Sports and Entertainment, 2006.

A.S. Barnes & Co. *American Sports Library: The Official Basketball Guide, 1941– 1942.* New York: A.S. Barnes, 1942.

Ashe, Arthur R., Jr. *A Hard Road to Glory: The African-American Athlete in Basketball.* With the assistance of Kip Branch, Ocania Chalk and Francis Harris. New York: Amistad, 1988.

Auerbach, Arnold "Red." *Basketball for the Player, the Fan and the Coach.* New York: Pocket Books 1953.

Auerbach, Red. *On and Off the Court.* With the assistance of Joe Fitzgerald. Toronto: Bantam Books, 1986.

Auerbach, Red and John Feinstein. *Let Me Tell You A Story: A Lifetime in the Game*. New York: Little, Brown, 2005.

Auerbach, Red and Joe Fitzgerald. *Red Auerbach: An Autobiography*. New York: G.P. Putnam's Sons, 1977.

Barbey, Daniel E. *MacArthur's Amphibious Navy: Seventh Amphibious Force Operations, 1943–1945*. Annapolis, MD: U.S. Naval Institute, 1969.

"Basketball's All-Time All-America." *Sport*, March 1955, 21–23.

Beckett Publications. *Good Sports: Athletes Your Kids Can Look Up To*. Dallas, TX: Beckett Publications, 1999.

Bee, Clair. *Chip Hilton Sports Series: Championship Ball*. New York: Grosset & Dunlap, 1948.

Bender, Jack H. *Basketball-Log*. St. Louis County, MO: Valley Publishing Co., Inc., 1958.

Berger, Arthur Asa. *Li'l Abner: A Study in American Satire*. New York: Twayne Publishers, 1970.

Bjarkman, Peter C. *Biographical History of Basketball*. Chicago: Masters Press, 2000.

———. *Encyclopedia of Pro Basketball Team Histories*. New York: Carroll & Graf, 1994.

———. *History of the NBA*. New York: Crescent Books, 1992.

Bloomfield, Gary. *Duty, Honor, Victory: America's Athletes in World War II*. Guilford, CT: Lyons Press, 2004.

Boddie, Charles E. "A Study of the Relation of an Urban Negro Church to its Community." Master's Thesis, Univ. of Rochester, 1949.

Boyle, Robert H. *Sport—Mirror of American Life*. Boston: Little, Brown, 1963.

Bradley, Bill. *Values of the Game*. New York: Broadway Books, 2000.

Breuer, William B. *Operation Dragoon: The Allied Invasion of the South of France*. Novato, CA: Presidio, 1987.

Browne, Ray B. and Marshall W. Fishwick. *The Hero in Transition*. Bowling Green University/Popular Press, Bowling Green, OH, 1983.

Buck, Jack, Bob Rains, and Bob Broeg. *Jack Buck: "That's a Winner."* Champaign, IL: Sports Publishing LLC, 1997.

Caldwell, Howard. *Tony Hinkle: Coach for All Seasons*. Bloomington: Indiana Univ. Press, 1991.

Campus Confessions, directed by George Archainbaud (1938); Paramount Pictures, Hollywood, CA.

Caponi-Tabery, Gina. *Jump for Joy: Jazz, Basketball, and Black Culture in 1930s America*. Amherst, MA: Univ. of Mass. Press, 2008.

Carter, Craig and John Hareas, eds. *Sporting News: Official NBA Guide Ultimate 2000–2001 Season Reference*. New York: McGraw-Hill Trade 2000.

Caudle, Edwin C. *Collegiate Basketball: Facts and Figures on the Cage Sport*, 1959 ed. Winston-Salem, NC: John F. Blair, 1960.

Chalk, Ocania. *Black College Sport: The early days of the Black professional athlete in baseball, basketball, boxing, and football*. New York: Dodd, Mead, 1976.

———. *Pioneers of Black Sport*. New York: Dodd, Mead, 1975.

Champaign-Urbana News-Gazette. *Fighting Illini Basketball: A Hardwood History*. Champaign, IL. Sports Publishing, Inc., 2000.

Christgau, John. *The Origins of the Jump Shot: Eight Men Who Shook the World of Basketball*. Lincoln: Univ. of Nebraska Press, 1999.

———. *Tricksters in the Madhouse: Lakers vs. Globetrotters, 1948*. Lincoln: Univ. of Nebraska Press, 2004.

Clary, Jack. *Basketball's Great Moments*. New York: McGraw-Hill, 1990.

Clodfelter, Michael. *Warfare and Armed Conflicts: A Statistical Encyclopedia of Casualty and other Figures, 1494–2007*. Jefferson, NC: McFarland & Co., 2008.

Coles, Howard W., comp. *City Directory of Negro Business and Progress, 1939–1940*. Rochester, NY: Howard W. Coles, 1940.

Converse Rubber Co. *Converse Basketball Yearbook*. Malden, MA: Converse, 1941–1952.

Cook, Kevin. "The Rochester Royals: The Story of Professional Basketball." In *Rochester History* 58, no.1 (Winter, 1996): 3–20.

Cousy, Bob. *American Sports Library: Basketball Is My Life*, rev. ed. As told to Al Hirshberg. New York: J. Lowell Pratt, 1963.

———. *The Killer Instinct*. With the assistance of John Devaney. New York: Random House, 1975.

———. *The Last Loud Roar*. With the assistance of Ed Linn. Englewood Cliffs, NJ: Prentice-Hall, 1964.

Cousy, Bob and Frank G. Power, Jr. *Basketball Concepts and Techniques*. Boston: Allyn & Bacon, 1970.

Cousy, Bob and Bob Ryan. *Cousy on the Celtic Mystique*. New York: McGraw-Hill, 1988.

Cronin, Joseph Collection. Joseph M. O'Brien Historical Resource Center, Naismith Memorial Basketball Hall of Fame, Springfield, MA.

Crowley, Joseph N. *In the Arena: The NCAA's First Century*. Indianapolis: NCAA, 2006.

Danielson, Dr. Don L., Myra Ness Edevold and Darlene Clemenson-Sawyer, comp. *A Window to the Past: A History of the Gonvick Area*. Gonvick, MN: Richards Publishing Co., 1985.

Davies, Robert. Scrapbook. Joseph M. O'Brien Historical Resource Center, Naismith Memorial Basketball Hall of Fame, Springfield, MA.

Delozier, Alan. *Seton Hall Pirates; A Basketball History*. Charleston, SC: Arcadia Publishing, 2002.

Dempsey, Jack in collaboration with Ned Brown. "Basketball's Li'l Abner," *Liberty*, March 21, 1942, 30–31.

Denaro, Dominick. *A Centennial Field Scrapbook: Memories of the minor league's oldest ballpark*. South Burlington, VT: Blue Fish Arts, 1995.

Derks, Scott, ed. *The Value of a Dollar: 1860–1999 Prices and Incomes in the United States*. Lakeville, CT: Grey House Publishing, 1999.

Devaney, John. *Bob Cousy*. New York: G.P. Putnam, 1965.

Dickey, Glenn. *The History of Professional Basketball* . New York: Stein & Day, 1982.

Douchant, Mike. *Inside Sports: Encyclopedia of College Basketball*. Richmond, TX: Gale Group, 1994.

Dunn, Joseph. *Sharing the Victory: The Twenty-five Years of the Fellowship of Christian Athletes*. New York: Quick Fox, 1980.

Dunning, John. *On the Air: The Encyclopedia of Old-Time Radio*. New York: Oxford University Press, 1998.

Eastman, E. Irvine (ed.). *World Almanac and Book of Facts for 1945*. New York: NY World-Telegram, 1945.

Egan, John. *The Vern Mikkelsen Story: The Original Power Forward*. Minneapolis: Nodin Press, 2006.

Eig, Jonathan. *Opening Day: The Story of Jackie Robinson's First Season*. New York: Simon & Schuster, 2007.

Enright, Jim. *Ray Meyer: America's #1 Basketball Coach*. With the editorial assistance of Isabel S. Grossner. Chicago: Follett Publishing, 1980.

Falla, Jack. *NCAA: The Voice of College Sports; A Diamond Anniversary, 1906–1981*. Mission, KS: NCAA, 1981.

Fisher, Donald M. "Lester Harrison and the Rochester Royals, 1945–1957." In *Sports and the American Jew*, ed. by Steven A. Riess, 208–40. Syracuse, NY: Syracuse Univ. Press, 1998.

———. "The Rochester Royals and the Transformation of Professional Basketball, 1945–57." In *International Journal of the History of Sport* 10, no. 1 (April 1993): 20–48.

Fountain, Charles. *Sportswriter: The Life and Times of Grantland Rice.* New York: Oxford Press, 1993.

Fury, David. *Chuck Connors: "The Man Behind the Rifle."* Minneapolis, MN: Artist's Press, 1997.

Gelman, Steve. *Bob Cousy: Magician of Pro Basketball.* New York: Bartholomew House/Sport Magazine Library, 1961.

George, Nelson. *Elevating the Game: Black Men and Basketball.* Lincoln: Univ. of Nebraska Press, 1999.

Gilbert, Eugene. *Advertising and Marketing to Young People.* Pleasantville, NY: Printers' Ink Books, 1957.

Gildea, Dennis. *Hoop Crazy: The Lives of Clair Bee and Chip Hilton.* Fayetteville: University of Arkansas Press, 2013.

Glickman, Marty. *The Fastest Kid on the Block: The Marty Glickman Story.* With the assistance of Stan Isaacs. Syracuse, NY: Syracuse Univ. Press, 1996.

Gogan, Roger S. *Bluejackets of Summer: The History of the Great Lakes Naval Baseball Team, 1942–1945.* Kenosha, WI: Great Lakes Sports Publishing, 2008.

———. *By Air, Ground and Sea: The History of Great Lakes Navy Football.* Kenosha, WI: Great Lakes Sports Publishing, 2013.

Goldaper, Sam. *Great Moments in Pro Basketball.* New York: Grosset & Dunlap, 1977.

Goudsouzian, Aram. *King of the Court: Bill Russell and the Basketball Revolution.* Berkeley: Univ. of California Press, 2010.

Gould, Todd. *Pioneers of the Hardwood: Indiana and the Birth of Professional Basketball.* Bloomingdale: Indiana Univ. Press, 1998.

Graham, Tom and Rachel Graham Cody. *Getting Open: The Unknown Story of Bill Garrett and the Integration of College Basketball.* New York: Atria Books, 2006.

Grasso, John. *The Absurd "Official" Statistics of the 1954–55 NBA Season.* NP: privately printed, 2005.

———. *Historical Dictionary of Basketball*. New York: Scarecrow Press, 2010.

Grundman, Dolph. *Jim Pollard: The Kangaroo Kid*. Minneapolis: Nodin Press, 2009.

Gunther, John. *Inside U.S.A.*, 50th anniversary ed. New York: New Press, 1997.

Ham, Eldon. *The Play Masters: From Sellouts to Lockouts—An Unauthorized History of the NBA*. Lincolnwood, IL: Contemporary Books, 2000.

Hartman, Sid. *Sid! The Sports Legends, the Inside Scoops, and the Close Personal Friends*. With the assistance of Patrick Reusse. Stillwater, MN: Voyageur Press, 1997.

Helyar, John. *Lords of the Realm: The Real History of Baseball*. New York: Ballantine Books, 1994.

Hobson, Howard A. *Basketball Illustrated*. New York: Ronald Press, 1948.

———. *Scientific Basketball for Coaches, Players, Officials, Spectators, and Sportswriters*. New York: Prentice Hall, 1949.

Hollander, Zander, ed. *Pro Basketball Encyclopedia*. Los Angeles: Corvin Books, 1978.

Holzman, Red. *Holzman on Hoops: The Man Who Led the Knicks Through Two World Championships Tells It Like It Was*. With the assistance of Harvey Frommer. Dallas: Taylor Publishing, 1991.

Holzman, Red and Harvey Frommer. *Red on Red*. New York: Bantam, 1987.

Hubbard, Jan, ed. *The Official NBA Encyclopedia*, 3rd ed. New York: Doubleday, 2000.

Hyman, Ralph. "The Davies Story: Hero-Worshipping Father Raised His Own Hero: Robert Edris Davies." *Rochester Times-Union*, March 10, 1955.

———. "The Davies Story: Bob Forsook Baseball for Cage Career." *Rochester Times-Union*, March 11, 1955.

———. "The Davies Story: Ike will be Coach Davies' Neighbor." *Rochester Times-Union*, March 13, 1955.

Inabinett, Mark. *Grantland Rice and His Heroes: The Sportswriter as Mythmaker in the 1920s*. Knoxville: Univ. of Tenn. Press, 1994.

Isaacs, Neil. D. *All the Moves: A History of College Basketball*. Philadelphia: J.B. Lippincott, 1975.

———. *Vintage NBA: The Pioneer Era, 1946–1956*. Indianapolis, IN: Howard W. Sams/Masters Press, 1996.

Katz, Milton S. *Breaking Through: John B. McLendon, Basketball Legend and Civil Rights Pioneer*. Fayetteville: Univ. of Arkansas Press, 2007.

Keetz, Frank. "'We Really Liked to Play Basketball': The Rochester Royals in Schenectady, NY, 1946–1949." Schenectady: privately printed, 2002.

Keiderling, Kyle. *Shooting Star: The Bevo Francis Story; The Incredible Tale of College Basketball's Greatest Scorer.* Toronto: Sport Classic Books, 2005.

Kelly, J.F., Msgr. *Memoirs of Msgr. ("Doc") J. F. Kelley.* Locust, N.J.: J.F. Kelley, 1987.

Kennedy, Stetson. *Jim Crow Guide: The Way It Was.* Boca Raton: Florida Atlantic Univ. Press, 1990.

Kerr, Johnny and Terry Pluto. *Bull Session: An up-close look at MICHAEL JORDAN and courtside stories about the Chicago Bulls.* Chicago: Bonus Books, 1989.

Kirkpatrick, Rob. *Basketball Hall of Famers: Bob Cousy.* New York: Rosen Publishing Group, 2001.

Koppett, Leonard. *Championship NBA—Official 25th Anniversary.* New York: Dial Press/Associated Features, 1970.

———. *The Essence of the Game is Deception: Thinking about Basketball.* Boston: Little, Brown/Sports Illustrated, 1973.

———. *24 Seconds to Shoot: The Birth and Improbable Rise of the National Basketball Association.* Kingston, NY: Time, Inc., 1999.

Lazenby, Roland. *Jerry West: The Life and Legend of a Basketball Icon.* New York: ESPN, 2010.

———. *The Lakers: A Basketball Journey.* New York: St. Martin's Press, 1993.

———. *Michael Jordan: The Life.* New York: Little Brown, 2015.

———. *The NBA Finals: A Fifty-Year Celebration.* Indianapolis: Masters Press, 1996.

———. *The NBA Finals: The Official Illustrated History.* Dallas: Taylor Publishing, 1990.

Levey, Stanley. "The Cities of America: Rochester, N.Y.," *Saturday Evening Post,* March 18, 1950, 38–39, 122–25.

Lipsyte, Robert. *Sports World: An American Dreamland.* New York: Quadrangle/New York Times Book, 1975.

Lipsyte, Robert and Peter Levine. *Idols of the Game: A Sporting History of the American Century.* Atlanta, GA: Turner Publishing, 1995.

Liss, Howard. *The Winners: National Basketball Association Championship Playoffs,* new, enlarged ed. New York: Delacorte Press, 1971.

Lloyd, Earl and Sean Kirst. *Moonfixer: The Basketball Journey of Earl Lloyd.* Syracuse: Syracuse Univ. Press, 2011.

McCallum, Jack. "A Hero for All Times," *Sports Illustrated,* Jan. 7, 1980, 50–56, 58–60.

McCallum, John D. *College Basketball, U.S.A. since 1892.* New York: Stein & Day, 1978.

McKelvey, Blake. *Rochester on the Genesee: The Growth of a City,* 2d ed. Syracuse, NY: Syracuse Univ. Press, 1993.

———. *Rochester: An Emerging Metropolis. 1925–1961.* Rochester, NY: Christopher Press, 1961.

McKenzie, Mike. "Bob Davies: A Pioneer in the Backcourt." *Basketball Digest,* Jan. 1975, 58–61.

Macknowski, Johnny. *Dynamics of Basketball: The Dawn of a New Era Is Breaking Through.* Knoxville, TN: Publishing & Printing, 2000

Marcus, Jeff. *Biographical Directory of Professional Basketball Coaches.* Lanham, MD: Scarecrow Press, 2003.

Martin, Barry S. "A Look Back in History: NBA Yesterday; 1950–51 Rochester Royals," *Hoop,* March 1991, 72, 74, 76.

———. "Trotters made history in Schenectady." *Albany Times Union,* Feb. 23, 2005.

Menville, Chuck. *The Harlem Globetrotters: Fifty Years of Fun and Games.* New York: David McKay, 1978.

Messenger, Christian K. *Sport and the Spirit of Play in American Fiction: Hawthorne to Faulkner.* New York: Columbia Univ. Press, 1981.

Meyer, Roger. *Al "Digger" Cervi: Star Player, Great Coach, Hall of Famer.* Boxboro, MA: self-published, 2001.

———. *The First "Mr. Basketball": The Legend of Bobby McDermott.* Boxboro, MA: self- published, 2000.

———. *Rochester Seagrams History 1936–1937 to 1944–1945.* Boxboro, MA: self-published, 1997.

Michener, James. A. *Sports in America.* New York: Random House, 1976.

Mikan, George L. and Joseph Oberle. *Unstoppable: The Story of George Mikan, The First NBA Superstar.* Indianapolis: Masters Press, 1997.

Mill, Alvin H. *Sports on Television.* Westport, CT: Praeger, 2008.

Mokray, William G. *Ronald Encyclopedia of Basketball.* New York: Ronald Press, 1963.

Morison, Samuel E. *History of United States Naval Operations in World War II.* 1 *The Battle of the Atlantic September 1939–May 1943.* Boston: Little Brown, 1964.

———. *History of United States Naval Operations in World War II. 8 New Guinea and the Marianas March 1944–August 1944.* Boston: Little Brown, 1964.

———. *History of United States Naval Operations in World War II. 11 The Invasion of France and Germany 1944–1945.* Boston: Little Brown, 1957.

Mullin, Bernard J., Stephen Hardy and William A. Sutton. *Sport Marketing,* 3rd ed. Champaign, IL: Human Kinetics, 2007.

Myers, Jim. "Black History: Royals signed black pioneer," *Rochester Democrat & Chronicle,* Feb. 2, 1986.

Myrdal, Gunnar. *An American Dilemma: The Negro Problem and Modern Democracy (Twentieth Anniversary Edition).* New York: Harper & Row, 1962.

National Collegiate Athletic Association. *Official 2007 NCAA Men's Basketball Record Book.* Indianapolis, IN: NCAA, 2006.

Neft, David S. and Richard M. Cohen. *The Sports Encyclopedia: Pro Basketball,* 5th ed. New York: St. Martin's Press, 1992.

Nelson, Lindsey. *Hello Everybody, I'm Lindsey Nelson.* New York: William F. Morrow/Beech Tree Books, 1985.

Nelson, Murry R. *The National Basketball League: A History, 1935–1939.* Jefferson, NC: McFarland, 2009.

Nelson, Roger. *The Zollner Piston Story.* Fort Wayne, IN: Allen County Public Library Foundation, 1995.

Newell, Rob. *From Playing Field to Battlefield: Great Athletes Who Served in World War II.* Annapolis, MD: Naval Institute Press, 2006.

Nolan, Michelle. *Ball Tales: A Study of Baseball, Basketball, and Football Fiction of the 1930s through 1960s.* Jefferson, NC: McFarland, 2010.

Officer, Lawrence H. and Samuel H. Williamson. "Purchasing Power of Money in the United States from 1774 to Present." Chicago: Measuring Worth, 2013

Oriard, Michael. *Dreaming of Heroes: American Sports Fiction, 1868–1980.* Chicago: Nelson-Hall, 1982.

Overacker, Ingrid. *The African American Church Community in Rochester, New York, 1900–1940.* Rochester, NY: Univ. of Rochester Press, 1998.

Padwe, Sandy. *Basketball's Hall of Fame.* Englewood Cliffs, NJ: Prentice-Hall/ Associated Features, 1970.

Pallette, Philip. *The Game Changer: How Hank Luisetti Revolutionized America's Great Indoor Game.* Bloomington, IN: Author House, 2005.

Patterson, Wayne and Lisa Fisher. *100 Greatest Basketball Players.* New York: Crescent Books, 1989.

Peterson, Robert W. *Cages to Jump Shots: Pro Basketball's Early Years.* New York: Oxford Univ. Press, 1990.

Pierce, Richard B. *Polite Protest: The Political Economy of Race in Indianapolis, 1920–1970.* Bloomington: Indiana Univ. Press, 2005.

Pluto, Terry. *Tall Tales: The Glory Years of the NBA, in the Words of the Men Who Played, Coached, and Built Pro Basketball.* Lincoln: Univ. of Nebraska Press, 1992.

Porter, David L., ed. *Biographical Dictionary of American Sports: Basketball and Other Indoor Sports.* New York: Greenwood Press, 1989.

Purdon, Eric. *Black Company: The Story of Subchaser 1264.* Washington, DC: Robert B. Luce, 2000.

Rader, Benjamin G. *American Sports: From the Age of Folk Games to the Age of Televised Sports,* 3rd ed. Englewood Cliffs, NJ: Prentice Hall, 1996.

———. *In Its Own Image: How Television Has Transformed Sports.* New York: Macmillan/Free Press, 1984.

Rampersand, Arnold. *Jackie Robinson: A Biography.* New York: Ballantine, 1998.

Ramsey, David. *The Nats. A Team. A City. An Era: The Story of Professional Basketball in Syracuse, 1946–1963.* Utica, NY: North Country Books/Pine Tree Press, 1995.

Rappoport, Ken. *Tar Heel: North Carolina Basketball.* Huntsville, AL: Strode Publishers, 1979.

Reynolds, Bill. *Cousy: His Life, Career, and the Birth of Big-Time Basketball.* New York: Simon & Schuster/Pocket Books, 2005.

Rice, Grantland. *The Tumult and the Shouting: My Life in Sport.* New York: A.S. Barnes, 1954.

Robertson, Oscar. *The Big O: My Life, My Times, My Game.* Emmaus, PA: Rodale Press, 2010.

Rochester Royals. Scrapbook. Joseph M. O'Brien Historical Resource Center, Naismith Memorial Basketball Hall of Fame, Springfield, MA.

Roeder, Bill. "Bob Davies—Royal Playmaker," *Sport,* Feb. 1948, 50–53, 87.

Roselius, J. Chris. *Sports Stars with Heart: Tim Duncan, Champion on and off the Court.* Berkeley Heights, NJ: Enslow Publishers, Inc., 2006.

Rosen, Charley. *The First Tip-Off: The Incredible Story of the Birth of the NBA.* New York: McGraw-Hill, 2008.

——. *Scandals of '51: How the Gamblers Almost Killed College Basketball*. New York: Seven Stories Press, 1999.

Russell, Bill. *Go Up For Glory*. As told to William McSweeny. New York: Coward-McCann, 1966.

Russell, John. *Honey Russell: Between Games Between Halves*. Washington, DC: Dryad Press, 1986.

Ryan, Bob. *The Pro Game: The World of Professional Basketball*. New York: McGraw-Hill/Rutledge Book, 1975.

Sachare, Alex. *The Naismith Memorial Basketball Hall of Fame's 100 Greatest Basketball Moments of All Time*. New York: Pocket Books, 1997.

Salzberg, Charles. *From Set Shot to Slam Dunk: The Glory Days of Basketball in the Words of Those Who Played It*. New York: E.P. Dutton, 1987.

——. Tape recording and edited transcript of Bob Davies interview, Coral Springs, FL, 1986.

Sargent, Jim. "Arnie Risen: Remembering the 3-Time Champion Pivotman," *Ragtyme Sports*, May 1996, 38–45.

——. "Jack Coleman: An NBA Rebounding Giant," *Sports Collectors Digest*, Nov. 1, 1996, 152–54.

Sarmento, Mario R. "The NBA on Network Television: A Historical Analysis." Master's Thesis, Univ. of Florida, 1998.

Savage, William W., Jr. *Comic Books and America, 1945–1954*. Norman: Univ. of Oklahoma Press, 1990.

Schleppi, John. *Chicago's Showcase of Basketball: The World Tournament of Professional Basketball and the College All-Star Game*. Haworth, NJ: St. Johann Press, 2008.

Schoor, Gene. *The Pee Wee Reese Story*. New York: Julian Messner, 1956.

Schumacher, Michael. *Mr. Basketball: George Mikan, the Minneapolis Lakers, and the Birth of the NBA*. New York: Bloomsbury, 2008.

Sharman, Bill. *Sharman on Basketball Shooting*. Englewood Cliffs, NJ: Prentice-Hall, 1968.

Shouler, Ken, Bob Ryan, Sam Smith, Leonard Koppett and Bob Bellotti. *Total Basketball: The Ultimate Basketball Encyclopedia*. Wilmington, DE: Sport Media Publishing, 2003.

Smith, Page. 8 *Redeeming the Time: A People's History of the 1920s and the New Deal*. New York: McGraw-Hill, 1987.

Smith, Robert Ross. *United States Army in World War II: The War in the Pacific; Triumph in the Philippines.* Washington, DC: United States Army Center of Military History, 1991.

Smith, Ronald A. and Jay W. Helman. *A History of Eligibility Rules Among Big-Time Athletic Institutions.* Overland Park, KS: NCAA, 1990.

Smith, Seymour, Jack Rimer, and Dick Triptow. *A Tribute to Armed Forces Basketball, 1941–1969.* NP: privately printed, 2003.

Sporting News. *Official 1971–1972 National Basketball Association Guide.* St. Louis, MO: Sporting News, 1971.

Stafford, Edward P. *Subchaser.* Annapolis, MD: Naval Institute Press, 1988.

Steinberg, Rafael. *Time Life World War II: Return to the Philippines.* Alexandria, VA: Time-Life, 1980.

Taylor, Charles Wimbert. "A History of Intercollegiate Athletics at Franklin and Marshall College." Master's Thesis, Franklin & Marshall, 1962.

Thomas, Ron. *They Cleared the Lane: The NBA's Black Pioneers.* Lincoln: Univ. of Nebraska Press, 2002.

Thornley, Stew. *Basketball's Original Dynasty: The History of the Lakers.* Minneapolis, MN: Nodin Press, 1989.

Tower, Oswald. *Spalding's Athletic Library: Official Guide Basketball, 1940–41.* New York: American Sports Publishing Co., 1940.

Treadwell, Theodore. *Splinter Fleet: The Wooden Subchasers of World War II.* Annapolis, MD: Naval Institute Press, 2000.

Triptow, Richard F. *The Dynasty That Never Was: Chicago's First Professional Basketball Champions; The American Gears.* NP: privately printed, 1996.

Vincent, Ted. *Mudville's Revenge: The Rise and Fall of American Sport.* New York: Seaview Books, 1981.

Wade, Wyn Craig. *The Fiery Cross: The Ku Klux Klan in America.* New York: Simon & Schuster, 1987.

Warfield, William. *William Warfield: My Music & My Life.* With Alton Miller. Champaign, IL: Sagamore Publishing, Inc., 1991.

Westcott, Rich. *The Mogul: Eddie Gottlieb, Philadelphia Sports Legend and Pro Basketball Pioneer.* Philadelphia: Temple Univ. Press, 2008.

Wideman, John Edgar. *Brothers and Keepers.* New York: Holt, Rinehart & Winston, 1984.

———. *Hoop Roots.* New York: Houghton Mifflin, 2001.

Wind, Herbert Warren. "Bob Cousy: Basketball's Creative Genius." *Sports Illustrated,* Jan. 9, 1956, 42–46, 56–58.

———. "Bob Cousy: The Man and the Game." *Sports Illustrated,* Jan. 16, 1956, 28–32, 56–58.

Winters, Maj. Dick. *Beyond Band of Brothers: The War Memoirs of Major Dick Winters.* With the assistance of Col. Cole C. Kingseed. Detroit: Gale Cenage Learning, 2006.

Wolff, Alexander. *Sports Illustrated: 100 Years of Hoops.* Birmingham, AL: Oxmoor House/Time Inc, 1995.

———. "Lost History: The NFL's Jackie Robinson," *Sports Illustrated,* Oct. 12, 2009, 60–71.

Woodward, C. Vann. *The Strange Career of Jim Crow: A Commemorative Edition.* With a new afterword by William S. McFeely. New York: Oxford Univ. Press, 2001.

Work Projects Administration Writers' Program. *American Guide Series: Pennsylvania: A Guide to the Keystone State.* New York: Oxford Univ. Press, 1940.

———. *American Guide Series: Indiana: A Guide to the Hoosier State.* New York: Oxford Univ. Press, 1941.

Wormser, Richard. *The Rise & Fall of Jim Crow: The African-American Struggle Against Discrimination, 1865–1954.* New York: Grolier Publishing/ Franklin Watts Division, 1999.

Wright, Bradford W. *Comic Book Nation: The Transformation of Youth Culture in America.* Baltimore, MD: John Hopkins Univ. Press, 2001.

Zaloga, Steven J. *Operation Dragoon 1944: France's other D-Day.* Long Island City, NY: Osprey Publishing, 2009.

LIST OF ILLUSTRATIONS

INDEX

Abdul-Jabbar, Kareem, 4, 228

African Americans baseball players, 105, 110, 112, 115–16

African Americans basketball players, 11–12, 76, 101n8, 105–17, 188–89

Amateur Athletic Union (AAU), 56, 59

Amoco Gas endorsement, 183, *184*

Anderson, Forrest, 56

Anderson (IN) Duffey Packers, 145, 147, 154, 157

Anthony, Susan B., 110

Arizin, Paul, 4, 59, 185

"Armstrong, Jack" (fictional character), 16, 95, 183, 241, 242

Auerbach, Red, 198; on Davies creating behind-the-back dribble, 3–4, 89n19; on sixth man position, 192; on Zollner Pistons Northside High School court, 84

Austin, I. Jr., 110

Barkley, Charles, 247

baseball teams, 15, 17, *31*, 54, 59–60, 157; African Americans on, 110, 112, 115–16; Burlington Cardinals, *31*, 38–39. *See also* Seton Hall baseball team

Basketball Association of America (BAA), 81, 82, 93, 98, 146–53; Davies as marquee attraction, 147

Battle, Mark, 110

Beahon, George, 134, 173, 233

Beard, Ralph, 58, 167, 170, 176–77

Bee, Clair, 35–37, 41, 177, 224, 228, 240; Chip Hilton series of, 4, 239, 241–46, *243*, Davies relationship with, 245

Beech-Nut gum endorsement, 193, *194*

behind-the-back dribble, 1–4, 38, 40, 82; Cousy's version of, 2, 27, 89n19, 170; Davies' version of, *26*, 27, 33, 225; Honey Russell on, *33*

Note: Page numbers in italics indicate photographs.

ABOUT THE AUTHOR

BARRY MARTIN, a native of Webster, New York, saw Bob Davies play for the Rochester Royals. Martin is a Phi Beta Kappa graduate of the College of William and Mary, holds a master's degree in American History from the University of Washington, Seattle, and graduated from the University of California Berkeley School of Law. He is a retired Administrative Law Judge. Martin has spent seven years doing extensive research, including interviews with Davies' family members and former NBA players. The author and his wife, Carolyn, reside in Sacramento, California.

COLOPHON

DESIGN
Marnie Soom

TYPEFACES
Palatino Linotype and Trade Gothic

PRINTING AND BINDING
Thomson-Shore
Dexter, MI

 green
press
INITIATIVE

RIT Press is committed to preserving ancient forests and natural resources. We elected to print this title on 30% post consumer recycled paper, processed chlorine free. As a result, for this printing, we have saved:

6 Trees (40' tall and 6-8" diameter)
9 Million BTUs of Total Energy
1,512 Pounds of Greenhouse Gases
6,170 Gallons of Wastewater
519 Pounds of Solid Waste

RIT Press made this paper choice because our printer, Thomson-Shore, Inc., is a member of Green Press Initiative, a nonprofit program dedicated to supporting authors, publishers, and suppliers in their efforts to reduce their use of fiber obtained from endangered forests.

For more information, visit www.greenpressinitiative.org

Environmental impact estimates were made using the Environmental Defense Paper Calculator. For more information visit: www.papercalculator.org.